Kinship in

Kinship in Bali

Hildred Geertz and Clifford Geertz

The University of Chicago Press ▼ Chicago and London

HILDRED GEERTZ is an associate professor and chairman of the Department of Anthropology at Princeton.

CLIFFORD GEERTZ is professor of social sciences at the Institute for Advanced Study in Princeton.

The University of Chicago Press, Chicago 60637
The University of Chicago Press, Ltd., London

© 1975 by The University of Chicago
All rights reserved. Published 1975
Printed in the United States of America

Library of Congress Cataloging in Publication Data
Geertz, Hildred.
  Kinship in Bali.

  Includes bibliographical references.
  1. Kinship—Bali (Island) 2. Bali (Island)—Social life and customs. I. Geertz, Clifford, joint author. II. Title.
GN635.B3G42   301.42′1′095986   74–11621   ISBN 0–226–28515–4

For Erika and Benjamin
part of our life . . .

Contents

Illustrations

Tables

Preface

The fieldwork upon which this analysis is based was conducted in the principality of Tabanan, August–December, 1957, and in the principality of Klungkung, April–July, 1958, and this is the period of reference in the following pages. It was supported by a grant from the Rockefeller Foundation, administered by the Center for International Studies, Massachusetts Institute of Technology, Cambridge, Massachusetts. In the first portion of the fieldwork, the authors lived with a Brahmana (priestly caste) family in the town of Tabanan; in the second, with a commoner family in the village of Tihingan. Balinese vocabulary varies greatly from place to place. Terms reported here are by and large those current in the Klungkung area, but the reader should be aware that there are many alternate forms, and that often the same word has rather different meanings in different areas. We are indebted to Paul Friedrich, David Schneider, and Nur Yalman for critical readings of earlier drafts of this study, to James Boon for extensive advice and help throughout, and to our research associate, E. Rukasah, for assistance in gathering the data.

1

Culture, Kinship, and the Search for the Dadia

Balinese kinship customs and practices are, on first encounter, puzzlingly irregular and contradictory. The ethnologist can find very little agreement among his informants on many basic substantive issues, such as what forms of groupings of kinsmen the Balinese recognize, or what the essential structural characteristics of these groups are thought to be. Two fully cooperative and intelligent Balinese from the same village may give completely variant accounts on matters that the ethnologist believes to be crucial to his formulations. They may give strikingly different descriptions of the organization of the same concrete group of kinsmen, or they may even use completely different terms to identify that group. On a more abstract level, the same two informants may give entirely different lists of the various kinds of kinship groupings that they know about.

If the ethnologist attempts to solve his perplexities by ignoring analyses by Balinese of their own kinship relations and by painstakingly collecting information on actual groupings of kinsmen through genealogies and censuses, he finds new and equally puzzling inconsistencies. For instance, he might find that some persons belong to large, organized kingroups which have corporately owned common property, a social unity and identity recognized by the rest of the village, and an authority structure of leaders and members, while others within the same village have no such kingroups and are organized, instead, only into loosely related networks of elementary families.

He would find, further, on studying the corporately organized kingroups, that the members of only some of them have any detailed knowledge of their genealogical relationship, while the members of others have no interest in their forebears earlier than their own grandparents, nor in tracing their precise relationships to living persons whom they recognize as kin; that the memberships of some corporate groups are sharply localized while others have members scattered over a wide area in many different villages. These variations cannot be explained by regional differences, for Bali is a small island, and all Balinese share the same general beliefs, the same overall world-view, the same broad ideas on how their society is, and should be, arranged.

It is clear, then, that the first theoretical problem presented by the study of Balinese kinship is that of discerning some underlying principles which can account for this highly variable set of kinship practices. Allied to the task of finding unity in diversity—if there be any—is that of explaining the occurrence of each variant form of kinship organization. While these are, of course, essential issues in any study of social organization, they appear to be more pressing and difficult in the case of Bali.

Our main strategy for uncovering such an underlying order in Balinese kinship practices has been to make an analytic separation between the cultural dimension of this order and the social structural. By "the cultural dimension" we refer to those Balinese ideas, beliefs, and values which are relevant to their behavior as kinsmen—ideas, beliefs, and values that are abstracted from and distinguished from the actual regularities in that behavior, from the concrete interpersonal relationships which obtain "on the ground" among particular kinsmen. The relevant ideas, beliefs, and values are those having to do with, for instance, the perceived nature of the connection between parent and child, or between deceased ancestors and living persons, or between individuals who share (or think they share) a common parentage or common ancestry. Taken together, these assumptions form a culturally unique conceptual framework that the Balinese use to represent, to understand, and to organize their social relationships with their kinsmen.

A brief discussion of Evans-Pritchard's classic analysis of Nuer kinship may help to clarify this distinction.[1] Evans-Pritchard demonstrates in considerable detail that Nuer ideas of descent provide what he calls the "idiom" of the political structure. The fundamental cultural premises underlying the Nuer kinship "idiom" are the agnatic principle of exogamous lines of descent through males, together with the principle of segmentation, by which he means the Nuer assumption that all descent groups which are related through a set of full brothers are therefore socially equidistant and that all such groups can also be seen as one larger group united through the single father of the fraternal set.

Evans-Pritchard then goes on to show how this idiom is used by the Nuer to perceive or describe the relationship not only between consanguineal kin but also between whole villages, and even between larger territorial areas. That is to say, each village is thought of as a lineage segment which has kinship-like relations of "cousin-ship" with neighboring villages. And each such set of villages, while in segmentary opposition to *its* "cousins"—that is, to those village-sets which are seen to be in an identical structural "lineage" position— ally themselves as part of a larger maximal "lineage," against more distant territories. And, finally, the whole of a Nuer tribe is thought to be composed of the descendants of one ancestor, to be therefore a single comprehensive lineage. In actual fact, as Evans-Pritchard shows, such agnatic relationships do not obtain among all the members of any one village, nor between whole villages and territories, nor are the Nuer under any illusion that they do. The whole schema is a way of looking at and guiding a partly ordered complex of on-going social interactions.

Evans-Pritchard's use of the term "idiom" is close to our more explicit concept of the "cultural dimensions of kinship." In Bali, how-ever, in contrast to Nuerland, the case is not one of an entire society being organized in terms of a kinship idiom, but rather of conceptions of kinship being integrated with even more fundamental conceptions, stemming especially from the realms of religion, residence, and social rank, into a comprehensive cultural pattern. The Balinese "idiom" of kinship is not an autonomous system at all, but an integral part of a more inclusive "idiom," or "culture pattern," in which it plays a criti-cal but far from dominant role.

The Balinese pattern—a structure, essentially, of significant sym-bols—is very general and flexible in form. Because its elements are global and imprecise, it is easily interpreted in different ways by per-sons with different points of view. It does not describe the whole of Balinese kinship practices and institutions or even account for most of them, and therefore it permits considerable variation in its name.

It should be clearly understood, therefore, that we do not employ the concept of culture pattern here as a causal force but rather use it interpretatively—as a means for bringing together as aspects of a single structure of meaning what are apparently diverse social ex-pressions. It makes it possible for us to say, as the Balinese do, that the different kinds of kingroups that we found are all variations on a set of common ideational themes, themes which permeate and inform the whole of Balinese life.

We will, in chapter 5, the conclusion of the book, attempt to formulate these themes in exact and concrete terms and to develop the implications, some of them radical, such an approach to the study of "kinship" has for our view of the subject generally. Seeing "kinship systems" (a notion we shall, in fact, attempt to bring into some disrepute) against the background of the overall structure of symbols in terms of which a people organize their lives, leads, we shall try to show, to an analysis at once less formalistic and more faithful to the particular shape and pressure of those lives. Kinship, as Fred Eggan remarked many years ago now, has work to do: turning away from views of it as a complex of sentiments, a set of rules, or a table of categories to a consideration of it as a part of a way of being in the world, an expression of a view of what life is like and how persons ought, as a result, to treat with one another while passing through it, can give us a clearer idea of just what that work is and just how it manages to get done.

But all this—the Balinese conception of kinship, its elements, and its social consequences, as well as its fit with other Balinese views of religion, politics, status, or whatever—cannot be discussed separately and explicitly until the concrete description of the operation of kinship symbolization in Balinese life is itself complete, and it is to that that we now proceed.

The Search for the Dadia

What follows, then, is a study of Balinese social structure centering around the use of the symbols of kinship in organizing domestic and public life. Within this framework, we will be mainly concerned with three things: the formation of social groups and networks and the manner in which, once formed, they operate; the relationships of power and influence, that is, with domination, dependence, compliance, and cooperation; and the ways in which persons and groups can and do act to defend and so far as possible enhance their general social position within Balinese public life.

Such an aim leads one, or anyway led us, with great rapidity to a focus on a particular, and peculiar, social institution called, in most parts of Bali, the *dadia*. In certain respects this study is one long attempt to understand this institution, to grasp the nature of the group or groups for which the word "dadia" and its analogues stand.

None of the established categories of kinship analysis in anthropology—"lineage," "clan," "sib," "kindred," even the more recently popular "ramage" and "ambilateral descent group," seem properly to translate it, while at the same time none of them seem entirely off the mark, just ill-fitting, awkward, not quite right. The dadia, a term we shall henceforth use untranslated, is—or, anyway seems to be when first you look at it—an agnatic, preferentially endogamous, highly corporate group of people who are convinced, with whatever reason, that they are all descendants of one common ancestor. But such a description hardly completes the term's characterization. Indeed it rather truncates it, for one of the most interesting, and from a theoretical point of view most challenging, features of the dadia as a "kingroup" is its contingency, the fact that it does not necessarily form wherever there is a large enough group of agnatically related kinsmen. There are many Balinese who have recognized patri-kinsmen who never organize themselves, never incorporate into a dadia, never pull themselves together as any sort of kingroup at all. It was, as already mentioned, this "sometimes/sometimes not" quality of the dadia which created much of our puzzlement during the initial phases of fieldwork and which was, alas, but a harbinger of deeper puzzlements to come.

We found, or more exactly had forced upon us against our preconceptions, that the reasons for the emergence or nonemergence of a particular dadia from among a particular pool of kinsmen were multiple and only loosely interrelated, and had precious little to do with any autonomous operation of "kinship principles." First, there is the nature of the internal structure of the dadia as a corporate body, a structure which enables it to respond with extraordinary sensitivity to pressures of circumstance. Under various conditions, it can form, expand, contract, even dissolve. and does so with relative ease and flexibility. It is, in a word, adaptable. Second, it is multiplex. The conception that the Balinese have of the nature of kinship and of groups formed out of kinship connections classifies together as one entity several quite disparate—to foreign eyes—organizational forms. Indeed, dadias are such that about as strong an argument could be made that they are religious groups, or microcastes, or local factions, as that they are kingroups, and so the forces propelling their creation and maintaining their force have as much to do with notions about the nature of ultimate reality, the foundations of social rank, or the conflicts in interest among co-residents as about who has issued procreatively from whom. And, third, the dadia is set within, and in a sense in opposition to, what one can only call the general community, against which it is constantly seeking to assert itself and by which it is constantly being restrained, even undermined.

Taking this last point first, which is preliminary to grasping the others, by "community" we mean here at least two different things. There is the community that the commoners look toward, their villages or hamlets. And there is the community that the gentry, descendants of the nobles, kings, and priests of pre-twentieth-century Bali, look toward, the broad regional community of the "state," or as we shall call them, the principalities or kingdoms.[2]

By "gentry" we mean those persons whom the Balinese refer to as *triwangsa*, the "three (upper) castes." As we will try to show, the Hindu concept of "caste" is inappropriate and confusing when applied to Balinese status distinctions, but the Balinese themselves, less interested in precision, nonetheless use it to explain their own system to themselves. In these Hindu terms, the triwangsa represent all those of Wesia, Satria, and Brahmana status, as set against the Sudra, the commoners, who are all the rest of the Balinese.

Bali's gentry make up no more than ten percent of the population, but they are scattered, if unevenly, throughout most of the island's villages. In the nineteenth century, some of the gentry played important political roles, for Bali was ruled, or anyway presided over, by a group of competing kings and lords, each sovereign over a varying proportion of the commoners. Each king had a court of noble relatives and followers, who lived either near him or were placed in more distant villages in charge of outposts of the realm. In addition to these gentry who were active politically, there were many more who were not, who traced their aristocratic origins back to even earlier kings and lords. And finally, the Brahmana priests and their kinsmen, who are considered to be even higher, in spiritual terms, than the ruling groups, are also included in the gentry category.

To what extent the gentry and the commoner are true "status groups" in the Weberian sense—that is, to what extent they have separate spheres of interaction and distinct subcultures—is a much debated matter. Some writers have implied that the gentry are quite distinct, others tend to ignore the difference.[3] We take, and not merely out of caution, an intermediate position. The higher gentry of the capital towns certainly move, and have long moved, in circles quite aloof from commoners, although since they continually bring in commoner wives, their mothers and maternal relatives are, more often than not, commoners. But the lower gentry are nearly indistinguishable, in interaction patterns and way of life, from the commoners among whom they perforce live. When one is writing about Balinese religion, art, drama, ethos, or most kinds of economic activity, the distinction between gentry and commoner is at best peripheral and most often irrelevant.

But in the area of kinship the distinction is crucial. Among the gentry, the dadia takes the form of a nonlocalized corporate group, which is held together by an explicit table of father-to-son successions linking numerous people into a broad, region-wide web. Among the commoners, on the other hand, the dadia is a spatially restricted, though no less corporate, group within which any sort of genealogical linkage is virtually ignored and, beyond a generation or two, unknown, membership being determined by immediate patrifiliation. Institutions such as preferential endogamous marriage, virilocal residence, and unigenitural succession are present in both the gentry and commoner contexts, but the operation of these institutions is quite different in each. The gentry do not call their kingroups "dadia," but use other more elevated terms—*batur* is one of the most common— in keeping with their higher social position. Nonetheless, for all their surface differences, we shall try to show that gentry and commoner kingroups are but variants of a single underlying type, and that the principal reason for the variation in kingroup organization lies in the fact that the "community" has a different locus, makeup, and significance for gentry and commoners and that the effort on the part of individuals and groups to attain political power and social prestige consequently takes on quite different forms for the two groups.

The world of the commoners is that of the village or hamlet. The competition for prestige and position is largely confined within this quite narrow field. For commoners, the dadia serves as an effective means to gain and maintain personal and group ascendancy on a constricted social stage. The world of the gentry, on the other hand, is made up of other gentry, wherever they may reside. In nineteenth-century Bali, the competition among various gentry groups for the political allegiance of the commoners was conducted in terms of the noble dadia groups, but the broad field of all of Bali, or one or another of its major subregions, had very different characteristics for the struggle for position than did the small field of the commoner village. With the colonial administration and the subsequent establishment of the Indonesian Republic, the political position of the gentry has changed considerably, but the structure of their kinship groupings still reflects the earlier political situation.[4]

In any case, the dadia remains a central institution of Balinese society, and the struggle to understand it—what it is, how it is formed, how it operates—is critical to a comprehension of what "kinship in Bali" amounts to as a social force. The search for the dadia is, at bottom, a search for what the symbols that pertain to family life in Bali are, mean, and do.

Balinese Society: An Overview

Bali is a very fertile island. It has plenty of water, an equable tropical climate, and rich soils, making possible both the intensive cultivation of wet rice and the support of a large population. Famines and crop failures have been rare, and until the present century only disease and warfare prevented overcrowding. There were nearly two million people living on Bali in 1958, and the bulk of them were concentrated on the slopes and plains of the southern portion, within an area of no more than eight hundred square miles in extent. In this region, the heartland of Balinese culture, population densities commonly exceed one thousand persons per square mile.

In the center of the island, somewhat toward the north, is a group of mountains, volcanic cones interspersed with crater lakes, which provide a steady supply of water even through the marked five-month dry season, enabling irrigation farming during almost the entire year. Rivers radiate down from the mountains, each one paralleled by steep ridges, corrugating the landscape. Except in the narrow coastal plain, the ridges and river ravines make travel difficult from east to west, although it is fairly easy to go from the shore to the interior. The villages and towns are huddled on top of the ridges; roads and paths run mountain- and sea-ward along them, and the rice-paddies step down in terraces on either side.

Bali, historically, has been quite effectively cut off from the rest of the world. Located on the southern edge of the Indonesian archipelago, with the mountains on its northern side, Bali's back is turned on the commercially busy Java sea. Its harbors are few and small, the southern coast is lashed by heavy seas, and the Balinese people have never been particularly attracted to either sailing or fishing. Until recent years the land itself has been rich enough to make the population self-sufficient.

The last cultural importation of major significance (prior, that is, to the past twenty-five years) was completed at least five hundred years ago, and probably considerably earlier. This was the influence of Indian culture, at first direct, then, after the eleventh century, filtered through Hinduized Java, Bali's nearest neighbor. When in the fifteenth century the great Hindu-Javanese kingdom of Madjapahit fell to the onslaught of Islamized coastal sultanates (the traditional date is 1478), many of its princes, scholars, and priests fled to Bali, bringing with them a vast store of religious lore and classical literary manuscripts, and—so the court chronicles declare—established themselves as Bali's cultural political elite. This event, however, probably had more of a reinforcing than a revolutionary impact on Balinese society (though the Balinese themselves think otherwise), for the Javanese immigrants and whatever cultural innovations they brought were soon absorbed. After that time Bali was largely left alone to follow its own course of growth, and was bypassed by both the flood of Islamic belief that covered much of the rest of Indonesia and by the subsequent colonial intrusion which so markedly transformed the archipelago from the seventeenth century on.

Direct Dutch administration was not imposed on south Bali until the first decade of this century, and even then its impact was small, being largely limited to the construction of a supravillage government. The Dutch government sought to conserve traditional Balinese culture and discouraged both new commercial agriculture and Christian missionary activity. However, the forces which were set in motion by the colonial government have been carried forward more rapidly by the Republic of Indonesia since 1950, and some of those forces, notably popular education and increased political and commercial contact with the outside world, are beginning to transform traditional society. For the most part, however, Balinese material technology, values, and social organization, especially at the village level, remain but barely changed from what they were in the nineteenth century.

Religion

Balinese religion is a highly revised version of Hinduism, a variant which stresses the latter's ritualistic and dramatic aspects over its philosophical and mystical ones. It is by no means merely borrowed but contains many elements unique to Bali and omits many that are important in India. Despite these historical ties with a sophisticated world religion, with a philosophical and poetic sacred literature, and despite the fact that in Bali itself there is a high-ranking hereditary priesthood—the Brahmana *pedandas*, who are dedicated to the intellectual preservation of the ancient religion—there are few signs in

Bali of a distinct separation between bearers of the Great Tradition, the world religion of Hinduism, and various little traditions. There is no formation of social groups based on their relatively greater adherence to a sophisticated folk theology as against a folk animism, as is found, for instance, in India or even in Java.[5] The distinction between gentry and commoner is fundamental in Balinese social structure, but it is not paralleled by an equally sharp cultural distinction: both gentry and commoner, as well as Brahmana priest and layman, hold much the same religious beliefs and participate in much the same rituals.

In very general terms, Balinese religion can be characterized as "public," "social," and "civic." Worship is, by and large, collective and external, a matter of visible dramatic actions. Private silent prayer, inward contemplation, and personal religious speculation are all unusual, though they of course occur. There is, in the general population, but sporadic concern for either theological or ethical reflection, for spiritual ecstasy, for divine communion, or for personal feelings of worshipful awe, and to the degree such interests are present in Bali among individuals with a special bent for them, they are covert, implicit, unverbalized, and, at least until recently, socially unimportant.[6]

Ceremonies are frequent, elaborate, and involve lengthy preparations. The most common form is the temple festival, in which the gods are formally entreated to descend into the human realm for a few days, during which time they reside in a temple and are feted as honored guests.[7] The temple is gaily decorated, there are joyful processions to meet the gods, dances and dramas are performed for their diversion, gamelan orchestras play, and, most important, all sorts of foods, each carefully decorated in traditional ways, are ritually offered to the gods. Every detail of these culinary offerings is rigidly prescribed, and the slightest deviation is thought to invite the anger of the gods. While everyone participates in the making of the offerings, their actual presentation to the gods is carried out by temple priests or by high Brahmana priests. The food must be first sanctified by the priest, by the ritual sprinkling of holy water. This holy water is later sprinkled over those members of the congregation who desire it, to spiritually "cleanse" them.

Purification through sanctified water is considered by the Balinese to be one of the central pillars of their religion; in fact, they often call it the "holy water religion" (*agama tirta*). The notion of spiritual uncleanliness is equally important: contact with death, menstruation, physical deformity, sexual intercourse, insanity, sexual perversion, are all dangerously unclean. Such pollution (*sebel*) is a kind of irreverence, an insult to the gods. Anyone in such a contaminated condition may not enter a temple for fear of bringing disaster onto the entire congregation.

Thus, the gods are proud, they strictly uphold the rules for proper respect for their superior rank, and their displeasure falls not on the individual transgressor but on the temple group as a whole. But the rules are fairly clear, and if one is properly cautious and circumspect, one need not worry. And the gods like to laugh and they enjoy fine music and dance: one can have a great deal of pleasure at the gods' festivals. The atmosphere at a temple ceremony is neither fearful nor solemn, but happily busy, matter-of-fact, and, for the uninitiated Westerner, bewilderingly without focus.

Despite the insistence by thoughtful Balinese that their religion is really monotheistic, their gods, or the manifestations of their one god, are myriad. There are many different kinds, some of high rank, some of low. There are demons in addition to the gods—and the manner of their placation is somewhat different—but their exact moral status is unclear, for some demons are thought to be the "servants" of the gods, while others are thought to be the evil "aspect" of a normally benevolent spirit. The concepts of good and evil are not really relevant to the Balinese system, for neither gods nor demons are felt to be directly concerned with human ethical behavior as such. They appear to be much more intent on enforcing the appropriate deference due them. Few of these spirits have a very distinct personal identity; they are not usually referred to by a name but rather by the designation of the altar or temple at which they are worshipped.

Another significant trait of the Balinese deities is their great physical mobility. Supernatural beings are thought to be traveling around— "blowing through the island like the wind"—stopping at many different temples. They may even enter human beings, causing the well-known Balinese trance phenomena.[8] A god who is most closely associated with some particular temple may have special altars or small temples to him in many quite distant places. These lesser altars and temples are often called *pasanggrahan*, a word also used for a king's temporary rest house where he stops when on tour away from his palace. We will refer to these pasanggrahan altars and temples as "way-station temples."

Apart from the temples and their celebration, there are also a great many other kinds of religious activities and practitioners: the dragon-and-witch dramatic trance ritual, the Brahmana priests, the rituals to exorcise demons from village and houseyard, personal life-cycle rituals of all sorts, the funeral and cremation ceremonies, curing and witchcraft, and spirit mediums.[9]

Social Organization

As noted, religion is not mere creed in Bali; nor is it mere piety. It is a public fact—there are few areas of human life which are not felt to be permeated with transcendental significance. The entire social structure is suffused with religious concern, and almost every kind of social relationship, from the most collective to the most personal, is either necessitated by or validated by ritual. A full study of Balinese religion would entail close investigation of virtually every aspect of the society—from farming and marketing methods to government and kinship. And conversely, any study of Balinese social structure must take as its baseline the Balinese religious concepts and ceremonies.

The religious basis: the temple system as a social matrix. Mere statistics on the numbers of temples in Bali illustrate their social importance: there are, conservatively, over twenty thousand temples, and this number does not include the houseyard temples of which there must be at least three hundred thousand, nor the countless minor altars found at crossroads, springs, great trees, individual rice paddies, and so on.[10] This in a population of—in 1960—about two million. Every adult has specific and demanding ties to more than one temple, often to as many as ten. The upkeep and ritual attention required by all these temples involves the almost daily participation of everyone, and most of the renowned Balinese dancing, music, and plastic arts derive their vitality from their roles in the temple celebration.

Every temple, whatever its function or size, is the center of activities of a specific corporate social group. It is a permanent, well-organized association with commonly owned property. In addition to carrying out the regular ritual festivals connected with the temple, the group is responsible for the physical maintenance of the temple, for its decoration with renewed stone carvings and colorful cloth banners, for its cleanliness, and for the provision of small daily or weekly offerings. The priest of each temple is usually chosen from among its members, either by hereditary succession, popular election, or divine intercession via the trance of one of the worshippers. The size of a congregation (*pemaksan*, from *paksa*, "obligatory work") may range from but a few people, as in the case of a houseyard temple, through several hundred up to tens of thousands, as in the case for a few temples representing almost the entire population of Bali. Since the duties of the congregation are generally considerable, there is usually, in addition to the priest, a secular chairman or council in charge of the coordination of work and of the group's treasury.

Temple groups have certain structural features which, no matter what kind of social function the congregation performs, directly influence their form. First, temple membership is exclusive; that is, only those who are members may worship there. One cannot, as in Islam and Christianity, stop in at any temple and pray; for this privilege, in Bali, one must be in some sense a regular member of the congregation. Of course, it is not too difficult to become a member of most Balinese temples. One may learn, for instance, from a dream or a spirit medium that one ought to be worshipping there, or one may move to a new village and automatically take over the obligation to attend the local temples. But there are always specified grounds on which the obligation rests.

Second, the entire congregation as a corporate whole is responsible for the adequacy of its ritual observances. Any lapses are thought to bring retribution upon the group as a whole or on every person in it, not merely upon the person who made the original error or transgression. This feature of group responsibility gives a considerable degree of coerciveness to the group's power over the acts of its individual members, a highly charged pressure for conformity in particular matters.

Lastly, there is the "way-station" relationship between a temple and its branch temples, in which the god of a central temple makes flying visits to certain other ones. This is almost entirely a ritual relationship, and is not necessarily paralleled by social obligations. The establishment of a way-station temple, for instance by a migrating group, is completely optional, as is setting up an altar within a local temple for the god of a more distant one. Such a way station is merely a matter of convenience for the worshippers, to save them the trouble of long journeys to fulfill their ritual duties. However, the way station principle can affect the manner in which social groups can be linked, most especially, as we shall see, kinship groups, for it provides a tangible means for symbolizing group relationships of increasing inclusiveness where such symbolization is desired.

The social groups which are formed around any temple usually have other functions besides worship, such as community welfare, social control, agricultural cooperation, indication of rank, political

allegiance to a king, and so on. We will discuss immediately below
the various types of temple groups in turn, according to their secular
functions; and in the process of this discussion all the major aspects
of traditional Balinese social organization will be touched upon.
Temple groups to be described are: the *désa adat*; the hamlet; the
irrigation society; the title group; the kingdom; the group that centers
around a Brahmana priest; the club; and the kingroup.[11]

It is important to keep in mind as these various types of temple
groups are examined, that no two of them within a community have
exactly the same membership in terms of concrete individuals. There
is never (or hardly ever) a precise identity in social constituents between any two of these temple groups. For instance, a given village
and the particular agricultural society for the rice fields near it are
rarely, if ever, composed entirely of the same people, for the agricultural society will draw on members of other villages, and some of the
villagers will not be part of the agricultural society.

Again, Balinese social organization cannot be understood if it is
thought of as a number of distinct village communities, each a
bounded monad with an independent internal structure, each repeating the form of the next. Rather it must be seen as a complex pattern
of interpenetrating groupings. If a simile can give any clarification,
the overall social organization is not like a repetitive wallpaper de-
sign; rather it is like an intricately embroidered texture, with many
overlapping and irregular interpenetrating shapes, with few sharp
junctions or edges. We will now take up each of these groupings, one
by one, seeing each one in terms of the temple at its focus.

The desa adat and its congregations. One type of temple group
which is of fundamental importance in Balinese social organization is
the *désa adat*.[12] In most cases, this group is not a single society, but
consists of a number of cooperating congregations which support together a set of related temples. The temples of the desa adat are
called collectively the *Kahyangan Tiga.*

Kahyangan Tiga means literally "the three great temples," and the
term stands for a set of three temples which are thought to protect
the general welfare of the residents of the locality immediately surrounding them. There are several hundred sets of Kahyangan Tiga
temples scattered over the island. While ideally they come in sets of
three, in actuality they vary from two to four, or even more, per set.

The first temple of the ideal three is called the *pura pusèh*, which
can be translated as the "[village] origin-temple" (*pura* means "temple"; *pusèh*, "navel"). Various gods are worshipped in the village

origin-temple, but the main ones are an anonymous host of deified predecessors of the present inhabitants of the village. The second temple is called the *pura dalem,* the "[village] death-temple," which is usually located next to the cemetery. In this temple, the gods in their evil aspects are placated, together with the still-dangerous souls of the newly dead of the village, who have been buried in the cemetery but have yet to be disinterred and then given the proper holy cremation by means of which the dead spirits are transfigured into deities. The third temple in the trio is called the *pura balé agung,* "the temple of the great council [of the gods]." This temple is primarily concerned with the fertility of the farmland in its neighborhood, most notably the irrigated rice-land. Because of its agricultural emphasis, the great-council temple usually has, in addition to its local congregation from the settlements lying near it, also the support of one or more irrigation societies (*subak*) from the nearby rice fields.

Every local community (or, more precisely, every houseyard) in Bali belongs to a Kahyangan Tiga set. A few atypical villages possess a perfect set of three temples which are worshipped by a single unitary congregation. But the greater number of Kahyangan Tiga congregations are subdivided in various ways and embrace more than one community. In many cases there are several death-temples, each with its own congregation, to a single origin-temple and great-council temple. Often the worshipping unit has only an origin-temple and a death-temple, while the great-council temple is absent or is located inside a courtyard of the origin-temple.

One extremely important function of the Kahyangan Tiga set is essentially legal: in most pura puseh a written charter is preserved, a set of rules for behavior, some narrowly ritual, others more broadly moral, which must be followed by the members of the congregation.[13] The areas of social life which may be regulated by such a charter include: burial, cremation, and the length of periods of mourning according to social status, closeness of kinship to the deceased and so on; requirements for membership in the component hamlet councils; modes of public announcement of marriage and inheritance settlements; prohibition of various specified acts which are considered defiling to the temple's territory. The document also details the particular fines to be levied for infraction of these rules. The regulations are sacred, and it is extremely dangerous to transgress them, for the wrath of both the gods and the demons will be brought down upon the entire populace of the desa adat. The physical manuscript itself, a set of incised palm-blades (*lontar, rontal*), is an object of worship in itself, and may not be exposed to human view except under ritual conditions.

No two such charters are the same, and the differences in content of the rules can be considerable. For instance, in one desa adat a man may be required to retire from the hamlet council when his youngest son enters adulthood and takes a seat on the council; in the next adjacent locality he may have to step down at a much earlier age, when his eldest son reaches maturity. The consciousness of the differences between the rules of one desa adat and the next is very strong and bears with it an intense awareness of "we" versus "they."

In many parts of Bali there is a traditional official at the head of each desa adat, who is in charge of its sacred charter and of the temple or temples with which it is associated. He is usually called the *bendésa adat* and is consulted by anyone in the component congregation who is in doubt about the application of a rule. He has no power, however, to enforce his judgments; such power lies only in the hands of the component communities, represented by the hamlet councils, which sit in judgment on wrongdoers and levy fines or other punishments.

As a social form, the desa adat serves primarily symbolic functions—it is a stretch of sacred space. It stands for the consensus of customary regulations which holds within a particular locality and for the attention of the gods to the welfare of those settled in that locality. But as a community, in the sense of a certain density of reciprocal social obligations among members, the desa adat does not as a rule have the immediate social importance of its components, the hamlets. It defines sociality; they produce it.

The hamlet and its citizens. As the implementing organ of the sacred demands of the desa adat, the hamlet (*banjar*) becomes the main organization responsible for local regulation, for the preservation of general moral behavior, and, thus, for the general public welfare. For the Balinese commoner, the hamlet is the most important single set of people in his life, outside of family and kingroup. It is his primary community: he lives from birth to death in it, the land for his house is (in most cases) lent to him by the hamlet, he usually marries within it, his work groups (such as for harvesting) and musical-dramatic clubs are mostly recruited from within it. The ritual work required by the temples of the Kahyangan Tiga and the many mortuary ceremonies are very time-consuming and are all under the aegis of the hamlet. Festivities of a lesser, more private form, such as weddings, tooth-filings, and those connected with infancy, are usually invitational, and the guests are, by and large, members of a man's own hamlet.

In most of our theoretical discussions in this book about commoner social organization, we mean by the term "community" that group more precisely termed the "hamlet" or banjar, as in such phrases as "the opposition between kingroup and community." Nevertheless, there are so many exceptions to this identity of banjar and community, so many other sorts of groups which may play the role of "the community" in a commoner's life, so many sharp limitations on the power and functions of the hamlet, that it is far from resembling the ideal-types of Redfield's "small community" or of Goris's and Korn's "village-republic" (*dorpsrepubliek*).[14]

The hamlet council, or *krama banjar*, is made up of all adult men who are citizens of the hamlet. Each member must have a woman partner. Usually this is his wife, but, in the absence of a wife, a sister, mother, or daughter may fill the place. Should he not have such a partner, he normally cannot be a member of the council, for many of the duties of a council member require women's work, such as the manufacture of offerings for temple ceremonies. The definition of "adult" varies in different desa adats: in some cases a man achieves majority when he marries, in others when he has his first child, and in a few places only at the death of his father, whose place he then takes. In the latter type of hamlet, the council is much smaller, there is a limited number of seats, and only one of a set of brothers occupies a seat at a time, the others merely assisting him with the work of the hamlet. Similarly, the rules for retirement from the council vary from desa adat to desa adat.

The hamlet council meets regularly, usually every thirty-five days, on a day sacred to the origin-temple. The meeting is held in a courtyard of the temple, although if there is a *balé banjar*, a structure built especially for holding such meetings and for dramatic performances of various sorts, it may be held there. The meeting opens and closes with various rituals, and discussion is held in a very dignified manner. The authority of the hamlet council is based on unanimity; no decision is made until the entire group has thoroughly discussed it, both in the formal meeting and outside it. If there is any vocal opposition to a proposed course of action, it is usually abandoned, at least for the moment.

The group chooses one or more chairmen, usually called *klian banjar* ("the elders of the hamlet"), who have no independent authority but merely expedite the group's wishes, oversee the work, and collect the contributions for the treasury. These posts are rotated within traditional periods of time, periods varying from banjar to banjar. The chairmen may also have several assistants, with various titles and tasks, such as announcing to villagers scheduled work or providing ceremonial betel for the meetings. These assistants are, like the klians themselves, chosen by rotation, and their number depends on the size of the hamlet or the degree of factioning within the hamlet which might make necessary a representative from each segment.

A hamlet council is variable in size, but it rarely has more than seventy-five households as members. If the population within its domain grows, it is usually split eventually into two or more hamlets. These splits may be on territorial lines, a common one being into "northern group" and "southern group." But it may as likely be on a nonterritorial basis, with, for instance, every other household in the settlement being arbitrarily assigned to the new hamlet.

The hamlet council has a considerable amount of property. Very often it has authority over houseland occupancy, and it has the power to grant or take away the right of a family to live on a certain plot. This gives the council a powerful lever for social control, an ultimate sanction of ostracism, and a tight rein over the selection of new members of the community, a power which it does not hesitate to use.

The public secular buildings, as well as the temple or temples entrusted to it, are also the property of the hamlet council. Such structures as the hamlet meeting hall (the *balé banjar*), the circular pit for cockfights (*wantilan*), and the market sheds must be erected by and maintained by the council. In addition, all roads and paths running through the hamlet are its responsibility. Many hamlets own an expensive set of gamelan instruments, which when not in use in local ceremonies are frequently rented out to other groups or individuals.

Much of the work connected with these undertakings is done by the members of the hamlet themselves. Strict records are kept of amount of work put in, and fines are imposed for those who miss or are late on the job. However, financial outlays are made possible in a variety of ways. The hamlet may levy a tax on the rice harvested from its members' land: the hamlet council as a group harvests the crop, and that fraction of it which would have been paid them for their labor is placed directly in the hamlet granary for later sale. Some hamlets own a plot of rice land, a wagon, or even a bus, the rentals for which also go into the hamlet treasury.

Burials and cremations are matters of high sacred concern to the hamlet. At a death, the entire hamlet council is required to come to the bereaved family's courtyard, equipped with tools for making the litter and digging the grave. Roll is taken and fines imposed for those who do not attend. However, in many villages where gentry are present, the gentry may be excused, for religious reasons, from the death rituals but not from the other activities of the hamlet council. In such cases, the cremation activities are said to be carried out by a separate organization, usually called the *patus*, which is virtually the same in membership as the hamlet council but with the omission of certain gentry. This "second order" distinction between the banjar and the patus illustrates the extent to which Balinese social structure can be functionally specific, with each purpose and each set of rules being formally portioned out to a separate organization.

The irrigation society and its members. The arrangements for sharing of labor and costs of irrigation and of agricultural ritual obligations are all completely independent of village governmental structure and of both the traditional and the present-day state political apparatuses. Irrigation is accomplished through an ingenious and ancient system, reference to which can be found in Balinese texts as far back as the first millenium A.D. Because the rice terraces are situated on the slopes of the river ravines, in many cases high above the stream, the rivers must be tapped at considerable distances upstream from the fields and the water led down over the irregular terrain to each set of rice fields, often miles away. Each major dam and sluice on a river, together with its set of canals, tunnels, aqueducts, and lesser sluices, is built and maintained by an association of the owners of the land which is being served, such an association, along with the land over which it has control, being called a *subak*. Membership in a subak follows automatically from landownership (plots may be bought, rented, held in pawn, or inherited) or from possession of sharecropping rights on land within the irrigation section. Subaks are generally small. One subak that we studied had 70 hectares and 197 members and another had 159 hectares and 439 members. These were both of moderate size.

The subak, too, is basically a temple group having at the center of its concern the worship at a set of temples. The sacred aspect of the irrigation society is what gives it its strong authority over its members, for any transgression or omission is felt to be supernaturally threatening to all members and their crop. Several of the temples are located at the major sluices, and one stands somewhere near the middle of the rice fields. It is usually on the grounds of this central temple that the irrigation society holds its monthly meetings, much like the banjar. The society as a unit also usually participates in the support of a temple in a nearby settlement, called the pura balé agung, one of the Kahyangan Tiga temples.

The group is usually drawn from different settlements in the surrounding area, and the members of any one hamlet generally belong to several different irrigation societies. The societies, thus, are usually composed of persons of differing social rank, gentry side by side with commoners, but within the society itself each man's social status and influence is the same as that of everyone else. Decisions are reached by consensus in the meetings and are enforced by the members themselves, with punishments by fining, or, ultimately, expulsion. Heads (*klian subak*) and other officers are chosen by election or rotation. In addition to maintenance of the physical irrigation system, the irrigation society controls timing of cultivation processes during the course of the year, and, perhaps most important in the eyes of its members, each society is responsible for religious observances in the several agricultural temples and altars in its domain.

As explained, there are a fairly large number of irrigation societies along a single river course. Consequently, there are opportunities for cooperation among the connected irrigation societies, for instance in the rituals performed at the river's head before the beginning of the planting season. Conversely, there may also be opportunities for conflict between societies, for example, when water is scarce. In the past when quarrels arose between irrigation societies, a paramount king or several influential lords were sometimes requested by the farmers to arbitrate, as disinterested observers—not as sovereigns. The real power of the nobility over the irrigation societies was as weak as that extended over the hamlet councils. Today the provincial government has a similarly insulated relationship toward the irrigation societies. While it has attempted to take a slightly more active role, in the synchronization of planting so that water is not wasted, in building large dams and sluices, and in extending agricultural advice, it too has had to remain outside as merely an interested onlooker with little direct influence over the societies.

The title group and its titlebearers. The distinction that Balinese make between pure status (one's prestige based on inherited title) on the one hand, and political power as measured by the possession of subjects or of office on the other, is of profound importance. Wealth, talent, and personal behavior are also irrelevant to social rank and to the degree and type of deferential behavior one merits. Nearly every

Balinese, commoner as well as gentry, has a title of some sort for which he proudly, even touchily, demands proper recognition.

But, though titles are treated with utmost seriousness, there are extensive areas of social life which are unaffected by them and by the relative prestige of the participants. The main fields in which title has impact are etiquette and marriage. Seating arrangements, posture, and style of speech are all directly affected by the relative rank of the titles of the actors. Marriage is sharply regulated by title: if it is at all possible one should marry someone of the same or equivalent title, and in no case may a woman marry a man with a title lower than that of her father. In earlier times, when a woman of the gentry married beneath herself, the punishment was death or banishment. Today it is ostracism by her family, by the gentry, and by her village as a whole.

Because of the narrowness and specificity of this system of prestige stratification, the term "caste" when applied to Balinese social organization is only roughly appropriate, and in some ways misleading. While the Balinese terms for some of the customs concerned and some names for ranks have been borrowed from India, the actual system is quite different. There is no intricate division of labor, no reciprocal exchange of goods and services according to ascribed membership in different status groups. The titles are not generally associated with occupations and, with the exception of the Brahmana priests, possession of a title never entails exclusive right to an occupation. While possession of the same or similar title can become the basis for formation for certain kinds of organized groups (most particularly, the corporate kingroups we shall discuss at length below), titles in themselves do not signify membership in any such group. Further, the relative rank of titles is far from fully agreed upon by all. There are very few customs of ceremonial avoidance between persons of different title, and, with the exception of foods which have been offered to ancestral gods in certain rituals and which may be later consumed only by the worshipper and his family, there are no restrictions on commensality between holders of different titles.

The titles are broadly classified into two general categories, the titles of gentry and the titles of commoners. The first set are referred to as Triwangsa, "three peoples," for it comprises the titles borne by the three upper "twice-born" ranks of Brahmana, Satria, and Wesia. Such people are also often called *anak jero*, "insiders," meaning those who dwell inside the walls of palaces. Correspondingly, individuals bearing the other category of titles, those of the common peasants, are popularly referred to as *anak jaba*, "outsiders." These lower-bracket titlebearers make up about nine-tenths of the Balinese population.[15]

One of the main differences between gentry and commoner titles is that the gentry are addressed by their title, while commoners' titles are used only in reference. That is, the name of each member of the gentry is always preceded by his or her title, Gusti, Dewa, Ida Bagus, and so on. Commoners, however, rarely mention their titles, which are employed only when there is a need to indicate someone's precise social location. In fact there is considerable ambivalence of feeling among commoners about their titles, for each one thinks privately that his title is really superior to those of the others and he can usually recite mythological history as "proof" of this fact, while at the same time there are strong resentments against fellow commoners who act superior, who appear to try to lift themselves above the rest. As a result the whole matter of commoner titles is somewhat subterranean, and in some areas of Bali, especially western Bali, where the social structure is simpler and less rigid, many families claim to have "forgotten" their titles or not to have any at all. In most of central Bali, however, every member of each village knows the titles of all the others in his village.

Gentry and commoners live side by side, although there are some hamlets which are composed exclusively of one or the other. Those villages—today's district capitals are among them—where a powerful noble or king once had a court often now have a very high proportion of gentry, while villages which were remote from such power centers have very few or none. Everyday social intercourse between gentry and commoners is usually unaffected by prestige differences, as long as the forms of etiquette are observed. However, in certain respects the attention of the gentry is turned outward and away from the village, toward the affairs of gentry in other villages or in the court, while commoners' interest is turned inward onto strictly local matters. In many areas gentry, particularly those of high title, do not participate in hamlet council decisions or projects, but hold themselves aloof. Endogamy within the title group is interpreted quite differently by gentry and commoners, the former being much more strict, choosing wives from a distance rather than break the rule. Commoners on the other hand, if they find that title-endogamy is impossible, generally prefer to marry another member of the same hamlet. The consequence is that gentry familial ties are widespread and regional, while commoner kin ties are confined to the hamlet of residence. These differences, of which more will be made below, were especially functional to the contrasting roles that gentry and commoner played in the traditional political system, with the gentry serving as a horizontally integrating network which interpenetrated the highly localized commoner groups.

Titles are borne by individuals, they do not refer to solidary groups. They can, however, serve as the pretext or basis for the formation of such a group. For instance, in villages where there are sizeable proportions of gentry, various organizational recognitions of title distinction may arise: the gentry of assorted titles may have a special temple in addition to regular local temples, or the village death-temple may be divided in half, with one side of the temple reserved for gentry worship and the other for commoners. Many gentry usually attend ceremonies at the family temple of the local paramount lord, claiming distant familial connection. Commoners often travel miles twice a year to worship at a temple of their title. Such acts are, however, individual, and there is very little feeling that all persons with the same title, no matter where they live, necessarily have any special duties or rights with respect to one another.[16]

The kingdom and its subjects.[17] When the Dutch entered Bali early this century, the complex indigenous political system that they found was basically not territorial in nature. The many small competing kingdoms were dependent for their strength on personal ties between lords and their commoner subjects irrespective of their landholdings or place of residence. Nor were the boundary regions between kingdoms clearly defined. Usually they consisted of intermediate areas where villages or even subjects of different kings were scattered in among each other, living side by side.

Within each king's domain, the power over subjects was further subdivided among a group of lords and then further among groups of lesser lords. In actuality most peasants were not subject directly to a king but to a lesser lord who then gave his (conditional) loyalty to one of the higher lords. Each such lord or noble was sovereign only within the range of this personal influence, and each was a threat to all others, even to his nominal superiors. Some gentry had been granted their subjects directly by a king or lord, but others held them by virtue of inheritance or from conquest and therefore quite independently of any higher authority. A king or lord who could command the loyalty of a large group of brothers and cousins had a distinct advantage over his competitors, for he could entrust them with power with less fear of betrayal. Nonetheless, wars of brother against brother, and cousin against cousin, were not uncommon.

The political system of the traditional Balinese state was essentially one of multiple interconnected networks of personal, but at the same time sharply limited, ties between superior and subordinate. These networks took the form of highly unstable pyramids of authority; at the apex of each was a king, prince, or lord. Such a system, based as it was on constant reassertion of personal dominance, encouraged political machination, palace intrigues, and war.

The relationship between the state, as represented by these lords in their constant maneuvering for power, and the villages was not a simple one. It was not true, as has been argued by a number of writers, that the lords characteristically treated their subjects with barbaric cruelty and unbridled economic exploitation. Nor was it true, as—somewhat illogically—has also been maintained by the same writers, that the two groups, the gentry and the peasants, lived in worlds of their own, insulated from one another.[18]

A lord's power over his subjects was sharply circumscribed by customary law. He had the right to expect the subject to fight in war for him, but these "wars" were commonly short, fighting often stopping at nightfall or, sometimes, with the first death in battle, and only rarely did they involve extended campaigns. They were fought on foot, using only knives, spears, and bludgeons. Much more important as an obligation than the military service, was the subject's duty to participate in the heavy preparations for the lord's periodic religious rituals, which were accompanied by great feasts and dramatic displays. Each subject was expected to supply a certain amount of produce, but he was fed well in return; he had also to do a certain amount of work, but he then became part of the enthusiastic audience at the show. These religious rituals and artistic performances remain today a climactic part of Balinese life. In fact, it is not inaccurate to state that, in traditional Bali, ritual did not so much support the political system as the reverse: the political system buttressed and made possible a good deal of ritual activity.

These various traditional political nets—the kings, lords, and their subjects—even though they were not territorial in makeup, nonetheless had the characteristics of temple groups. Each important royal or lordly family maintained its kingroup temple in a style that moved it out of the purely familial realm into the public political world. Subjects, dependents, and retainers, as well as family members, participated, in various ways, in all the major ceremonies and obligations of the temple. In addition, there are a good number of temples whose congregations consist of the entire kingdom, commoners and gentry alike. These temples are still maintained today, even though the kingdoms as political entities have long been abolished. The great temple of Besakih, on the high slopes of the volcanic mountain Gunung Agung, is essentially a cluster of such kingdom-temples, each supported by a different region of the island of Bali.

Despite the deep-going ritual allegiance that commoners paid to their kings and lords, the political influence that the gentry had over village affairs was limited. Lords who had subjects in a particular village did not interfere in affairs that were considered to fall under the sovereignty of the hamlet council. Only in cases involving members of different hamlets, cases which were so difficult that the hamlets involved felt they could not handle them, was a lord called in to arbitrate. The strict autonomy of the hamlet, in regard to the kings and lords, was ensured by the fact that the subjects of each lord were usually dispersed over the countryside, rather than clustered together in a single locality. Ordinarily, no lord held as subjects the entire population of any one village or even of one hamlet. In any single village, the various members would typically owe fealty to a number of different lords. Thus the power and influence of even a very powerful lord over village affairs was sharply curtailed by the presence of subjects of competing lords. Even the paramount lord of an area, the "king," did not hold a majority of the people in his region as personal subjects, but was able to make claims on their loyalty only by way of the lesser lords.

Villagers, in nineteenth-century Bali, had ties of other sorts to the nobility, obligations which strained against rather than reinforced their political ties as subjects to their lord, for these ties were usually to lords other than the one to whom they were subject. One was the paying of taxes on rice land, or, more accurately, on the water used to irrigate the rice. The unit of area taxed by one lord was a set of rice fields which were irrigated from a single source of water. The lord was usually granted the power to tax by the paramount lord in the area, and took the tax in the form of a share in the harvest. As has been mentioned, the landholders within such an irrigation section, even a small one, were rarely people from only one village, and not very many of them were likely also to be subjects of the lord to whom they paid the water tax.

The second kind of tie that some villagers had to a lord, before this century as well as today, was that of sharecropper. This was, traditionally, a strictly economic arrangement, and the lord did not have, or even prefer, to choose his own subjects for tenants, but tended to select someone who lived near the rice field in question or who was an exceptionally good worker. There appears to have been no particular tendency for subjects and share-tenants to be the same persons.

Consequently, a peasant often had important relationships with as many as three different lords, one to whom he was subject, one to whom he paid tax, and a third for whom he worked. Obviously, this kind of crosscutting distribution of subordinate roles limited the power of those in the superior positions.

Today in Bali, these kingdoms, with their spreading networks of obligations and privileges, are not merely a memory in the minds of the older men. While the fundamental political structure was progressively transformed, by the Dutch in the 1910s and 1920s, and by the republican government in the 1950s, into a modern bureaucratic administration, many elements persist, affecting the way this administration functions. The presence of the traditional relationships of authority and prestige is felt, however, most particularly in contemporary social stratification and in kinship behavior.

Among the first governing acts of the Dutch was the abolishing of the peasant subjects' obligations to the gentry, the elimination of all duties of a ceremonial, military, and taxpaying nature. However, the institution of sharecropping remained. In some principalities a good deal of the personal rice land of the paramount lord was confiscated at the conquest; but most of the gentry were permitted to retain their land, and it was this land which continued to be parcelled out for sharecropping to the peasants. The periodic great ceremonies and festivals of the gentry, formerly made possible through the support of their subjects, were of such central value to all Balinese that the gentry did not give them up. In place of the subjects' contributions to the prince's ceremonies, the sharecroppers on his land are now required to give, in addition to their agricultural labor, certain amounts of work and produce. Thus a new kind of "feudal"—or "feudal-looking"—tie, one based on rights to work on the lord's rice land, rather than on the radically nonterritorial subjecthood of former times, emerged and continues to be of high social importance.

Another significant modern carry-over from the traditional political structure lies in the area of social stratification. In the nineteenth century a sharp distinction was made between gentry who actually wielded political power and those gentry families that merely held Triwangsa titles. The former gentry-with-power were granted a great deal more respect than the others, a respect which their descendants continue to receive in the present day. These families provide much of the personnel, at all levels, in the present-day bureaucratic administration, and in general grandsons of the lesser lords and of the kings' viziers continue today to have more wealth, power, and influence than other Triwangsa whose grandfathers were not politically important in the ancien régime.

The republican government and its citizens. In place of this involved and knotted set of traditional political arrangements, the Dutch sought to create a thoroughly rationalized territorial government.

Adjacent hamlets were grouped into a unit (the *perbekelan*) we will call the government village. Over each government village a headman was appointed, called in most localities, the *Perbekel*, who was chosen for his ability to read and write Indonesian. The traditional lines of allegiance between hamlets, for instance, the sphere of the desa adat, or any other such ties, were often ignored in delimiting these new units, which were formed according to territorial proximity and ease of access. Consequently, the government village usually consists of parts of several desa adats, and any single desa adat is distributed among several government villages. At first the Dutch even attempted to include the surrounding rice fields under the authority of the government village, following the Javanese pattern, thus breaking through the traditional separation of hamlet and irrigation society. This rapidly proved unworkable, and by the early 1920s the effort to fuse banjar and subak by administrative edict was abandoned.

The headman, the Perbekel, today is still appointed by the government, as the lowest rung in the central Indonesian administration. His duties are confined primarily to communicating government decisions and propaganda to the villagers and to maintaining such records as a register of birth and deaths. Since he is chosen for literacy and for capacity to deal with the bureaucratic structures of the new Indonesia, he is often quite young, and he may be from a family marginal to the established power lines of the village. As Perbekel, he has no official authority within the component hamlets, while in his own hamlet he has only the single vote of a member of the hamlet council.[19]

Above the level of the government village, the Dutch set up a new series of territorially nesting administrative units—the district (a number of government villages under an officer called a Punggawa), the regency (several districts united under a head, who was the former paramount lord retitled the *Zelfsbestuurder*, "independent governor"), and the province (the island of Bali, plus the Lesser Sunda Islands). The nine regencies were drawn up roughly along the lines of the major principalities as they existed at the time of Dutch takeover, with considerable regularization of boundaries and some arbitrary regrouping of smaller lords into the new system.

After Independence (1950), the same general pattern was retained, but some new institutions were added. An elective council was set up for each regency, called the *Dewan Perwakilan Rakyat* (Council of Representatives of the People). Elections were held and each rural area sent a representative. In most regencies, the paramount lord, now called the *Rajah*, continued to be administrative head with the alternative title of *Kepala Daerah Swapraja* (Head of the Region of the Regency), but in Tabanan and Singaraja, for local reasons, the rajah abdicated. In these two areas, the chairman of the Council of Representatives was named administrative head.

There was also an attempt to rationalize the system of subaks, the irrigation societies, into a formal hierarchy of responsibility and control. The government appointed a head of each subak, called *Klian Subak*, whose main duties are the maintenance of adequate records of sales, inheritance, and pawning of land, and the collection of annual taxes on rice production. The Klian Subak is parallel to the Perbekel Desa in importance and influence: he can be exceedingly powerful locally, but he also can be little more than a clerk. He works closely with the village headmen in the villages in the immediate area. The official in charge of the group of subak heads is called the *Sedahan*, and he in turn is responsible to the government irrigation office, headed by the Sedahan Agung. These officials do not have any real authority over the internal organization of the subaks; their main concern is with the collection of taxes.

The Brahmana priest and his clients. The topmost set of gentry titles is the Brahmana. It is from among the Brahmana that the high priests (*pedanda*) of Bali come, the guardians of the sacred knowledge of ritual detail, philosophy, and mythic history, ultimately of Sanskritic origin but preserved in revised form in the holy writings which are sometimes in Sanskrit, most often in old Javanese and in Balinese. The office of high priest is usually passed down from father to the son of his choice, and there is considerable training and spiritual preparation required for the position. There is generally only one pedanda in a large extended family of Brahmanas, and the rest of the family do ordinary labor as farmers, artisans, teachers, clerks, merchants, or even day laborers.

The temple system and the high Brahmana priestly network are almost completely separate and independent. Every temple has its own priest (*pemangku*) or even a group of priests, but these are usually commoners, although non-Brahmana gentry also may serve as temple priests. Brahmana high priests are never in charge of a particular temple (with the exception of their own family temples), but they are often called on to officiate at important ceremonies in the temples, and no ritual, large or small, can be carried out without some holy water procured from a high priest. The temple priest or household head must petition to a Brahmana priest for this sanctified water before every ceremony.

Nearly every family, gentry or commoner, has a traditional, usually inherited, relationship with a particular high priest, from whom they obtain the sacred water, various specially prepared offerings and ritual or general moral tutelage. The Balinese terms for the relationship, *siwa* for the priest and *sisia* for his follower, mean "teacher or preceptor," and "student" or "follower," in the eastern connotations implied in the Indian term *guru*. But for most Balinese this tie to a priest is not one of "student-follower" but rather "client," for their dependence on the priest is almost utilitarian. The pedanda is the source of sacred water for ceremonies and the reciter of the holiest prayers. For a small minority of those commoners who have a serious or thoughtful turn of mind, or who are passing through some moral crisis, the priest may have great spiritual authority; the kings and princes of traditional Bali each had a specific priest as their religious and ritual guide. The "students" of a priest have a diffuse obligation to aid him in material ways, to help him build a new house, for instance, or to assist at large ritual festivals that he or his family hold, much as do the subjects of a lord. When a priest is cremated, his "students" have the right, in many parts of Bali, to bring to the ceremony their own uncremated dead, thereby avoiding large expenditures. Consequently, a priest's cremation may be attended by thousands of persons, the majority of whom take part in the ceremony.

The relationship structurally parallels the traditional political tie between lord and subject, for it has the same radically nonterritorial character. A priest has no parish but rather serves a number of families who live scattered over an extremely wide region. Neighboring families usually are dependent on different priests. In many parts of

Bali one's priest is assigned according to one's houseyard (as is the lord to whom one is subject), so that even brothers and cousins may have different priests. The tie is dyadic or individual, that is, a follower of a priest is not as such a member of an identifiable group and, except for the rare cremations, a priest's "students" never come together at the same time.

The club and its members. It should be clear by now that the overriding principle in Balinese social structure as a whole is one of functional specificity for every group. That is to say, the premise "an independent group for every purpose, and only one purpose per group" is pursued in Bali almost to the limits of its potentialities. Various social functions, which in many traditional societies are performed by a single coherent set of institutions, are, in Bali, each provided with a separate autonomous social apparatus.

Even when new or temporary needs for working together arise, Balinese do not normally employ one of their already existing social groupings, but instead usually establish a new one. Elementary school districts, burgeoning in Bali since Independence, for example, rarely coincide with any previous territorial division. The same is true for the formation of groups with more traditional interests, such as dance troupes, work groups, associations of artisans, or societies for singing and interpreting the traditional poetry.

The generic term for an organized group of any kind in Balinese is *seka*, which means literally "to be as one." The term is normally applied to all those groups already described: the hamlet council is often called the seka banjar; various temple groups are referred to as the seka of that temple; the irrigation society is a seka subak; and so on. In a seka all members have equal rights and duties, irrespective of their status positions elsewhere. In most of the groups described above decisions are reached unanimously in meetings of the whole and leadership is nominal and nonauthoritative, a situation made possible by the fact that each seka is not part of a larger organization but exists independently, free of other social ties or influences.

These traits of egalitarian, consensual decision-making and autonomy from other institutions are equally characteristic of the voluntary organizations found in every village which crystallize around special or temporary interests. There are voluntary seka for keeping the village coconut trees free of marauding rodents, groups for thatching roofs, groups for playing gamelan orchestras, groups for arranging cockfights and for the commercial activity which accompanies them, groups for carrying goods back and forth to market, groups for the support of modern producers' or sellers' cooperatives, and so on. The membership of these special-interest societies usually further cross-cuts those of the other forms of organization, thus even further complicating and tightening the tangle of Balinese social structure.

The kingroup and its members. We will reserve most of our discussion of kinship relationships and groupings for the body of the book and make only a few remarks at this point. In the light of the foregoing description of Balinese social structure, the reader might predict that kingroups should have the same radical dissociation from other kinds of social ties that are generally characteristic of organization in Bali. This is indeed the case. Every kingroup of whatever scope stands essentially alone, jurally free from even closely related kingroups. The Balinese image of a kingroup, whether the group is a nuclear family or a large corporate dadia, is that of an independent seka, an autonomous organization within which every member is equal. Gentry kinship groups have, to a greater extent than those of commoners, a hierarchic form, connecting several related subgroups, but even the royal dadias more closely resemble voluntary organizations, in their internal structure, than do their counterparts in other societies.

Another trait of Balinese kinship that derives from its position in Balinese society as a whole is that it must coexist with a number of other, equally salient structures. Kinship is merely one mode of ordering rights and duties which must adjust to the counterbalancing pressures and pulls of other modes. In this respect Balinese kinship contrasts with those tribal systems, such as the Nuer, in which the reckoning of descent is the primary basis of organization in the larger society on the one hand, and on the other with those more developed peasant or industrial systems, such as our own, where kinship plays a clearly secondary role in the general pattern of social integration. While this process of adjustment between kinship institutions and the other such structures of the society is of course present everywhere, it takes on a peculiar form in Bali, a form which the remainder of our discussion is dedicated to clarifying.

Cases in Point: Two Principalities and Three Villages

This discussion of the main forms of Balinese social organization has provided only the formal outlines of their society, the institutional constants within which their social life moves. These forms are parameters, not variables; they set the enduring framework within which many other forms of social relationship fit: friendship patterns, modern political parties, ancient power struggles among the gentry, economic ties such as landownership and sharecropping, or commercial ventures and wage-work, gambling alliances and rivalries in cockfighting, witchcraft threats and suspicions, artistic innovations and virtuosity, and so on.

No one Balinese community, large or small, can serve as a concentrated representative of the others. Each one is slightly different in social organization, each seems to typify most clearly the structural possibilities of only one or two of the organizational forms described above, and to slight the others. This, we cannot too strongly stress, is not a consequence of cultural variation between different regions or between different status groups. Below the level of the often bewildering surface variations, the agreement among all Balinese on ideational matters, on beliefs, values, social definitions and perceptions, and so on, is profound. Nonetheless, the researcher is forced to move from community to community, minutely comparing them, not so much to factor out the "chance elements" which make each one idiosyncratic, as to try to learn, in each case, what fundamental principles it exemplifies and illuminates.

In our case, the bulk of our work was carried out in two principalities (or, as they now are called, Swaprajas): Tabanan, on the western edge of the south Balinese heartland; and Klungkung, in the eastern part of that heartland. In Klungkung attention was concentrated on three villages which form adjacent segments of the perbekelan of Tihingan, several miles northwest of the present town of Klungkung. There were other communities—around twenty-five of them—that we surveyed, or even lived in briefly; but these two principalities and three villages were the ones which we came to know most intimately, the places where we lived during our fieldwork, and from which we have drawn the greater part of the illustrative material for the ensuing discussions of Balinese kinship.

Tabanan. In 1908, Tabanan was the seat of a flourishing principality with considerable influence over a region nearly thirty miles in diameter. In 1958, it was the capital of a lively local division of the Republic of Indonesia which sent representatives to Parliament in Djakarta, students to universities in Java and the United States, and dancers and musicians on world tours.

Modern Tabanan is (by Balinese standards) a busy commercial town, with a daily market through which passes a fairly large stream of food products destined for other parts of Bali and Indonesia and textiles imported from overseas. There are one or two export firms (shipping out cattle, pigs, and coffee) which are run by Balinese, several blocks of retail stores owned by both Balinese and Chinese, a book store, gas station, some small industrial establishments, two high schools, and a host of governmental offices. The villages surrounding Tabanan are reached by good roads, along which buses, trucks, cars, and bicycles move easily. In the center of the town is a large open public square, where once the palace of the king of Tabanan, the Cokorda, stood. In 1908 the principality was invaded by Dutch troops, who razed the palace to the ground, imprisoned the Cokorda and the crown prince (both of whom then committed suicide), exiled the remaining close kinsmen of the king, and established a modern colonial administration.

In the old Tabanan, the Cokorda and his relatives, the lords, together with their retainers, were, in their own persons, the governmental apparatus. The Cokorda had monopolistic control over a fairly lucrative foreign trade in which tobacco and coffee were grown in Chinese plantations in the nearby highlands and exchanged for imported opium and textiles. He also had an extensive system of agrarian taxation and large personal holdings of rice land. Most of the nobility lived in compounds adjacent to the royal palace, although a few were stationed in distant villages as representatives (and also potential competitors) of the king. Many villages had lesser gentry who had the function of intermediating between peasants and court. Gentry kinship groups, articulated by descent and marriage, were in this context of supreme importance in the structure of the state.

In Tabanan today the nobility and gentry are no longer paramount but their influence is still extensive. Civil offices, while open to persons from all social strata, are, to a large extent, filled by members of the nobility. And the new world of export and import firms, of banking and small industry is, to a large extent, dominated by nobles. The massive ceremonials for which the gentry are famous are still held, although the cremation held in the 1930s by Puri Kaleran was said to be the last of the really grandiose ones, for after that the electric wires strung around the town impeded the passage of the funerary towers.

During the period of fieldwork in Tabanan, from August to December, 1957, we lived in the home of a Brahmana family, a barber with a college-educated son. Our initial research interest was in modern urban economic life, and our investigations threw us primarily, but not solely, into Tabanan's gentry circles. From them we gathered systematic information on their social organization and, by means of family chronicles, genealogies, and personal recollections, considerable data on the patterns of kinship and politics of the late nineteenth century. We worked without interpreters and visited many of the villages in the surrounding area. In addition, several detailed surveys of village life were made by our Indonesian research assistant, Mr. E. Rukasah.

Klungkung. It soon became clear, however, that we needed additional counterbalancing material, not only on the peasants and commoners but also, since Tabanan is a vigorous and progressive region, on the nature of a more conservative, less modernized kingdom. When the opportunity arose, we took up residence in the village of Tihingan, in the former principality of Klungkung, where we stayed from April to July, 1958.

Our perspective on Tabanan was, to some extent, from inside the ranks of the gentry; that on Klungkung was, also only in part, from the side of the peasantry. In Tabanan we studied mainly the noble houses of the court itself, while in Klungkung our work was mainly among village-dwelling commoners, and in consequence those gentry with whom we had the greatest contact were poor villagers, with the exception of certain very high nobles and Brahmana priests in the capital with whom we sought interviews. In Klungkung we had good opportunities to observe the social relationships of the commoners who had familial connections with the gentry.

The Klungkung region has even less commerce than Tabanan, being primarily a rice- (and in poorer areas, maize-) growing economy. The town of Klungkung, like Tabanan, has a market, government offices, stores, and so on, and, as in Tabanan, the urban population is at least fifty percent nobility and gentry, who live inside crowded walled compounds near the center of town. Some of the villages near the town are heavily saturated with noble, gentry, and priestly residents, while many others are entirely commoner in composition.

Klungkung has been, according to tradition, the cultural summit of Bali. The princes and holy men of Madjapahit, fleeing from Java in the fifteenth century, were said to have landed on the shore nearest Klungkung and to have established their first kingdom nearby. The Klungkung lords are the direct descendants of these Javanese immigrants and therefore are considered of higher rank than all other Balinese lords. Partly because of this responsibility of cultural leadership and consciousness of superiority in rank, Klungkung is a culturally conservative region.

In the thirties the Dutch returned the kings of the seven largest principalities to their thrones, but with considerably circumscribed and changed powers. The Indonesian Revolution in 1945–48, and the subsequent establishment of the Republic meant even further erosion of the power and status of the king. In Tabanan, the struggle between political parties grew so intense that, with the loss of the old unquestioning acceptance of traditional lines of influence, the Cokorda, a grandnephew of the 1908 sovereign, voluntarily relinquished his throne. In Klungkung, on the other hand, the old order survived and even, in substance though not in form, grew stronger. In 1958, the king of Klungkung still headed the government of the principality, and while he had the official title of "Chairman of the Council of People's Representatives," he was ordinarily called by the honorific "Dewa Agung" ("Great God"). And, in Klungkung much more than in Tabanan, the rank order of the lord's kinsmen according to traditional rules tended to determine their level of attainment in the hierarchy of the new bureaucracy.

Tihingan, Pau, and Penasan. The three villages of our study lie within the sphere of influence of the Dewa Agung in Klungkung. Their residents were subjects of his or of his lords. An hour of difficult walking, through rice fields and down into a deep ravine, takes one from Klungkung to Tihingan, for the court capital lies on one broad ridge and Tihingan on the next parallel one. There is today a more circuitous route by road, longer to walk but only ten minutes by car when passable. Tihingan is the name both of the central hamlet and also of a larger set which includes the two others, comprising the government village.

The relationships between the three villages can be seen from the maps. Map 1 shows sharply distinct patches of houseland, connected by a road and surrounded by terraces of rice paddies with two small rivers running down the ravines on either side and other villages a literal stone's throw away. The sea is about ten miles south, the volcanic cone of Gunung Agung, Bali's holy mountain, about twenty miles north, and both are visible from vantage points nearby.

The three villages are strung along the crest of the sloping ridge, the one on the uphill side being Pau, the next lower Tihingan, the last, on the seaward side, Penasan. Pau has (1958) a population of about 630, Tihingan 720, and Penasan 690.

There are five blocks of rice fields, subaks, in the immediate vicinity of the three villages. Those who own land in these subaks come from

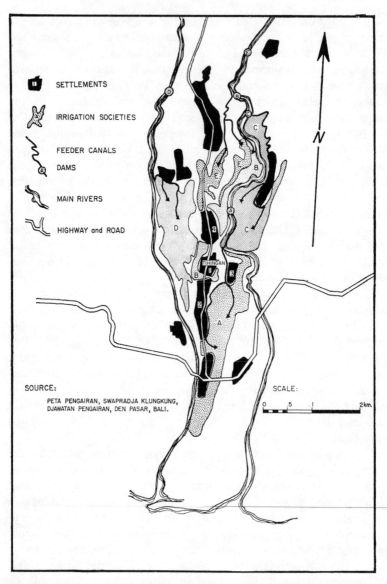

SETTLEMENTS

IRRIGATION SOCIETIES

FEEDER CANALS

DAMS

MAIN RIVERS

HIGHWAY and ROAD

SOURCE:

PETA PENGAIRAN, SWAPRADJA KLUNGKUNG,
DJAWATAN PENGAIRAN, DEN PASAR, BALI.

SCALE:

0   .5   1   2 km.

1. Banjars and subaks in the Tihingan area (simplified). From Clifford
Geertz, "Tihingan: A Balinese Village," *Bijdragen tot de Land- Taal- en
Volkenkunde* 120, n. 1 (The Hague: Martinus Nijhoff, 1964), p. 4.

all around the area; for instance, in subak A next to the village Penasan, about one-fourth of the land is owned by Penasan residents, about five percent by Tihingan hamlet residents, and the remaining seventy-one percent of the land is held by people coming from thirty-six other villages.

The reason that we are introducing all three villages is that they contrast, in some aspects rather neatly, in their social and economic composition and, correspondingly (we shall argue), in kinship organization. Although they lie near one another, each separated from the others by scarcely twenty yards of open fields, and although there are many crosscutting ties that bind them variously together (temple worship, governmental administrative arrangements, subak cooperation) each one of the three has its own quite distinct character.

Pau is a village of comparatively prosperous, freehold peasants, a village with few status distinctions, either in traditional titles or in wealth. It has only a few large landholders, the richest owning no more than five hectares (around twelve acres), and relatively few with no land at all. Most of the landless have enough work as share-croppers in the fields of their kinsmen or fellow villagers, and their rights to these tenancy holdings are well protected by custom. Of the 125 household heads, only two are not farmers; one of these is the proprietor of the village coffee stall, and the other ekes out a living buying and selling the peanut and vegetable crops of his neighbors. No one commutes to the nearby town of Klungkung for employment, and everyone does almost all their daily shopping in a tiny market held on the road in the middle of the village. Highly self-sufficient socially, its members have few ties with anyone from nearby hamlets. They have a reputation for sober, even dour industriousness; they rarely hold cockfights, for example, or gamble at those which the men of Tihingan and Penasan avidly follow.

Tihingan, on the other hand, is sharply stratified into the rich and the poor. Its rich men, "rich" only in a relative sense, of course, are better off than those of Pau, and its poor are poorer. It is also the only village of the three that has gentry residents, but they are by no means well-to-do. There is a Brahmana House with a highly respected but not wealthy priest at its head. There are also two large families of low Satria status, with the gentry titles of Sang and Gusti. The first perbekel of Tihingan (1900–31) had been a man from one of these families, and his son later briefly held the post during the postwar Dutch occupation of Bali, 1948–50. In 1958, however, the family was without office, landless, and most of the men were only occasionally employed as unskilled brick makers or sharecroppers.

The gentry of Tihingan live in the hamlet but do not take great part in its affairs. Those from the Brahmana house, in particular, do not participate in the hamlet council meetings and are not permitted to enter the village death-temple. Their dead are buried in a section of the cemetery set aside from the commoners. The Satria are drawn into the hamlet to a greater degree. While they also have special arrangements for funerals, they are members of the hamlet council, and one Satria man was serving as priest in the Pura Puseh, the origin-temple of the village.

Tihingan's economic elite is a small number of commoners, highly skilled craftsmen, blacksmiths who forge delicately tuned gamelan orchestra gongs and xylophones. While traditionally the craft may have been the sole prerogative of one commoner title-group, the Pandé ("Blacksmith"), this monopoly must have broken down at least a century ago, and today gamelan forges are found in several different, competing, title-groups. The master blacksmiths are independent entrepreneurs, but they need helpers whom they employ at day-wages or by the piece. These helpers are almost always poorer members of the same title-group. Some of the blacksmiths own, individually, more rice land than the wealthiest Pau farmer, but while the smith may work one small piece of his land himself, most of it is let out in various sharecropping arrangements. The middle group of farmers who both own and work their land, the "yeomenry" who predominate in Pau, is a very small group in Tihingan. Only fourteen percent of Tihingan's households are entirely dependent on agricultural labor for support. Another thirty percent are completely without access to land, either as owners or workers. These last are Tihingan's poor: they work as unskilled laborers in brick, tile, and cigarette factories in the town, as occasional helpers in the forges, as seasonal migrants to coffee plantations in the hills. Tihingan also has a modern white-collar contingent, a group of nine young men who commute to town to teach school or to work as government clerks. Finally, there are several people who make most of their living in traditional callings: the priest, two curers, the three stone- and wood-carvers who make temple ornaments. This occupational and economic variegation gives Tihingan its peculiar character but does not make it untypical of Bali. Rather it is a representative of a very frequent kind of Balinese village, that with a craft specialization.

We lived in Tihingan during the fieldwork, in the home of a blacksmith who farmed some of his fields himself. From Tihingan we walked up to Pau and down to Penasan to interview and observe. But, of course, the material that we gathered in Tihingan, coming in as it did at all hours and from the many sources that actual participation brought to us, was of greater depth, precision, and detail. It was a fortunate accident for the present study that Tihingan turned out to be a hamlet in which kinship plays so large a part, for it enabled us to study at close hand the patterns of Balinese kinship in their most fully developed form.

Penasan, the third village, provides a still different example of Balinese community. It is much poorer than either of the others, both in land and in other resources. In general characteristics it is more like Pau than it is like Tihingan, for it has no gentry, no highly skilled craftsmen, and no broad chasm between the haves and the have-nots. But while seventy percent of the Pau household heads own land, only forty-seven percent of Penasan's do. And while the average size of holding for Pau is seventy-three *are* (about 1.8 acres), the average for Penasan is only about fifty *are* (1.2 acres). The most comfortable families of Penasan are poorer than most in the Pau and Tihingan elites. And, while Pau has a class of landless laborers, it comprises only about thirty percent of the total, while for Penasan the corresponding group is over fifty-three percent.

Penasan, like Pau, is a village of farmers, but since most of Penasan's men have insufficient land of their own to support themselves, they must supplement their income with sharecropping or wage-labor. Most of the tenants of the wealthy Tihingan blacksmiths live in Penasan. Although it is actually no nearer than Pau to the town, Penasan has a large number of commuters who trudge an hour in and out of Klungkung for the chance to work for a few rupiah a day as "factory" workers, making soap, bricks, and tile by hand, or as coolies carrying burdens in the market. Nearly all of Penasan's and many of Tihingan's unmarried girls go daily to Klungkung to roll cigarettes for a Chinese merchant, while only a handful of Pau's girls have been permitted by their more old-fashioned and less needy parents to do this. This heavy reliance on wage-labor has had a number of repercussions on Penasan's social structure. Since the demands of wage-work are different from those of farming, conflicts arise with the duties of the members of the hamlet council—duties, such as harvesting, which are geared to the agricultural calendar. Thus, the authority and capacities of Penasan's hamlet councils are being gradually eroded. This is a specific instance of a more general tendency of Penasan's people to give up older practices for modern ones. In fact, the members of the Penasan hamlet councils eight years ago adopted a new rule regarding the time at which an older man may retire from citizenship. While in Tihingan and Pau a man must continue to shoulder the rather heavy responsibilities of hamlet membership until his youngest son is married, in Penasan he may withdraw much sooner, at the marriage of his first son. Tihingan people strongly disapprove of this laxness, but Penasan people consider it a progressive innovation.

Two other examples further illustrate the differences in atmosphere between the three villages. One concerns burial customs. Traditionally in Bali, nearly everyone except high Brahmanas are buried at death, and their bodies are disinterred at a remote later date for cremation. Also traditionally, burial may not take place except on certain magically auspicious days. If death occurs on one of these days, the body is buried immediately; if not, it may have to be kept above ground for as long as a week. In a tropical, humid climate, this is a disagreeable and unsanitary custom, and there has been some pressure from the Ministry of Health to abandon it. Of the three villages, Penasan is the only one which has made the change; the other two villages are watching apprehensively to see if there will be supernatural retribution. In Tihingan the suggestion has come up several times in hamlet council meetings but has always been strongly opposed by the conservative faction. In Pau the idea has been considered unthinkable.

The second example concerns the customs surrounding the birth of opposite-sex twins. Traditionally, if a commoner has such a birth, the mother, infants, and father are forced to leave the hamlet for a month, to live in an improvised shack in the fields south of it, and to go through a ritual taboo period. All temples in the village are closed. For considerations of the health of the mother and newborn children, the government has also pressed to give up this custom. A reason that some modern Balinese find more compelling is that the custom is seen as a holdover from what they call the feudal period, for it applies only to commoners. A birth of opposite-sex twins to a gentry woman is thought to be great good fortune, while the same birth to a commoner woman is thought to represent an insolent presumption which is magically dangerous. Persuaded by the new egalitarian ideology of the republic, the hamlet council of Penasan voted to give up the custom. In Tihingan only one faction was in favor of abandoning it, and on the birth of such twins about five years ago to a woman of the progressive faction no taboos were observed. But Tihingan's conservative wing did not accept it, and they themselves observed the taboos against entering their own temples and posted a notice on the village death-temple prohibiting anyone from entering. In Pau the issue has never been raised.

In describing these three villages and, to an even greater extent, in our analysis in the chapters below, we have been constantly plagued with terminological difficulties surrounding the word "village." In part this is because there are no precise English equivalents to the various Balinese words for rural communities. The translation problem is made more difficult by the fact that the English words, such as "village," "community," "hamlet," "neighborhood," all have connotations of territorial location, boundedness, and diffuseness of function which make them highly misleading. On the other hand, there is no single, general Balinese word which covers all the varieties of concrete communities that are found in Bali. The most general term is *désa* (usually translated "village"), but in Balinese it has several distinct meanings; in addition the term desa is also found in Indonesia, and in other languages of the archipelago, with even more, slightly different, meanings.

The fundamental reason for our semantic struggles is that almost all Balinese communities are crosscut and parcelled out according to the several planes listed above, and their affiliation with neighboring communities are so numerous that it is difficult to specify a structural locus for "the" Balinese village community. In any concrete instance it is not so difficult to identify a set of persons as belonging to a single bounded community within which the bulk of their most significant and enduring primary relationships are found. In common-sense terms there is no doubt that Tihingan, Pau, and Penasan are all "villages," although their formal structures are quite different.

Some maps may make the difference in social organization of the three villages clearer. Map 2 shows the three communities plus a small fourth one, Mengguna, which make up the perbekelan, or administrative village of Tihingan. The perbekel has four assistants, called *pengliman*, whose bailiwicks in this instance correspond to the four settlements. Either the perbekelan complex or the unit under each pengliman could be called the village. Another definition of the village, often found in the literature on Bali, is that of the combined congregations of the three temples, the Kahyangan Tiga. Map 3 shows the distribution of these temples and the local limits of their congregations for the four villages. Of the three villages, only one, Pau, has all three temples. The activities associated with worship at the village temples are directed by a chairman, called the *klian désa*, and the

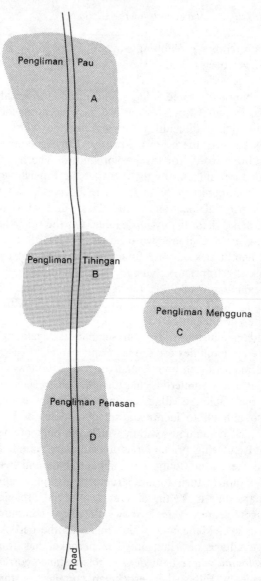

2. The Perbekelan of Tihingan, showing the territories of the four assistants (pengliman) to the Perbekel.

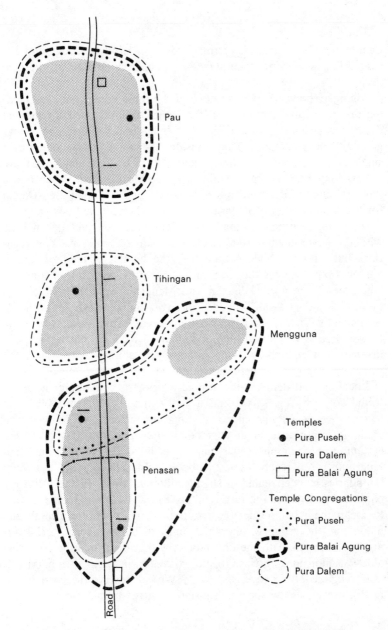

Temples
● Pura Puseh
— Pura Dalem
□ Pura Balai Agung

Temple Congregations
⋯ Pura Puseh
▪▪▪ Pura Balai Agung
--- Pura Dalem

3. The temple congregations in Tihingan, Pau, Penasan, and Mengguna.

unit of people is generally termed the *désa adat*. Meetings and the assembling of offerings take place in a public pavilion called the *balé désa*.

Tihingan, however, has only two of the three village temples, lacking the Pura Balai Agung. Nonetheless it considers itself a complete desa adat, and has a klian desa and a bale desa. Penasan and Mengguna are more complex. They consider themselves to be joined as a single desa adat, for they share a single Pura Balai Agung. But there are two separate sets of the other two temples, a Pura Puseh and a Pura Dalem for Penasan and Mengguna, and a Pura Puseh-Dalem for the southern end of Penasan, a neighborhood called Sangging.

A strong case can be made for identifying the "village" neither with the governmental subdivision nor with the religious congregation, but with the civic community, the hamlet council or krama banjar. Map 4 shows the location of these divisions in the four villages. In this respect, Tihingan and Mengguna each consist of one unified banjar. Penasan is divided into two banjars, each with a meeting pavilion, bale banjar, and a number of banjar heads, or klian banjar. Pau is composed of four banjars, which are not territorially distinct, their members living interspersed among each other, but which have separate meeting pavilions and heads.[20]

Locating and defining the Balinese primary community is not a trivial concern, for, as we shall try to show, it is the interplay and tension between community and kingroup which is of fundamental dynamic importance in understanding the operation of the kinship system. For commoners the hamlet tends to be endogamous, and kingroups rarely reach out past its bounds. In each concrete case these boundaries are delineated in slightly different ways. In the following chapters we will use the term "village" in a diffuse and general way to mean the rural residential group of primary importance to the individual, the group within which most of his significant social ties are concentrated, with the understanding that there may be considerable variation in its precise formal structure, in terms of administration, religious observance, and so on. We will reserve the term "hamlet," however, as the specific translation of the term "banjar."

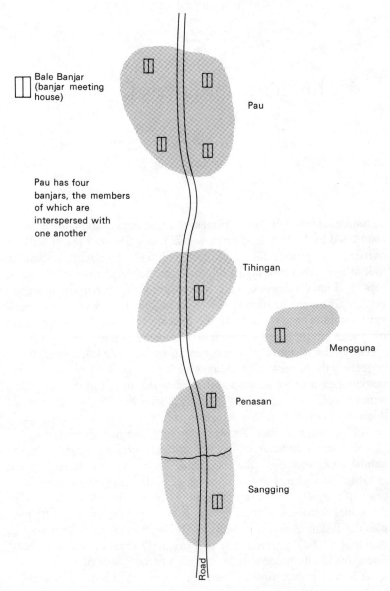

4. The banjars of Tihingan, Pau, Penasan, Sangging, and Mengguna.

2

Kinship in the Private Domain

As one enters a Balinese village, the first impression is of a cross-road lined by high, blank, brick walls. The walls are broken only by narrow, inhospitable doorways, each with a short staircase leading up to it, often with a foot-high sill to restrain the wanderings of chickens, pigs, and small children, and, a few feet inside the door, a second brick wall placed in such a way so as to shield from view the court-yard within. These walls mark the division between the public world of village affairs and the private world of the family.

The Balinese hold that what goes on within their houseyards is the concern only of those directly involved; what goes on outside, in the marketplace and coffee shop at the crossroad, or out in the rice fields, is the concern of the public. The distinction between the domain of domestic matters and that which is civil or public is very explicitly institutionalized in Bali. As we have seen, the public domain is or-ganized into a number of sharply distinct entities: the hamlet, the temple congregations, the irrigation societies, the large descent groups, and so on. Each of these is a jurally independent corporate unit with legally circumscribed spheres of action. Although most of the actual members of these groups may be physically the same peo-ple, the Balinese perceive limits of jurisdiction of every grouping as distinctly as if they were made up of entirely separate sets of people. The same clarity holds also for the lines between any of the organiza-tions in the public domain and the realm of the domestic family group.

Dividing our description of kinship institutions and practices in terms of the private or domestic domain and the public or civil do-main is therefore more than merely analytically fitting. The composition of the household, arrangements for the provision of economic needs, decisions about inheritance, about marriage, about child-rearing, all are primarily private matters. The hamlet intrudes only as a legal witness of contracts, such as adoption and marriage, which are likely to lead to disputes over inheritance among kinsmen. The congregation of the village death-temple is concerned only that the family provide for the proper disposal of the dead. The corporate descent groups, the dadia, are similarly distinct entities which can encroach very little on the autonomy of the domestic familial group. The houseyard walls therefore represent a fundamental social divide between domestic affairs and those of the society at large.[21]

Houseyard and Household

In one corner of every houseyard is a gardenlike, roofless temple, a low brick wall enclosing a few flowering trees and a set of wooden or carved stone altars. One of these altars has three compartments, one for the highest god, Batara Guru, procreator of all Balinese, one for the very distant, anonymous ancestors of the residents of the houseyard, and one for those immediate ancestors who were personally known by the living and who have been properly cremated. This houseyard temple may be merely a way station to a more inclusive temple elsewhere, or it may be the only one that the family knows of. In either case it is the temple of the family origin-point, the *kawitan*, "the source, beginning, or origin."[22]

A houseyard group may consist of a single household or it may be subdivided into several households—the groups of people who share a single kitchen and food supply. The term for household, *kurèn*, meaning "kitchen," "hearth," indicates its most fundamental definition. These households, however, are all paternally related to the ancestors whose spirits are worshipped in the houseyard temple, and they share together the obligation to care for the temple.

Residence in a houseyard and the duty to worship in the houseyard temple are transmitted by the principle of patrifiliation: from father to son. The term "patrifiliation" is used here in preference to "patrilineality" for it is a set of dyadic connections, not linear descent, which binds the group together. The heads of the component households in a houseyard live there because their respective fathers lived there before them, not because they are all members of a patrilineage. In practice, of course, this set of household heads are related through their fathers, usually being no further distant than uncle and nephew or than first cousins, and thus the line of males is given spatial definition.

Residence at marriage is virilocal. The women who have come to live in a houseyard no longer worship at their own parents' houseyard temple, and after their own deaths their spirits are enshrined in their adopted houseyard temple, even when they have no descendants.

Aside from its function as supporter of the houseyard temple—holding a twice-yearly ceremony, plus a number of minor ceremonies, and the building and repair of altars in it—the houseyard group has few other special social functions. In precolonial days the political ties to the hundreds of petty Balinese lords followed houseyard lines. All those dwellings in one houseyard owed fealty to a single lord, while those of other houseyards, although of the same village or kin line, as often as not owed loyalty to a different one. This tie has now largely disappeared in any specific or explicit form, but the similar houseyard-based tie to Brahmana priests persists.

The household, or kuren, is, on the other hand, the fundamental unit of membership in almost all aspects of hamlet social organization. Whenever any collective work is undertaken in the hamlet—road repair, temple renovation, rice harvesting—each household must send one adult representative (or sometimes one male and one female, depending on the sort of work involved). Each household is awarded one seat, occupied by the male household head, in the hamlet council at which all important hamlet decisions are made, and each has one vote in electing hamlet officials. Ritual obligations and irrigation society duties fall upon the household rather than upon individuals as such, as does hamlet taxation and responsibility for hamlet security (night watch and the like). The household is also usually the landowning unit, so that in the typical case rice is grown on household land, is stored in the household granary, and ultimately cooked in the household kitchen.

How many nuclear families make up a single household varies considerably, but the majority contain only one or two nuclear families plus some dependent adults such as parents or siblings. One household encountered had over forty-five nuclear families, all kinsmen and followers of a Brahmana priest, all sharing the same rice supply and the same kitchen. Such size, however, is extremely unusual.

The number of persons in a houseyard, consequently, also has a wide range of variation. Larger houseyard units, containing up to twenty households, are characteristic of the higher gentry. Probably ninety percent of the houseyards in Bali hold less than six nuclear families, no matter how they are organized, and the mode is probably around two or three nuclear families per houseyard.

The Ground Plan of the Houseyard

The houseyard-household social distinction is reflected directly in the physical ground plan of the houseyard, for each component household has a specified set of buildings, the spatial layout of which delineates the relationships among their inhabitants. The construction of such a yard is not a matter left to individual taste but follows exact prescriptions in the ancient Balinese palm-leaf law-books, the lontar. These sacred writings distinguish between different types of buildings, give the proper dimensions, methods of construction, and uses of each, prescribe their spatial relation to one another within the houseyard on the basis of traditional cosmological ideas, relate who is permitted and who is not (for reasons of status) to build various kinds of them, outlines the ceremonies attendant on their construction, and so on. Consequently all houseyards are laid out on a fundamental pattern.

The main types of buildings prescribed are the one-roomed windowless walled house, or *mètèn*; the open, roofed pavilion, or *balé*; the kitchen shed, or *paon*; the rice-barn, or *lumbung*; and the temple, or *sanggah*.[23]

The windowless house is the only completely walled dwelling structure in the houseyard, and as such is used as a sleeping place for married couples, younger children, and adolescent girls, as a place for the storage of heirlooms and other valuables, and for certain ceremonies such as the seclusion of an adolescent girl at first menstruation or before the tooth-filing ritual. The pavilion is used for a sleeping place for adolescent boys and unmarried men, as an everyday household work place or sitting room, as a display site for a corpse after death, and as the place for the performance of a number of personal rituals. A small altar is usually placed up under its eaves for the spirits of those dead who have not yet been cremated. The lower portion of the rice barn is also used for sleeping and domestic work. In theory every household should have a walled house, a pavilion, a kitchen, and a rice barn of its own. Actually, however, only the kitchen is always separate, and the number of pavilions, walled houses, and rice barns varies with particular circumstances. Some general plans of different houseyard designs will clarify the matter (see fig. 1).

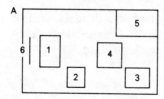

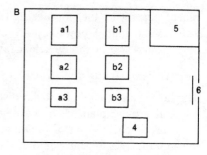

Houseyard (*karang*) A,
with one household (*kurèn*)
  1. Sleeping house (*mètèn*)
  2. Kitchen (*paon*)
  3. Rice barn (*lumbung*)
  4. Pavilion (*balé*)
  5. Houseyard temple (*sanggah*)
  6. Houseyard door (*pemesuwèn*)

Houseyard B
  Household a (informant)
    a1. Sleeping house
    a2. Pavilion
    a3. Kitchen
  Household b (informant's father's
  brother)
    b1. Sleeping house
    b2. Pavilion
    b3. Kitchen
  Shared by entire houseyard
    4. Rice barn
    5. Houseyard temple
    6. Door

Fig. 1. Types of houseyard plans

The first plan gives the basic pattern in its simplest form. It shows
a single-household houseyard, belonging to an ordinary peasant in a
village in the Klungkung area. Living in the houseyard, in addition to
the household head, are his younger unmarried brother, his wife, and
his three young, also unmarried, sons. The temple is in the northeast
corner, nearest to the sacred mountain, Gunung Agung, in the center
of the island, while the kitchen and rice barn, the profane elements,
are located, as usual, to the south. The walled house and pavilion face
one another, as they are required to do, toward the northern edge of
the yard. The simplicity of this layout is, however, atypical, and plans
B and C of two-household houseyards represent more common patterns.

In houseyard B—from a village in the Tabanan area—there are
two households, each with its own walled house, pavilion, and kitchen,
but the two share a common rice barn (which is, however, divided
internally to keep stores of the two families separate). The two
households are headed by a man and his paternal uncle, and roughly

Houseyard C
  Household a (informant)
    a1. Sleeping house of informant
    a2. Sleeping house of
        informant's married son
    a3. Kitchen
  Household b (informant's younger
  brother)
    b1. Sleeping house
    b2. Kitchen
  Shared by entire houseyard
    4. Rice barn
    5. Pavilion
    6. Door
    7. Temple

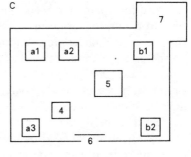

Houseyard D
    a1—i1. Sleeping houses of nine descen-
          dants of three brothers (i.e.,
          brothers and first cousins)
    a2—i2. Pavilions of these nine households
    a3—i3. Kitchens of these nine households
    a4—i4. Rice barns of these nine households
        5. Houseyard temple (shared by
          entire houseyard)
        6. Door

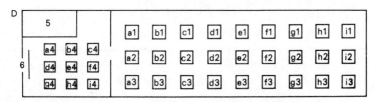

the same arrangement of buildings occurs as in A above.

Houseyard C, from the town of Tabanan, belongs to a highly proletarianized tailor and his market-trader younger brother and is somewhat less neatly laid out, but it still follows the general pattern. Here
there is an extra walled house for the tailor's married son, who remains, however, part of his father's household. A single pavilion and
a single rice barn are shared by the two households.

Finally, let us look at a large houseyard, D, from the Tabanan
countryside. Here the temple is in the northeast corner of the yard,
for the holy orientation point in this region is not Gunung Agung but
another sacred mountain, Batu Kau. There are nine households, the
heads of which are brothers or first patricousins to one another. (Some
of the households contain the families of married sons of the heads
as well, so that the total population of this houseyard is over fifty.)
Each household has a walled house, pavilion, kitchen, and rice barn,
though the rice barns are placed to the front of the yard rather than
to the south.

These four plans represent but a few of the many variations possible, for almost every houseyard is a little different from the next. But the general underlying pattern they demonstrate holds for almost all the houseyards of Bali. The major exceptions to this pattern are the palaces (*puri* or *jero*) of the former ruling lords and of the Brahmana priests (*griya*), where ceremonial and political considerations have reshaped the houseyard pattern to some degree. Aside from the fact that these palaces are often large sets of more than a dozen houseyards all surrounded by a common wall, they also usually have elaborate series of entry courts, dance and reception pavilions, greatly enlarged temples, and expanded kitchen areas for the preparation of ceremonial offerings (see below, "The Spatialization of Kinship," in chapter 4). However, the fundamental pattern of at least one walled house, pavilion, kitchen, and rice barn for each household in the complex persists, and there is always an origin-temple for the palace as a whole.

The Houseyard Cluster

When a houseyard becomes overcrowded and one or more of its households moves out, the group that leaves still maintains ritual ties with the temple of the original yard, which they continue to regard as their "origin point," or *kawitan*. Their new houseyard is provided with a temple too; or, as in the majority of cases, where the move is to a vacated yard, the existing houseyard temple is reconsecrated for its new users. This new temple is ritually subordinate to the temple of the first houseyard: it is considered a way station, or temporary stopping-off place for the gods and ancestral spirits whose primary locus is in the original temple.

The first, "original" houseyard temple is now called a *sanggah gdé* ("great houseyard temple") rather than simply a sanggah, and it is usually more elaborate and kept in better repair than those supported only by the members of a single houseyard. The members of the houseyard cluster as a group are also usually referred to as a sanggah gde, or as *sameton* ("one emergence") or *njama* ("siblings, kinsmen").

A houseyard cluster, then, is a group of houseyards linked together by their common worship at the temple in one of the yards, their mutual origin-point temple. Since temple affiliation is inherited from one's father or, in the case of a married woman, adopted from one's husband, these houseyard clusters, like the houseyard, are formed around groups of agnatically related men and their families. The houseyards in a cluster are usually located near one another but not necessarily so. The cluster may be scattered around within a hamlet or even, in the case of gentry, over a large region.

Houseyard clusters are not corporate groups. Under certain circumstances, a houseyard cluster may adopt some corporate features—elected leadership, common treasury, sometimes ownership of rice land to support rituals, and a permanent identity in the eyes of the community. These then become the corporate kingroups—dadia—discussed at length in the following chapters. We will reserve the use of the term "houseyard cluster" for those groups with few or no corporate characteristics.

Core and Periphery

The internal structure of the houseyard cluster group, the relationships between its component houseyards and households is primarily one of core and periphery. The original houseyard from which the new houseyards have hived off is referred to as the core (*kemulan*, literally, "beginning," "first") houseyard. It is here that the core temple representing the origin-point of the members of the entire houseyard cluster is maintained. Should the group continue to grow, a process of secondary dispersal takes place so that in some cases a fully developed pattern is produced of a set of subcores united by the central core.

Which households remain in the core houseyard and which disperse is mainly determined by a rule of unigeniture for inheritance of the houseyard and succession to the father's position as guardian of the houseyard temple, and to some of his political roles—that is, to his place in the hamlet council if he is a commoner or, in the past, to his position in the precolonial government of the nineteenth century if he was of the gentry. Only one son succeeds the father, and at least one—the same one—must remain in the houseyard. The others may stay to share it with him if there is room, or may move out to establish a houseyard of their own, older brothers generally leaving before younger. The remainder of the father's property, and especially his land, is divided equally among all the sons. The successor son (called the *sentana*) usually, though not inevitably, receives a slightly larger portion, for he must take the lead in his parents' cremation and in the upkeep of the temple. He has no genuine authority over his brothers and cousins, however. In most commoner villages it is the youngest son who succeeds the father, although in a few places a primogeniture rule is followed. There are also some villages, particularly in the more loosely organized western Bali, where the father chooses freely among his sons as to who will stay in the houseyard in his place.

The gentry rule is exclusively primogenitural. Gentry succession is made more complicated by the general practice of polygamy and the status of plural wives. The general rule is that the first son of the highest ranking wife succeeds his father, but there are many disputes on this issue. (See Chapter 4, on succession and inheritance.) For both gentry and commoners, once a man has inherited the place at the core of the group, his own successor should be not one of his brothers but one of his own sons. Only in those cases where he does not provide an heir does the core position revert to a collateral line, that is, to one of the brothers or their descendants. Many commoner families can be found in which a line of youngest sons—the youngest son of a youngest son of a youngest son, and so on—has held the core houseyard. And in the gentry, where considerable emphasis is placed on descent line, the usual sequence is one of a core line of eldest sons, descendants from an eminent ancestor, with a peripheral scattering of branch lines which have lower prestige. (See below, Chapter 4, the section on gentry descent.)

The Substitute Heir

No matter how a successor is selected, there must be someone to inherit the care of the houseyard temple. Not to worship one's ancestors suitably is to invite disaster. It is this feeling that lies behind the institution of "substitute heir," the naming of a man as heir who is not a direct lineal descendant where there is no son.

There are two ways in which this can be accomplished. First, if there are no offspring at all, someone, male or female, may be adopted and be given full inheritance rights. The second way is to bring a man into the origin group by marriage, if there is a daughter, or if the adopted person is a girl. However, the wife in these cases is the actual successor, the *sentana*, to her father, and she is considered for legal purposes to be a man. The man who marries her is considered for legal purposes a woman, and since he is marrying like a woman into an alien descent line he relinquishes all inheritance rights in his own family property and moves to his wife's family houseyard and joins her family temple worshipping group, allowing his children also to be members of it. This is essentially the so-called "borrowed man" pattern, found also in other parts of Indonesia.[24]

The general Balinese term for the process of heir substitution is *nyentana*, "to become the legitimate heir." Substitution by adoption is called *pemerasan*, while a man who marries into an origin group is said to *nyeburin*, "to jump in." To minimize squabbling over the inheritance within the kingroup, the adopted heir is usually a brother's son, or a daughter's son; the man who is selected to marry a daughter to become heir is often also a brother's son or a more distant paternal cousin. In some hamlets there are rules prohibiting adoption or heir marriage beyond the limits of paternal ties. In any case, the nyentana form of marriage is quite prevalent. In Tihingan, a village in southeastern Bali, seven percent of the marriages over the last four generations were substitute heir marriages.[25]

Marriage

Aside from such special arrangements, the most desirable marriage choice is with one's parallel patri-cousin, one's father's brother's daughter.[26] Failing this, another member of the houseyard cluster is considered best. An endogamous marriage is a matter of considerable pride for the family, and its members turn to outside women only when cousins are unavailable or unattractive. The proportion of endogamous marriages that a family can attain varies with the strength and size of the household cluster group. In some cases it reaches as high as sixty percent. The other marriages, those between unrelated persons, are always somewhat awkward and tense in their accomplishment. There is usually sharp status-rivalry between kin groups—especially the large incorporated dadia—and a marital alliance between two such competing groups is accompanied by tension and excitement. Such a marriage cannot be concluded amicably; it usually involves elopement or wife-kidnapping, and can leave a residue of bitter feelings between the two groups that may last a whole generation. The wife in such a case is socially ostracized (at least temporarily) from her original group, and the husband's relationships with his affines are marked by hostility and avoidance. This is by no means always the case, of course, and peace is generally made by the time children are born of the union. Even marriages brought about under such dramatic circumstances, however, are remarkably stable. There are no legal restrictions against divorce, but it is quite uncommon.

Interpersonal Relationships in the Domestic Domain

Household, houseyard, houseyard cluster—all organized around paternally related kinsmen—these are the primary groups within which each Balinese has his most intimate and enduring relationships. These are the people with whom he lives, with whom he worships, works, and plays, and among whom he first seeks a wife. They provide a basic framework for interpersonal relationships among kinsmen.

The women of these family groups, even when born elsewhere and marrying in, are not second-class members but have full rights and responsibilities. The relationship between husband and wife is one of equality. Most of the activities that the Balinese consider important—those concerned with political citizenship and religious worship—require the joint participation of a man and a woman as a single unit. To a large extent, husband and wife make joint decisions. The custom of teknonymy, taking the name of the firstborn child, has the result that husband and wife are called by the same name, a practice which further emphasizes the unity of the conjugal pair. As noted, divorce is not frequent, especially among couples with children.

Balinese make no sharp conceptual opposition between masculinity and femininity, and the division of social roles or spheres of activity according to sex is blurred and weak.[27] Men do most of the skilled and heavy agricultural tasks, but women are necessary for all the rituals in the rice fields at each stage of the crop, and women can do minor farm labor, and can also own land in their own name and supervise men's work on it. Women usually care for the children and do the daily cooking, but men are often seen carrying young children on their hip, and men do most of the cooking for the large ritual feasts. In the dance and the drama, men can play female roles or women male roles with no sense of impropriety or oddness.

Relationships within the nuclear family are close and continue to be so after the children are adult. In fact it is usually the houseyard rather than the nuclear family alone which is psychologically the more significant unit for the individual. The families of a houseyard spend most of their waking hours not in the individual pavilions allotted to them but in the open yard itself. The men of the houseyard work together, the women share domestic tasks, and the children play together.

During the day, more distant relatives come in and go out of the houseyard, and its members go out into the public sectors of the village to meet their other kinsmen and neighbors, but as night falls each houseyard draws together again. There is a warm, intimate, and relaxed atmosphere inside the walls, an atmosphere which contrasts strongly with the restraint, coolness, and caution in the road, market-place, and village meeting hall. At sunset the family members bathe in the river along with the rest of the village, then return for a quick supper near the kitchen fire, and then sit, clean and full, close to-gether, arms about one another, chatting about the day's events. Someone picks a tune on a metallophone or a flute, the women plait palmleaf temple offerings, and the children drop off to sleep in some-one's arms.

The men of a houseyard often own a piece of rice land together, for inherited land is not supposed to be divided until after the crema-tion of its owner, and the cost of a cremation ceremony is now so high that years usually pass after a father's death before the proper rituals can be performed. Meanwhile his land should stay intact, and his sons may either live together as one household or, as is more common, they may work the land together and divide its produce equally and store it in separate rice barns. Or one brother may farm the plot of land as sharecropper to the sibling group as a whole. Each man may also have land of his own, given him by the father, or earned by his own efforts, or he may have some other source of in-come. Informal assistance, borrowing of tools or of work animals, is common. A father usually retains ownership of most of his land until his death, allowing his sons to use it, or to be sharecropper to him. At least one son, of course, stays within the father's household, work-ing and sharing with him directly. The relationship between the men of a family is therefore quite close, and it appears to be a comfortable, relaxed one, although serious quarrels, usually over inheritance, are not unknown. Such quarrels, however, are more frequent between half-brothers, cousins, or uncle and nephew than between full brothers.

The men of a houseyard may spend much of their free time to-gether but here a loose age-grading tends to break up the group. Boys of the village of roughly the same age play and often sleep in a group, and as they mature these play gangs become sets of bachelors who roam around together in the evenings, sometimes going to other villages to see a dance or a shadow play performance and to look over the girls or to gamble. Married men with familial responsibilities have less free time, but they too spend it outside the houseyard, going to cockfights, or sitting in a coffeeshop in the long hot noon-hours between trips to the fields, or squatting in the village crossroads comparing fighting cocks with their neighbors and members of their wider kingroup.

The women of the houseyard, on the other hand, stay close to home. Even though they may be of different households, they share a good deal of their domestic work: rice-pounding, going to the river for water, going to market, caring for the children, and, most especially, the incessant preparation of offerings for the temples. This last is primarily women's work, and since rituals, of varying degrees of elaborateness, occur on the average of one a week, there is always something to be worked on in the spare time. Young girls, as early as eight or ten years old, join their mothers in their daily work and are given additional duties in the temple ceremonies, bringing the offerings to the altars on their heads, representing the household in the prayers, dancing the solemn, graceful, sacred dance of reverence.

These work groups of women appear to be friendly and cooperative, even though they are composed of sisters-in-law, or mother- and daughters-in-law, or co-wives. The warmth of the relationship is in part due to the fact that the women of a houseyard or houseyard cluster are often cousins—for even when wives are not taken from within the paternal kin groups, there is a strong tendency to take them repeatedly from a single family. That is, if a man's paternal cousins are not attractive to him, he often turns to his maternal cousins for a wife, and his brothers may do likewise. (There is, however, a strong belief that it is dangerous for a brother and sister to take their spouses from the same sibling group; that is, for a man to take a wife from among his sister's husband's sisters.)

The group of women of an entire houseyard cluster often gather sociably in the afternoons. The high walls between contiguous paternally related yards are often broken by small, almost accidental, apertures, which although they are not given the formal recognition of a wooden lintel and the term "door," are still large enough for passage. In many cases the intervening wall may be omitted entirely between two houseyards, with a row of flat stones taking its place, to mark but not separate the two houseyards.

In sum, the personal relationships within the domestic realm of household, houseyard, and houseyard cluster are close, cooperative, and solidary. In descent terms, the ties that form their basis are successive links of patrifiliation, father to son. And with patrilateral endogamy, the women, too, are often indirectly members by birth in the group through their fathers or grandfathers. But it is neither filial loyalty as such, nor a sense of lineal roots, nor even common residence, which binds them all together. From the Balinese point of view, it is the temple in the core houseyard, representing their spatial and genealogical point of origin, which forms the center of the system. It provides the conceptual framework, the normative force, and the emotional anchor which prevents Balinese familes from disintegrating at each generation and enables them, when they find it desirable, to organize into larger and more permanent kingroups.

3

Kinship in the Public Domain
The Commoner Dadia

The Dadia Defined

Just as the tangible brick-and-mud walled houseyard symbolizes the separate existence of kinship within the private domain, so also there is a physical symbol for kinship's place in the public or civic world. This is the transfer of a houseyard temple out of its houseyard onto hamlet-owned land, and the erection there of a more permanent and elaborate temple enclosure. Hamlet council approval of such a move is obviously necessary, and the move represents, therefore, a quantum change in the social status of the kingroup. What was formerly a loosely connected set of houseyard groups engaged in private worship at the shrine of their common origin within the houseyard of one among them, now becomes a socially recognized permanent public entity, a group powerful enough to gain hamlet council consent to their taking the land, and wealthy enough to build an elegantly carved temple on it. The houseyard cluster has become a fully corporate kingroup—a dadia.[28]

The change has been determined not entirely, or even mostly, by processes internal to the kingroup, but by shifts in the relationship between that group and the larger community within which it is embedded. For the commoners this community is the village, for gentry it is the larger community of the region or kingdom as a whole. Commoner dadia are normally confined to a single hamlet or banjar. If a member family moves out of the hamlet, it ultimately severs its ties with the dadia, and any dadia that has members in two adjacent hamlets is always weak. Gentry dadia on the other hand are essentially nonlocalized, nonterritorial in nature, even though in many cases a large number of the core members of a particular gentry dadia may be found together.

One of the most important characteristics of the dadia—and one of the most difficult to handle conceptually—is the fact that dadia do not *necessarily* emerge when kingroups are large or long-standing enough. Not every Balinese family, especially of the commoner stratum, is incorporated into a larger organized kinship unit. In the great majority of Balinese villages, only a certain percentage of the population belongs to dadia, the remainder does not.

The proportion may range widely. In one village, Penasan, only forty-one percent of the population belongs to its three dadia, contrasting with its nearest neighbor, Tihingan, in which members of four dadia make up eighty percent of the commoners. Two other villages nearby, Pau and Mungguna, have respectively, four dadia accounting for sixty-eight percent and two dadia accounting for seventy percent of the inhabitants. Another example from the Tabanan area, where there has been a great deal more population movement, is the village of Blumbangan, where there are seven dadia accounting for sixty percent of the inhabitants. And, to complete the range of variation, there is a hamlet near the Klungkung-Gianyar border in which the entire populace belongs to a single dadia.

The forces determining the formation of a dadia out of an undifferentiated mass of houseyards and houseyard clusters are various. Wealth, which makes larger temples and more elaborate ceremonies possible, is obviously one such factor. One group of twelve houseyards may not form a dadia where another of eight does, the difference being simply that the one is poor and the other rich. The accidents of birth-rate in small groups, where an overbalance of males in a given generation can make for rapid growth of a group's size, and a similar overbalance of females can make for its rapid contraction, are also of importance. The strength of status strivings, which are in part a reflex of the caste (or "title group") composition of the village plays a role as well. Villages containing only a few commoner castes of nearly equal rank seem especially liable, for example, to develop strong dadia organization, because the struggle for local eminence in such communities tends to be keen. The relative strength of nonkinship organizations which can serve as corporate subgroups within the hamlet is also relevant. In some villages, for example, the expression of status rivalry may appear in the form of competition between dance, drama, and music groups formed on a voluntary, achieved skill basis rather than in the form of kin-based dadias, and such voluntary groups may take on broadly social, political, economic, and even religious functions as well.

Because the process of differentiation is one only of relative degree, it is sometimes difficult for the investigator to determine in concrete cases, especially among commoners, whether a kingroup has taken on enough suprafamilial functions and sufficient corporateness within the hamlet context to be considered structurally a "true" dadia. The building of a temple on public land is the best index, because the heightened ritual activity is usually correlated with heightened social solidarity. But it is not an infallible one, for a group may grow large, appear in hamlet life as an important economic and political unit, and yet still not have gotten around to moving its temple out of its original houseyard, merely renovating it *in situ*. The presence of a formally elected kin chief is another index of the emergence of a true dadia. In any case, there is high variation in size and degree of corporateness of kingroups found in any Balinese community. Balinese kinship units fall along an unbroken continuum from a pole of minimally cohesive families to a pole of fully organized, autonomous descent groups.

Differentiation: The Structure of Dadia Organization

In order to understand the structure of the dadia it is necessary to pause and, anticipating its detailed description, to contrast in abstract terms the Balinese system with those generally termed segmentary lineage systems. For the main characteristics of the latter, we may turn to a summary by Middleton and Tait:

The term 'segmentary' has been used in reference to several types of social systems, but the essential features are the 'nesting' attribute of segmentary series and the characteristic of being in a state of continual segmentation and complementary opposition. The series may be one of lineages, smaller ones nesting inside and composing larger ones, which in turn compose still larger ones, and so on; or it may be one of territorial groups (hamlets, villages, sections, tribes, nations), or of others. Subtraction or change in size of segments lead to a re-organization, although not necessarily to re-structuring. Analysis of the process involved in this re-organization within an unchanging total structure has led to the use of the term to refer to the second characteristic. This is the process of continual segmentation of the structure. The constituent units are all of the same order and segment (or merge, the complementary process) in response to various factors, one of which is the increase of numbers in a segment so that it splits into two or more new segments each of a population nearer the optimum population within a given system. A corollary is that within the structure coordinate segments which have come into existence as a result of segmentation are regarded as complementary and as formally equal, even if in actuality they are not so in population, wealth, or in other ways.[29]

It is the principle of complementary opposition which lies at the heart of a segmentary system and which is completely absent in the Balinese system. The identity of a Balinese dadia is not perceived in terms of its opposition to another dadia—that is, to a unit of formally equal political, ritual, or kinship status. The "nesting" characteristic of segmentary systems can be understood only in terms of complementary opposition, for each more inclusive unit must consist of two or more subsidiary segments, which together absorb its entire membership. That is, "nesting" for segmentary systems does not merely mean that there are units of increasing inclusiveness, but that the steps up are by means of alliance of several segments of equal jural status.

There can be, and generally is, very sharp competition between Balinese dadia, especially when there are more than one of nearly equal strength within a village. But, while such competition makes each of them more salient in the eyes of the outside world and more integrated internally, it is nevertheless not a structural necessity. This is seen on the occasion of the "death" of a dadia: no restructuring, no reorganization of the other dadia is required. Each stands alone, against the world of the community. The dadia is never seen as a building block out of which the larger community is constructed. A more accurate metaphor is that the community is a bounded field of unequally distributed forces, within which are found various areas of more concentrated and organized power, which have crystallized out, or differentiated out, of the field around them.

We have called the process of dadia formation in Bali "differentiation," a concept standing in contrast to "segmentation." Just as segmentation refers both to the nature of the overall structure of the system as well as to the process of internal subdivision of its units, so also differentiation can be seen at work not only in the relationship between dadia and community but also in the emergence within the dadia of what we have termed "subdadias." We will discuss the subdadia in more detail presently, but for the moment remark only that, just as the dadia does not owe its existence to competition with another dadia in the village, so also a subdadia is not in complementary opposition to any other subdivision of the dadia. It is merely a nucleus of dadia members which is more tightly organized than the others and which may have more power or ritual responsibilities than they. The subdadia exists as figure against the ground of the dadia, just as the dadia is figure against the ground of the local community.

The characteristics listed by Middleton and Tait—nesting, constant segmentation, complementary opposition—do not fully describe the structure of a segmentary lineage system. Its foundation is a specific type of cultural model, one based mainly on an image of a series of parallel genealogical pyramids. It is this image—of a father, a set of sons, and a series of sets of grandsons—which locates the points where segmentation can take place and from which the principle of complementary opposition is derived as a corollary of the notion of the equivalence of siblings within each set. Middleton and Tait discuss this model, which they term an "ideology":

> In the societies with which we are dealing there is an ideology by which certain social relations are expressed in terms of kinship. Relations conceived in this idiom may be concerned with the interests either of individuals or of aggregates of unilineal kin. In the former case the relations concerned are those of personal kinship, in the latter they are those of lineage. . . . Relations between local groups can be conceived in terms of relations between lineages, and are then seen in terms of the kin relationships between the apical ancestors of the lineages by which the local groups define their membership. . . . This is an abstraction, a concept used by the actors, and by ourselves in analysis, to express certain relations between aggregates of people composing local groups.[30]

Similarly, the principle of "differentiation" as it operates in Bali rests on a cultural model, but on one of quite different character. The Balinese "ideology" about kinship relations completely lacks any cultural image or assumption of long chains or lines of descent.[31] In the place of such a linear image, the Balinese paradigm has the two related concepts of "origin-point," and "origin-group" (both termed *kawitan*), which we have already encountered in our description of the houseyard and houseyard cluster. The "origin-point" is a locus which is both historical (an ultimate ancestral progenitor) and spatial (a particular temple location). One's tie to an origin-point is by virtue of one's father's affiliation, but no need is felt for the specification of a genealogical line of men linking the present members to the founding ancestors, as a charter for their legitimate membership in the origin-group.

The origin-group, correspondingly, is the group of living persons who all actively support and worship at the same origin-point temple. The most important structural characteristic of the origin-group is that it is viewed by the Balinese as an overarching social whole, an indivisible unit which has jural and ritual precedence over any parts of it. For commoners, the dadia is the organized actualization of an origin-group. While some commoners, such as the Pasek Gelgel, may consider themselves to be also members of a much larger, translocal origin-group centered on a temple outside the immediate community, this membership is of secondary importance to them ritually, and the aggregation of people who may come together at the "national" Gelgel temple annually is of no importance politically.[32] The effective origin is felt to be in the origin-temple in the hamlet where one resides. Thus, the dadia, even though it is localized, is identified with the origin-group, and as such, it, and never any of its parts, is the fundamental, sovereign kinship unit, in Balinese eyes.

In keeping with such an image of an all-enveloping whole with prior claim over lesser units, is another set of ideas, which purport to describe the relationships between the present members of a dadia. Rather than visualizing a tree of descent which defines the kinds and degree of kinship among its members, the Balinese think of a dadia as a seka (literally, "association"), an organization of the same sort as an irrigation society, a dancing club, and so on, in which all members are structurally equidistant from one another and from their common origin-point. In fact, they generally refer to the dadia group as a *seka dadia*. In a seka, there can be—at least officially—no distinctions of status. All are equal in power, rights, and responsibilities. A dadia operates under the same radically egalitarian principle. One of the houseyards in the dadia may be recognized as the core houseyard, the one in which the group's temple was first located, but the inhabitants of that houseyard have no special prerogatives within the kingroup as a whole. Similarly, a dadia headman—a klian dadia—has no special authority and acts more as the group's steward than its chief.

The leveling of relationships within a dadia is further aided by a rather striking absence of precise knowledge of genealogical kin ties among the members of commoner dadias. In addition to the profound lack of Balinese interest in antecedents, there is a mechanism which promotes genealogical amnesia. This is their elaborate teknonymic system (discussed in detail below), which systematically suppresses personal names, substituting teknonyms, not only at the parental but also at the grandparental and great-grandparental levels. As a result, kinsmen as near as second cousins can be totally ignorant of the nature of their tie to one another. They know (and care) only that they are kinsmen and members of the same origin-group.

When differentiation does occur within a dadia—that is, when a subdadia develops—the Balinese do not have in mind an explicit genealogical frame which could specify who shall or shall not be its members. A subdadia may crystallize around the core houseyard and the houseyards most closely related to it, but equally often it may center on another set of houseyards. The social forces which operate in the differentiation and maintenance of a subdadia are similar to those operating in the differentiation of the dadia itself. That is to say, a concentration of wealth and power among a few of the dadia members may give rise to a desire to symbolize their superior position by possession of a special temple.

The subdadia temple may be placed either inside one of the houseyards or on hamlet land. The subdadia group is generally one of closely related patri-kinsmen, who can trace their ties to one another. The claim to kinship within the subdadia group may, on the part of some of the younger members, be merely putative or contestable, but that is not the usual case. The temple for such a subdadia is often called a *sanggah gdé*, the same term that is used for a simple houseyard cluster temple, for although in contrast to the latter the subdadia is not autonomous but is a dependent part of a larger unit, its structure is similar in that it also is based on explicitly traced kin ties. Another common term for the subdadia is *paibon*, literally "of one mother," again indicating the emphasis on known descent from a single set of parents. The jural position of the subdadia vis-a-vis the dadia is always clearly subordinate. Although its members may include the elite of the dadia, it is never structurally dominant. Its members participate in dadia affairs only as individuals, never as subdadia representatives.

When the term "differentiation" is applied in turn to the subordination of the dadia to the village, there is a shift in level of discourse from the realm of largely kinship relationships to one of political. This shift is the same as that made in those African societies where the term "segmentation" and the cultural model of genealogical pyramids are applied to perceived relationships between and within territorial communities. The Nuer, the Tiv, the Dinka, and their like see political relationships in terms of agnatic hierarchies and complementary opposition. So also, the Balinese perceive their community, the hamlet, as an all-enveloping origin-group, which has jural and ritual precedence over those origin-groups which assert themselves as dadias within it. One of the temples usually supported by a village is the pura puseh, which is conceived to represent the ancestors of all the community members. As remarked earlier, *pusèh* means navel, or origin-point. Thus, for the Balinese, the larger entity is always the point of reference: first there is the village, within which dadias may differentiate out, and then the dadia itself is seen as the prior unit, within which subdadias are permitted their limited subsistence.

Dadia Formation, Expansion, Crystallization, Differentiation, and Decline: A Hypothetical Model

A hypothetical, idealized case history of the rise and fall of a commoner dadia may make the process of differentiation clearer.

In the first stage, diagrammed in figure 2 below, there is a typical houseyard cluster, containing a group of households whose heads are related by known and close patrilateral connections. The pattern of kin ties is not indicated in the diagram other than showing the presence of *known* relationships with a line connecting two houseyards. For simplicity, we will say that this houseyard cluster is inhabited by a set of five brothers and their families. There is a temple within each houseyard, and one of these, in the core houseyard (in the center of the diagram) is considered the houseyard cluster temple of the entire complex.

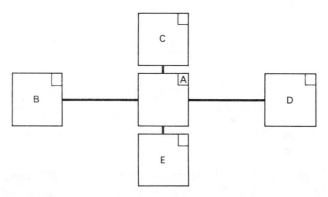

Fig. 2. Stage 1: a simple houseyard cluster. Five houseyards connected by known patrilateral kin ties, indicated by lines connecting the houseyards. The smaller squares in the upper right-hand corner of each houseyard represent family origin-temples. The origin-temple for the houseyard cluster is within the core houseyard at A.

Figure 3 shows the second stage, say three generations later, with the same five houseyards plus a new one, the six having just established a dadia temple for themselves, outside the original core houseyard. The group is now considerably larger; the houseyards are crowded, even though one new yard has been acquired for some of the overflow. The pattern of kin ties among them is no longer simple. Some of the household heads may be as distantly related as second cousins. Some of these, say the members of houseyards B and C, do not even know that they are cousins, considering themselves merely "kin." Others, of course, as indicated, still remember their ties. Since, however, the group is larger, and its wealth, status, and power have correspondingly grown, its members have decided to move their origin-temple out onto hamlet land and to assert themselves as a true dadia, with an elected chief and considerably more elaborate periodic rituals and dramatic displays.

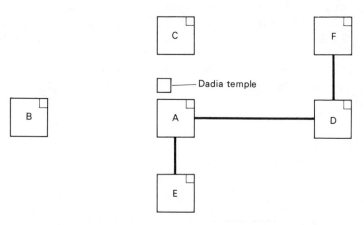

Fig. 3. Stage 2: a dadia. A group of houseyards, some of which are connected by known kinship ties, others unknown. There is a separate origin-temple for the entire group. The heads of houseyards B and C are patri-cousins, but they are unaware of the fact.

In stage 3, which would come no sooner than the fifth generation after the first stage of the simple houseyard cluster, the group as a whole is even larger and more affluent, and one segment has just established itself as a subdadia without the larger unit (see fig. 4). By this time all of the original ties between the five founding house-yards have been forgotten; most of the group members see them-selves as united only by a common patrilateral "origin," located some-where in the irretrievable past. In actuality some of them may be second patri-cousins, and many of them may have very close matri-lateral ties because of the practice of endogamy. Two interesting developments have occurred. First, a completely and genuinely un-related household (marked "G") has migrated into the village, an-nounced its common origin with the powerful dadia group, and has been accepted as a full member (how this can happen will be dis-cussed below). Second, the descendants of one man, in houseyard B, have multiplied substantially and rapidly, and simultaneously have captured a good many positions of influence: it is this group who have in turn elected a chief and built a more elaborate temple for their own use to symbolize their position as the inner elite within the general dadia. This temple is located in or near houseyard B, which is the core houseyard for the subgroup. It should be stressed that this subdadia could have appeared at any place within the dadia where there were traced collateral ties, and also that more than one such group might arise if the dadia were sufficiently large. In terms of genealogical structure, this subdadia group is almost identical with the houseyard cluster group of stage one. However, since it now lies within the context of a dadia instead of standing alone within the hamlet, its political and general social significance is very much greater than that of the earlier group. Classifying the two groups merely according to their formal internal constitutions would mis-

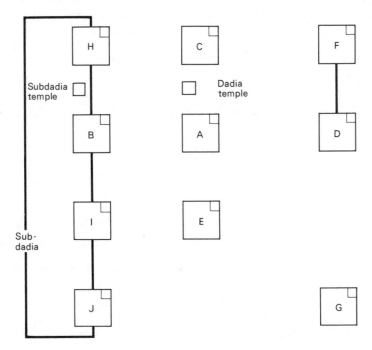

Fig. 4. Stage 3: a dadia with a subdadia. One set of houseyards, H, B, I, and J, have differentiated themselves from the rest of the dadia with a special temple to indicate their distinct status. The kin ties between them are known, while only some of the ties of the rest of the dadia group are known.

takenly gloss over this significant functional difference, which is derived primarily from the nature of the setting within which each is
embedded.

Finally, the fourth stage in this hypothetical history of a dadia
shows it some five generations further on (see fig. 5). During the
elapsed period the fortunes of the kingroup have rapidly declined, its
members have diminished through demographic accident and emigra-
tions, and other hamlet kingroups have claimed most of the vacated
houseyards. The few remaining households still strive to maintain the
dadia temple, but they cannot keep it properly in repair, nor can
they produce the lavish ritual displays that proclaimed their power in
its more affluent days. Their number is so shrunken that each new
generation has an acute shortage of male heirs to continue the line,
and a series of substitute heirs have been brought in from the outside
by marriage and adoption. The genuine blood link between the generations is replaced by various makeshift legal arrangements. This is
now what we may call a "ghost dadia," a mere houseyard cluster with
a white elephant of a temple to burden it. Unless the group's fortunes
shift, it is merely a matter of time before a rival kingroup will ma-
neuver to take over the temple, renovate it, and reconsecrate it to
this group's own ancestral origins.

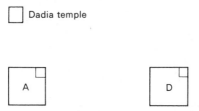

Fig. 5. Stage 4: a "ghost dadia." A dadia so shrunken that its members hardly
have the resources to maintain their temple, nor the male heirs to continue the
line without special means such as adoptions and matrilocal marriages.

The process of kingroup expansion and decline is, in actuality,
much slower than that suggested here by our "pure case" type construct. The dadia composition of most hamlets tends to be more or
less stabilized at some particular point, and fluctuation occurs within
a relatively persisting pattern. Dadias are not born every day, nor do
they easily die. The kingroups themselves may change size, and shifts
in their relative political status may occur; but a kinship-centered
hamlet with a high degree of dadia development tends to stay that

way, while a hamlet with a highly fractionated kinship composition can also be very stable. The building of new temples or the dismantling of old ones is at best a very slow process, so that the existing temple arrangement of a particular village forms a sort of concrete mold for its social organization, a mold which impedes change, requiring the various kinship units to adjust themselves within it.

Thus, in the short run at least, changes in kingroup forms tend to be of a "physiological" or "metabolic," rather than of an "anatomical" sort. The general pattern or organization changes slowly, but slight alterations are going on within this pattern constantly as particular dadias and subdadias wax and wane.

This general structural stability of hamlet kingroup makeup is apparent from statistics on houseyard occupancy over a fifty-year period from the village of Tihingan (see table 1). In 1957–58 Tihingan had eighty-seven houseyards, distributed among its four commoner dadia and a small number of unaffiliated family groups. Fifty years earlier these four dadia occupied, respectively, eighteen, twelve, eight, and ten houseyards; in 1957–58 they had twenty-six, fourteen, fourteen, and eleven houseyards. During that time only fifteen new houseyards were created, from former farmland, and the use of an older houseyard was transferred from one kingroup to another unrelated one in only fourteen cases. Of these fourteen cases of switches in houseyard occupancy, eleven were the direct result of a single, quite unusual occurrence—the enforced emigration of an entire gentry dadia after a pregnancy scandal. Aside from the removal of this one dadia, the dadia composition of the hamlet over the entire half century remained unchanged. One of the four was not so well entrenched at the beginning of the period as at the end and had no separate dadia temple; shortly after the end of the Japanese occupation, it built an imposing one. There were two ghost dadia in Tihingan in 1957–58; they were in about the same weak and anomalous condition fifty years earlier.

During that half century, Balinese population increased rapidly, and in the hamlet of Tihingan the increase was upwards of one hundred percent. The increase was almost entirely endogenous, for there were only fourteen households emigrating and only two immigrating in that entire time. The increased numbers were thus absorbed into the relatively fixed overall pattern through a kind of inward intensification and differentiation of it: the dadia and houseyard composition of the hamlet stayed the same, while there was some tendency for increased subdadia differentiation and a marked increase in the number of households per houseyard.

TABLE 1. CHANGES IN HOUSEHOLD/HOUSEYARD RATIOS OVER A
FIFTY-YEAR TIME SPAN. HAMLET OF TIHINGAN, KLUNGKUNG

	Ca. 1908	1957–58	% Increase
Number of houseyards	72	87	21
Number of households	88	137	55
Number households per houseyards	1.2	1.6	—
Percent of houseyards with two or more households	20	60	—

Types of Village Differentiation: An Empirical Model

The sequence of hypothetical stages in dadia growth and decline was
constructed not from family histories, which, given the blotting out
of genealogical history, are not available, but from an analytic juxta-
position of different kinds of contemporary kingroup constellations.
Most villages (that is, residential communities) contain kingroups of
all four kinds: the loosely connected houseyard cluster (stage 1), the
simple dadia (stage 2), the fully developed dadia with subdadia differentiated within it (stage 3), and the truncated ghost dadia (stage
4). However, the proportion of each kind of kingroup varies from
village to village, and the most highly developed form, the dadia enclosing one or more subdadia, appears rather infrequently, being most
common in villages where kinship is a focus of intergroup competition or in those communities in which there is a single kingroup
dominating the other unorganized families.

Since the community is the frame within which kingroup differentiation takes place, it is reasonable not only to construct a typology
of Balinese kingroups but also of villages. The criterion here is the
degree to which dadia have in fact differentiated out, that is, the
proportion of the population which belongs to dadia and/or subdadia,
and the significance of dadia in local social organization.

Villages with High Kinship Differentiation

The first type of community is one in which kinship plays a prominent, on occasion even dominant, role. The majority of the residents
are organized into dadia, and several of these dadia have developed
subdadia. An example of such a highly differentiated settlement is
Tihingan, where eighty percent of the population belongs to one of
the four competing dadia. The remaining families outside the leading
dadia play decidedly secondary parts in local political affairs, and
the only way they can get their voices heard is by alliance with one of

the stronger kingroups. The reason for Tihingan's high degree of kingroup organization is, in this case, economic, and there is a direct connection between its specialization in the manufacture of bronze percussion instruments for gamelan orchestras and the cohesiveness of its kingroups. Forging the larger gongs requires large groups of workers, which, in Tihingan, could be assembled most easily on a kinship basis, thus strengthening the already existing kin ties. Each of the four dadia has a large blacksmith's forge, a capital investment that unaffiliated families cannot afford, which requires large but spasmodic inputs of labor which they cannot command. There is intense and open rivalry among the dadia in instrument production. The dadia are in consequence steadily pressed to maintain their cohesiveness before the others and to retain or add as many members as possible. Tihingan is a special case, but it is one of many special cases—here a peculiar traditional relationship to the court, there an unusual ecological adaptation, over there a heightened development of intercaste rivalry—in which are found the elaboration of kinship as the basis of informal community organization.

Figure 6 is a schematic representation of this first type of village differentiation, one in which dadia and subdadia dominate the community.

Villages of Moderate Kinship Differentiation

Much more common is the second type of community, one of moderate differentiation, in which one or two dadia have emerged but subdadias have not. In such communities kingroups may play an important role in directing neighborhood social processes but not a dominant one. The other planes of social organization also play important parts in channelling alliances, and perhaps half the population remains outside of corporate kingroups. A settlement containing a strong gentry dadia might be of this intermediate type, for the aristocrats may choose to stay out of local political affairs or, conversely, they may completely monopolize all the leadership positions. In either case the effect on potential commoner kingroup development could be the same, for the commoner families would tend to be fractionated and weak. The mere presence of gentry in a settlement has no necessary or inevitable effect on community structure, for many small gentry families live far from the core group of their dadia and are without the support of a large, locally powerful kingroup. In such cases, the gentry family plays the same role within the community as a commoner houseyard or houseyard cluster.

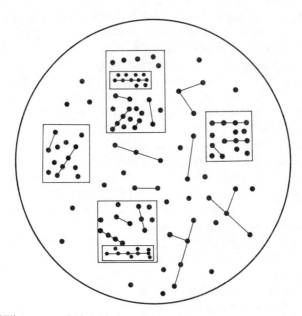

Fig. 6. Village type of high kinship differentiation. In this type the community is dominated by dadia and subdadia. The circle represents the total community membership, and the dots represent the component houseyards. Lines connecting dots indicate houseyard clusters. The squares represent dadia, and the smaller squares within them represent subdadia.

The settlements of Penasan and Pau are both examples of moderate kingroup development, although Penasan is considerably less differentiated than its neighbor. Pau has about seventy-five percent of its populace active in dadia, and nearly half of these are in one sprawling kingroup, with the rest in three small others. But the really powerful leaders of Pau are not dadia members at all, or at least had not been until recent years. In Penasan, in contrast, only about forty-one percent of the community is incorporated into dadia, and there are only three of them. But in Penasan, all the leaders are found within dadia groups, and in fact nearly all within one dominant dadia, and actually even in one elite subdadia within it.

Our general impression is that the intermediate type of village, with only a moderate degree of kingroup differentiation, is typical of the average unspecialized Balinese lowland rice community, although it is foolhardy to use such terms as "typical" or "average" in speaking of Bali and the Balinese. Certainly, most of the communities on which we had sufficient information were of this intermediate type.

Figure 7 shows schematically this second type of village differentiation.

Villages of Little or No Kinship Differentiation

A third type of community, representing the other end of the continuum in degree of kingroup organization, is one in which suprafamilial kinship structures are for practical purposes nonexistent, for no dadia have developed. Kin ties are operative only at the level of the houseyard cluster, and beyond this narrow, familial range are ignored and forgotten. Such a community is not necessarily atomized, however, for it will usually be organized in some other, nonkinship, terms. Subgroups in such settlements are formed on voluntary, caste, territorial, or other bases. Communities of undifferentiated kinship organization are probably more common in urban and suburban areas, but they may also be found in those parts of Bali—unirrigated regions, coastal areas, and the like—where social organization has long been looser than elsewhere. While we encountered several communities of this type, especially in southwestern Bali, we did not

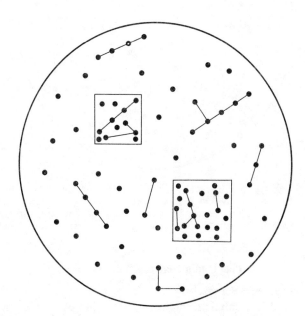

Fig. 7. Village type of moderate kinship differentiation. In this type there are only a few dadia and usually no subdadia. The circle represents the total community membership, the dots represent houseyards, and the squares enclosing them represent dadia.

make intensive, long-term study of one. Figure 8 shows an undifferentiated village in schematic form.

Distinguishing these three types of village according to the importance of kinship affiliation in shaping their social organization, will
provide a useful framework when we analyze the effects of the hamlet
context on the actual working of kinship institutions. For, as we have
stressed, the Balinese kingroup, of whatever form, must always be
seen as figure against the ground of the more inclusive community.
The internal dynamics of Balinese kingroups are sensitively responsive to their external setting.

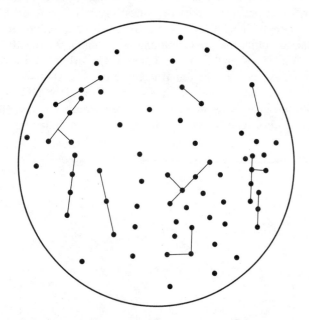

Fig. 8. Village type of little or no kinship differentiation. In this type there
are no dadia but merely independent houseyards and occasional houseyard
clusters. The circle represents the total community membership, the dots
represent houseyards, and the dots connected by lines represent houseyard
clusters.

The Dadia and the Title-Group

The dadia can be seen not only as a tentlike corporate kinship group
but also, in other analytic frameworks, as a kind of temple congregation, as a hamlet political faction, or as an organized local sector of
a dispersed title-group—an association of persons bearing the same
ranked title.

A good deal of the energy and momentum behind dadia development derives from the Balinese awareness that the prestige of the individual dadia members is intimately tied to the success of their dadia as a social actor on the local scene. Because the Balinese believe that all titles, commoner as well as gentry, have differential ranking, and that no two titles are precisely equivalent, the title system operates to distinguish and to set in opposition the various kingroups. In ordinary lineage systems with exogamic marriage rules, the function of marking the cutoff line between one lineage and another is performed automatically by the prohibition of marriage within the kingroup, thus establishing its boundaries. In the endogamous Balinese system, the patrifilially inherited title serves as the segregating factor.

Acquisition and Loss of Title

The link between title-group and dadia has another structural consequence, in the manner of recruitment of new members to the dadia. For, as we have indicated, actual or even plausibly traced descent is not the only possible basis for membership; common ancestry of a much more remote nature will suffice. Since title is inherited, all people bearing the same title regard themselves as stemming ultimately from the same ancestor, or as they most often phrase it, from some common "origin-point" (*kawitan*). This spot is usually marked with a large temple which is supported by persons of the same title from all over Bali.

Thus, if there is a dadia in a village from one title group, and another family with the same title moves in from elsewhere it will in most cases join this dadia, for although the new family is not local in origin and therefore almost certainly cannot be related to any of the dadia members in any even remotely traceable manner, it is nevertheless of "one origin" with them in the widest sense and consequently competent to worship the ancestor gods in their temple. As a result, if there are enough of them, all households of the same title-group in a village, related or not, may fuse to form one dadia, later comers being assimilated to the local core.

Furthermore, a household may acquire a new title or become a dadia member by ritual means. If an individual in the household or the household as a whole has met with a series of misfortunes— chronic illness, ineradicable poverty—the household head may visit a medium to discover why the gods are punishing him so. One answer the medium—who usually falls into a trance and permits the gods or their messengers to speak through him—often gives is that the client is mistaken about his origins. He should not be a member of, say, the Dukuh dadia as he at the moment is, for his ancestors were "really" Pemidilans. He is ill because he has been ritually neglecting his true progenitors. In such a case the household will almost certainly shift allegiance if it can convince those with traceable ties to it to go along with the change, for of course they must shift too. It is, actually, just the virtual absence of traced extended kin ties of any great range, even of a fictional sort, which permits the sort of compositional flexibility here being discussed, and in fact permits a man to think it possible he is mistaken about his own origin and thus about who his suprafamilial relatives really are. The shallow knowledge, deliberately enforced, of actual kin ties, and the basing of dadia membership on a vague concept of "common origin" allows the dadia to adjust with maximum flexibility to pressures from outside its immediate boundaries. In any case, as dadia eminence is correlated with size, any dadia will, other things being equal, usually be more than willing to accept new members. Nor will such members necessarily play a secondary role. In one village, the chief of the major dadia was a man who had entered by the entranced-medium route some ten years earlier.

A striking example of the way in which these apparently genealogically determined matters respond to wider social and psychological forces is provided by the case of a schoolteacher living in a small south Bali village. This man's father, although something of a rural intellectual, was poor. The son became, however, by means of his father's contacts in the colonial bureaucracy, one of the few Balinese who received an adequate education under the Dutch. After the war the teacher even went to the United States for several months for study and upon his return to Bali became a high school principal in a town near his village.

At one time, early in his career, the teacher had been in love with a girl bearing the title of Pasek Gelgel, a rather high commoner title. But as he was ostensibly without a title, it having been "forgotten" by his father (a result, the teacher now theorizes, of the father's shame over his poverty), the girl's mother would not permit the marriage to take place, regarding the young teacher as unworthy of her daughter. Some years later, after he had returned from the United States, married a patri-cousin, and became a high school principal, a respected position in postwar Indonesia, his family was troubled with a series of illnesses. Ultimately his father and one of his brothers both died within a space of a few weeks, necessitating the principal's return to live in the family houseyard he had left as a young student.

After these various misfortunes, he went to a medium, who informed him that he was neglecting his true origin-temple, though with the professional caution these practitioners often display, the medium would not commit himself as to where this was. A few weeks later the teacher heard someone outside the house call out to his two orphaned nephews, who "it just happened" were named "Pasek" and "Gelgel," and, with a shock of recognition, he realized that his true kawitan was the Pasek Gelgel all-Bali origin-temple at Klungkung. He went to this temple to pray and was instantly convinced of the truth of his revelation: "I had such a good feeling that I was sure I was right: I felt as if I had just come home after being a long time away." He immediately declared himself to be a Pasek, and so a member of the local Pasek dadia, and was accepted by his fellow villagers as such.

Here, psychological conflicts arising out of the damage to self-esteem consequent upon rejection as a suitor and out of the confusions of self-image due to increased cultural marginality have coincided with sociological strains arising out of rapid upward mobility and changes in the bases for ranking, and the solution found is a reorganization of the very framework of a man's suprafamilial kinship relationships. Becoming a Pasek Gelgel (or, to be fair, or anyway phenomenological, rediscovering the fact that he *was* a Pasek Gelgel) enabled him to solve all these various problems at a single blow: his self-image was restored, his marginality denied, and his new status legitimized. And it is the flexibility of the cultural conceptions underlying Balinese kinship structure—"origin point," "ancestor worship" and so on—which allowed, even encouraged, this solution.

However, common origin in itself does not give a person an unassailable claim to being a member of a dadia. In fact, persons with bonafide genealogically traced kin ties to the group can be expelled from a dadia, and this occurrence is not unknown. Such exiles will either remain independent of dadia ties or, less often, suddenly discover, with the aid of a medium, that they were mistaken about their ties in the first place (hence the conflict) and really belong with another local group.

An idea of the degree to which dadia membership is actually augmented on grounds other than descent can be gained from examination of table 2, which shows the grounds for recruitment and expulsion of members of the four commoner dadias in Tihingan. Klungkung is an area where there has been very little population

TABLE 2. DADIA COMPOSITION, SHOWING MEMBERSHIP RECRUITMENT AND EXPULSION ON GROUNDS OTHER THAN GENEALOGICAL DESCENT IN TIHINGAN

Dadia Title	Component Households by Related Clusters (family groups recruited or expelled on grounds other than genealogical descent are marked with *)	Number of Households in Cluster	Past Movement of Family Group and Grounds for Membership or Expulsion
Pandé	Cluster A (the subdadia)	21	
	B	9	
	C	1	Maintained by 2 generations of substitute heir marriages
	D	4	
	E	4	One substitute heir marriage in present generation
	F	1	One adopted heir, present generation
	G	1	Maintained by three generations of substitute heir marriages and adoptions
	H*	2	Newly immigrant to village; same title-group
	I*	2	Different title-group, an allied Pandé title
	TOTAL	45	
Pasek Kayuslem	A	13	
	B	7 (1)	One household had been expelled from the dadia ten years ago and was not affiliated with any dadia
	C	1	
	D*	1	Because of sickness joined Pandé dadia thirty years ago, was later expelled from Pandé for adultery, and recently rejoined Pasek
	E	2	
	TOTAL	24	

Kebun Tubuh	A		6	
	B		8	
	C		1	
	D		3	
	E*		4	Had been expelled from dadia twenty years ago; recently re-entered the dadia
	F		1	
	G		1	
		TOTAL	24	
Pulasari	A		3	
	B		3	
	C		2	
	D		3	Substitute heir brought in from another title group
	E		2	
		TOTAL	13	

movement, and only four households out of 106 were recent immigrants. The number of lines which have recently had to resort to substitute heir marriages and adoptions for their continuance are also indicated.

Title-groups which are themselves considered only remotely related to one another, can, if local economic and political forces encourage it, unite into one dadia. For instance, within the Pandé, a title-group found all over the island, there are a number of related titles, Pandé Tosan, Pandé Mas, and so on, each with a different all-Bali origin-point and temple, and which regard themselves as all "distantly connected." In the village of Tihingan, two of these Pandé groups are together in a single dadia, while in the immediately adjacent village of Penasan, the same title-groups are not. In another, more extreme, example, a houseyard cluster in Penasan with the title of Pasek Gelgel was ejected from its own dadia for local political reasons, and it subsequently joined together with three other completely different title-groups which were small but ambitious, to worship at the temple of one of these smaller ones, the Pura Ibu Daoh. The rationale for this rare arrangement of mixed-title fusion was that it had been ritually revealed that the ancestors of the four groups involved had, in times long gone, been stationed in that hamlet by the Klungkung king to guard the border against a neighboring hostile state. Thus, they considered themselves, in retrospect, bound together as brothers in a metaphorical sense. While they had a common public temple, and some among them considered themselves a dadia, there was not yet consensus on the part of the rest of the villagers as to their having actually achieved that status.

Another example of a nascent dadia was in the village of Pau. This one was even more recently organized, and in fact during the period of fieldwork was in the process of building a new temple. Two stone-carvers were working on it continuously for several months. The new temple was identified to us as Bendul Dadia. When its membership was closely examined, it turned out to comprise four title-groups and to include two of the most powerful men in the village, one of them the klian subak, and their sons-in-law.

From these examples it can be seen that the process of dadia organization and the title system are complexly interrelated with one another. The titles form a cultural classification system by means of which persons can sort themselves and their associates into distinct and exclusive categories. The temple system, based as it is on physical structures and corporate properties (often a plot of land in addition to the temple itself, and including, in a sense, the gods themselves of that temple) provides another classificatory system, one which groups people together more than it differentiates them. Thus the two—the title system and the temple structures—provide a fundamental matrix on which particular dadia organizations can be built and maintained.

How the title composition of a village, its temple facilities, and its dadia organizations intersect in empirical reality, can be shown by comparing the three villages of Tihingan, Pau, and Penasan. It can be seen in figure 9 that the three communities have quite different distributions of titles. Tihingan has far fewer than the others, so that its four dadias account for over eighty-nine percent of its commoner population. Penasan in contrast has a scattering of twenty different title groups, twice as many as the other two villages, and there are ten of these which have only one or two houseyards as members. In the diagram, those title groups which are considered by everyone to be dadias are indicated, together with the ambiguous cases cited above, the Pura Ibu Daoh in Penasan and the Bendul Dadia in Pau.

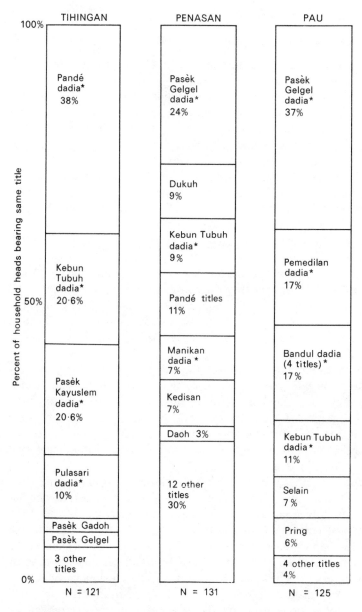

Fig. 9. Title-group composition of three villages, showing presence or absence of dadia organization. Dadias are marked with asterisks. (Based on a census of household heads. Tihingan percentages are calculated on the commoner population only.)

The Title System and Interlocal Ties

The all-Bali title or "origin-group" system also provides a framework within which relationships between dadia in different villages are organized. Such horizontal, castelike solidarity across village boundaries is, however, quite weak among the great majority of commoners and in many cases virtually nonexistent. There may be a general but not very intensely felt preference for title-group endogamy, if the much stronger preferences for hamlet and subdadia endogamy cannot be met. Sometimes a dadia in one village regularly sends a representative to the ceremonies of a same-title dadia in a nearby village as a gesture of friendship. Dadias often also send a representative to the ceremonies in the all-Bali origin-temple of their title group, an effort which may involve a journey all the way across the island.[33]

Although extra-village ties of this sort are of only marginal importance at best among the lower-ranking groups, horizontal unity tends, for reasons of politics and prestige we shall discuss in more detail below, to increase markedly as one moves up the stratification scale. Strong interlocal ties based on real or putative kinship among higher-status commoners, and especially among the gentry, which act to "lift" these groups up "above" the village social structure and organize them into a regional (and, at the very top, island-wide) aristocracy have long been of great importance in the overall, state-level integration of the Balinese social system. This contrast between a local and an interlocal focus of kingroup integration is, consequently, a primary mark of distinction between subordinate and superordinate in Bali.

There is another way in which dadia ties cross local borders, however. When a family (or group of families) emigrates to another village, usually a not too distant one, it may continue to attend the semiannual ceremonies in its home dadia and to contribute to the temple's support, even though it will be unable to participate in the other corporate activities of the kingroup. If this family grows in its new village, it may in time build its own dadia (assuming, of course, that it does not fuse with one already there), and in this case it will cut off connections with the old one. Almost every large dadia, especially now that urban migration is increasing, has a few of these recently dispersed adherents who turn up only for the semiannual ceremonies, and in villages where geographical mobility has been great a third or more of the villagers may have their dadia ties elsewhere. But such households have in any case little importance in the actual functioning of the dadia, being but ex-officio, for-ritual-only members. As will become apparent, the manner in which the dadia functions within the village organization makes it more or less impossible for it to operate as anything more than a strictly local group for most social purposes; though once more this is, as we shall see in chapter 4, not true for the gentry.

Teknonymy and Kingroup Flexibility

Clearly, this is a different kind of system from the classic segmentary systems with sharply defined corporate lineages of fixed membership. In societies with such kinship systems, the lineage members see themselves as more or less exactly organized in genealogical terms, the structure so organizing them stretching back through time, often fifteen generations or more. Of course, the idealized system as it appears in the minds of its members may not hold so consistently in fact—genealogies may conflict, individuals may forget, ignore, or manufacture ties, and lineage-clan systems reach varying levels of articulateness. But if the chain of kin ties is newly readapted to present contingencies, a new genealogy is fictionalized to legitimize it.

The Balinese (or, anyway, Balinese commoners) never see things this way. A man remembers his immediate ties generally only to the first- or second-cousin range, and is uninterested and unable to trace any further ones. All the ancestors beyond the great-grandfather level, and commonly sooner, are certainly forgotten and never fictionalized.[34] They are all, assuming they have been cremated, merged into the general category of "the gods," and it is ritually forbidden to use their names, even if they should by some quirk happen to be known. In a segmentary kinship system, an ancestral clan-founder stands at the root of the genealogical tree, the personal progenitor of everyone within the system; the Balinese rarely if ever know who began their local line, don't really care, and regard it as mildly improper even to want to know.

How then is that socially institutionalized genealogical amnesia accomplished, this "forgetting" of one's predecessors enforced?[35] Mainly through a rigorous, unusually systematized institution of teknonymy which progressively suppresses personal names and regularly substitutes what are essentially impersonal status terms.[36]

Outside of the immediate family, true kin terms are rarely used as forms of address or reference. In their place are the teknonymous terms, which are universally employed whenever a person has children. At birth each person is given a sex indicator, a birth-order title, and a proper name by which he or she is called until he marries and has a child.[37] Soon after he has a child people begin addressing and referring to him as "father of so-and-so," employing his child's personal name. The wife, likewise, becomes "mother of so-and-so," with the result that man and wife now have essentially the same name. It becomes extremely discourteous to use a person's childhood name instead of his teknonymous name, for to do so is to imply that he is still immature, and as a result a person's original name gradually fades from view. There is, in most cases, a second change of name, some years later when the couple have become grandparents. Their children now lose their childhood names in turn, and are referred to as "father of . . ." or "mother of . . ." their own child, while the grandparents' names shift to "grandfather of . . ." and "grandmother of . . ." the inserted name being that of the new grandchild. And finally, when they become great-grandparents, all the names again shift upwards, with the older couple now being called "great-grand-parent of . . ." the most recent offspring.

From the point of view of the individual, therefore, his name may shift as many as four times during the course of his life. Since not only a personal name is employed but also always a status term— "father of," "grandfather of," "great-grandparent of"—the name indicates each person's current familial status. From the point of view of a family group, there may be as many as three couples, all bearing the name of one small child, but with the status terms serving to indicate their lineal relationship to one another.

It is immaterial whether the child after whom all these adults are named is male or female. Since adoption of a teknonym occurs not overnight via a ceremony but gradually through the building up of a habit, the name is not firmly acquired until after the child has survived the perilous Balinese infancy. If the eponymous child dies after his parents have become firmly identified with his name, the teknonym is usually retained.

The grandparental and great-grandparental teknonyms, however, always follow the teknonym of a son and grandson. The result is that the chain of persons with related teknonyms is always a patriline, even though the youngest member of the line, the one after whom everyone is named, may be a girl. Which of a man's adult sons will be chosen as his intermediary namesake depends on a variety of contingencies. Probably most commonly, the teknonymous line is confined to one houseyard, with the grandfather being called after

the child of the son who remains in the houseyard. But circumstances alter cases, and other considerations may operate, such as
the greater prestige of one of his sons who has moved elsewhere so
that the grandfather continues to be identified with him and to use
his child's name.

An example from our field notes may make the entire naming
process more clear. Figure 10 shows some of the kinsmen of the
village head, the perbekel, of Tihingan, who is most commonly known
as Pan Loh, or "father-of-Loh." He is in his late thirties and has
several children, the oldest of which is a sixteen-year-old daughter
named Ni Wayan Loh, "Loh" being her personal name.

The perbekel's childhood name was I Wayan Suda, but this name
only appears in official records. His own father lives with him in the
same houseyard and until recently was called Pan Suda, or "father
of Suda," but now more and more is addressed as Kak Loh, or
"grandfather of Loh." The grandfather's own father is dead, but
reference to him (rare in any case, for Balinese do not like to speak
of the dead) is made as Kumpi Loh, "great-grandparent of Loh."
Pan Loh is the oldest son, and it is he who is succeeding his father,
not only by remaining in the houseyard with him but also by taking
his father's place as one of the most respected and powerful people
in the village. Two of his married brothers (Pan Sudiani and Pan
Darmarsih) have moved out of the houseyard, a third is newly wed
and continues to stay with his father and brother. Two sisters have
married out to other same-dadia houseyards, and there are nine
younger, unmarried brothers and sisters (not all of whom are shown
on the diagram) who, of course, remain at home. The diagram also
shows one of Kak Loh's brothers who also became a grandfather,
and the successive changes in his name.

The process of name-shifting is never cut-and-dried, however, for
there are many delays in change of usage. There are two main reasons
for postponing the renaming of a couple after they have become
grandparents. The first is that there is a general reluctance to take on
or award the grandparental teknonym while the person is still a
vigorous member of the community. Being a "grandparent" con-
notes a high status as wise elder, a person who gives advice and leaves
the "parents" to take action. Secondly, there is a strong element of
relativity in the conferring of a teknonym. A man's peers will tend to
call him by his "father of" name after he is a grandfather and even a
great-grandfather. The first ones to make the shift are always the
children. Thus, in our village, there was a very aged man who was a

Fig. 10. Balinese teknonymy, an actual case

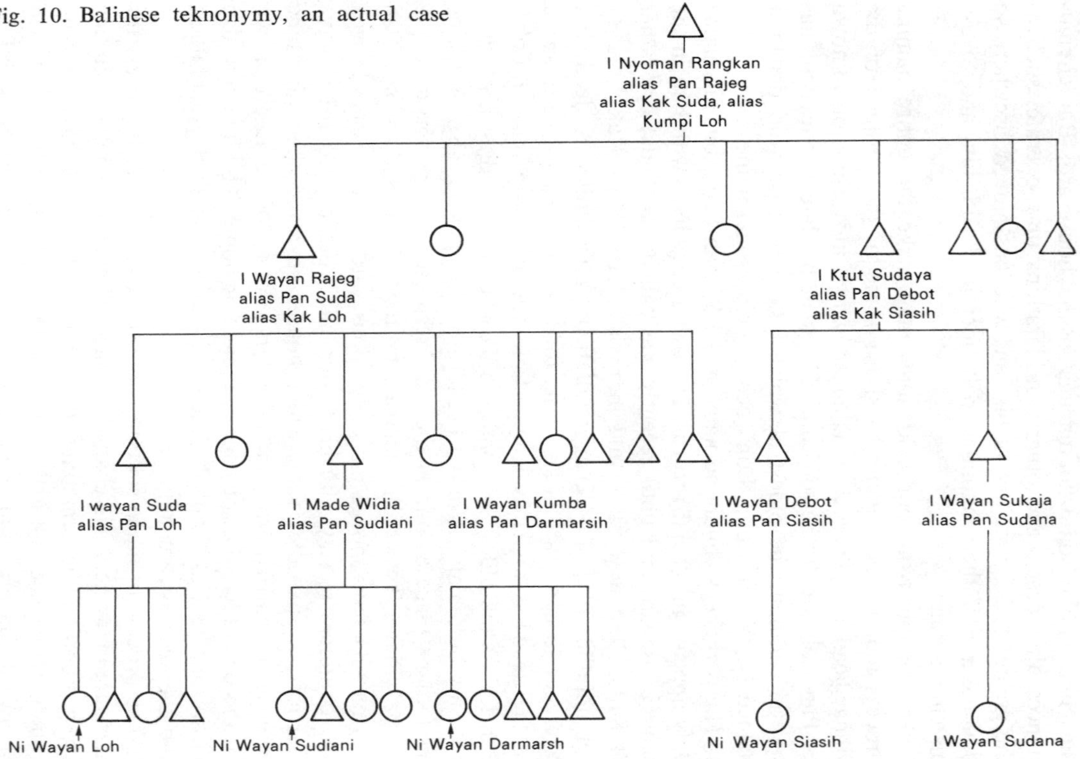

great-grandfather. One of his age-mates, another very old man, always referred to him as Pan Membah. The majority of the middle-aged villagers called him Kak Sukana. But the children called him Kumpi Puri, "great-grandfather of Puri," for little Puri was their playmate and the point of reference from which they saw him. It was obvious, however, that the number of those who might call him Pan, "father of," was rapidly diminishing, and the center of political balance in the village had already moved from his age-group to the next below, so that his actual social status was most nearly specified by the title "grandfather of," and that was indeed the one we most frequently heard.

This example leads us to consideration of an important function of the teknonymic system which is not directly related to kinship. This is that the set of four graduated status terms provide the outline for an informal series of age-grades within the village. It is the middle rank, the "fathers of," who are the backbone of the hamlet political structure. Those who are called "grandfather of" tend to take more passive advisory roles which, however, can be quite high in prestige and influence. And the "great-grandparents of" tend to be those who are dependent, senile, or physically weak. In a very few hamlets this correspondence between teknonymic title and social status in the village is fairly precise, for there a young man may not join the hamlet council until he has a child and at the same moment his father steps down from active membership in the council. In Tihingan, and probably most other hamlets, the correspondence was much less exact. There a young man joined the hamlet council at his marriage and stayed in it as long as he was capable of carrying out its rather heavy demands for physical labor. But even there the teknonymic generational categories served as rough indicators which were adjusted in everyday interaction to coincide with the community's real (but unnamed) social organizational layers of minors, active citizens, elders, and "retired" dependents.[38]

This parallel between teknonymous usage and hamlet role is by no means regular—nothing in Bali ever is. Insofar as it holds, however, the co-variation must be related to the importance that Balinese place on titles of address. In general, in Bali, the external forms of social intercourse, the manner of speech, and modes of etiquette are highly valued. In fact their system of social stratification as a whole is best understood neither as an arrangement of bounded social groups (a "caste" system), nor as a fluid ordering of persons according to their economic resources (a "class" system), but rather as several overlapping series of ranked honorific titles. As mentioned earlier, the pivotal distinction, symbolically, between gentry and commoners in Bali is that the former must always be addressed by their title, and the latter, while they do actually have inherited titles, may never be addressed by them. Teknonymy comes, for the commoners, to be a means of addressing one's equals respectfully and of avoiding the use of either personal names or honorific titles.

The members of the hamlet council are, so far as legal rights are concerned, all absolutely equal citizens; decisions are always reached unanimously in full meeting, and their leaders are never considered to be more than representative of the common will. Thus, to be a member of the hamlet council places the gentry in a chronically con-flictual situation, for their noble blood is a claim, however weak, to political and social superiority, a claim to membership in an exalted and nonlocalized aristocratic community above and outside of the hamlet. Mode of address in this situation becomes the weather vane for their social situation, summing up the various vectors of prestige and, correspondingly, shifting with changes in their social position.

Another important social consequence of the teknonymic custom is the social identification of man and wife, since they both carry the name of the same child. This is a matter of some importance in Bali where in fact the conjugal couple is usually considered to be an essential unit for most social purposes. Membership in any temple congregation, in the hamlet organization, in an irrigation society, all require the joint participation of a man and a woman, preferably husband and wife. The common appellation by a teknonym serves to underline this linking of man and wife together as a single unit.[39]

A third effect that teknonymy has is the stress it places on fertility in the conferring of social status, an implication which is in complete harmony with the Balinese value system. A man who has never had a child remains all his life a child terminologically. When all of his age-mates have become "father of" and "grandfather of," he retains his childhood name, and the shame of this is often very deeply felt.

Still a further implication in the system of teknonymy as it occurs in Bali is found in the image it provides of genealogical connections. The focus in teknonymy is the most recent addition to a descent line, not its progenitor. The patriline is thus defined in terms of its lowest member (generationally speaking) rather than its highest, in terms of the present rather than the past. It is not who one's ancestor is, or was, which is stressed, but who one's descendant is, whom one is ancestor to. It is a "downward looking" rather than an "upward looking" system, and a man sees himself, so to speak, producing structure below him rather than emerging from it above him.

But the most significant function of teknonymy for Balinese social structure is that of promoting genealogical amnesia, of systematically preventing any long-range genealogical knowledge from being preserved as a family tradition. Our thesis that teknonymy can be an active mechanism for suppressing such information is borne out by the fact that the Balinese gentry who do consider genealogies important enough to pass on from generation to generation, also do not, by and large, practice teknonymy.

Since in daily life a Balinese commoner hears only his father's teknonym, it becomes difficult for him to learn his father's personal name, and this ignorance is even more likely for his grandfather's and great-grandfather's names. Even while they are alive, one's ascendants' identities begin to disappear into indefinite generational categories, a fading which is merely completed after death with their ascent into a completely nonpersonalized divinity. It is extremely bad form for a son to ask what his father's personal name is, and unthinkable to use it should he happen somehow to know it, for his father, as all his living ascendants, should be viewed as half-way to a nonindividualized deification.

As a result, a Balinese villager will know the personal name of all those on the same generational level as himself and below, but not those on ascending levels. This means that only for the oldest men in the neighborhood—the great-grandfathers—will everyone living have an individual, absolute, fixed social definition, and this only in theory, for they often will forget a man's name after having called him "father of so-and-so" for a decade or more. When a man dies, he is in a sense inevitably lost to his descendants as a particular individual because none of them know his proper name. Thus a man cannot say to his own children "your great-great-grandfather" was so-and-so, because he doesn't know "who" in a personal sense he was, even though he may vaguely remember him as an actual living great-grandfather of himself. All he can tell him is that your great-great-grandfather was my great-grandfather, a simple and generalized tautology which contains information about kin-term usage but nothing about people. There is in fact no way older people can communicate to younger living people about a dead individual that the older knew as a man but the younger did not, in more than general terms as far as social identity is concerned. Of course, other characteristics about the man can be communicated—that he was wise, handsome, or came from North Bali—but the general loss of personal identity enforced by teknonymy usage tends to be part of a general cultural veil which falls over him in all his aspects. One should not expect to know much in detail about one's progenitors, living or dead, and to ask too many or too particular questions is to show a lack of breeding and piety.

In terms of kinship reckoning, this means that any tie which is based on a collateral relationship between two individuals both of whom were dead when the oldest living member of the kingroup was born is in principle untraceable. Or, put the other way around, any tie is intrinsically untraceable which is based on a common ancestor more than four generations ascendant from the oldest living member of the kingroup, assuming the life of a man and his great-great-grandchild rarely if ever overlap.

Figure 11 depicts in an idealized graphic form how teknonymy operates to erase knowledge of previous generations, and why four ascendant generations is the logically maximal time-depth of commoner kinship knowledge. Actually, four generations represents an absolute maximum range under ideal conditions in which the life of every individual overlaps with that of his great-grandchild, and the memory of sibling ties among the kinsmen one has known is perfect. Not only will most Balinese never know their great-grandfathers, and sometimes not even their grandfathers, as living men, but during the course of a long lifetime with many changes, they can easily forget facts of relationships they once knew. Thus, for instance, two men who are third or even second cousins could easily forget that their great-grandfathers were brothers, even if they once knew it. Indeed, their own fathers may have forgotten this fact themselves. Consequently the dissolution of traced kin ties typically occurs much more rapidly than in the model. Second cousins are often completely unaware how they are related, so that when their fathers die the specific nature of the tie can no longer be stated.

When one takes genealogies in a Balinese village, one can actually see the curtain of amnesia descending, for informants of older generations know the kinship links of younger men, who when they report their own genealogies regard themselves as related only in a vague and untraceable way. Thus a man's father may know who his son's second cousin is without the son himself being aware that this individual is his second cousin; and in most cases the father will never feel called upon to impart this information to the son. (See figure 12 for a specific example from our field notes.) For older men, the

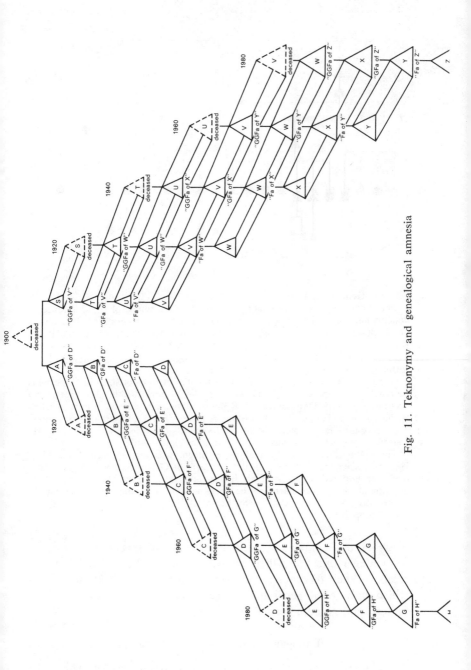

Fig. 11. Teknonymy and genealogical amnesia

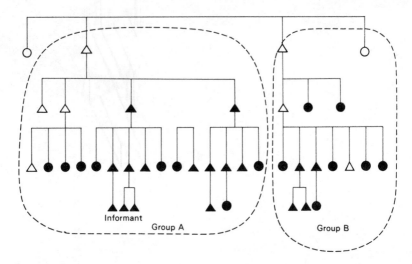

Fig. 12. Genealogical amnesia

The diagram presents an example, from our field notes, of the difference in kinship knowledgeability between persons of different generations. It shows a group of kinsmen who worship at a single subdadia temple within the Pasek Kajuslem dadia in Tihingan. The living are in black, the deceased in white. The genealogical connections were pieced together from a number of informants, none of whom knew the entire picture.

Group A indicates one young informant's picture of the limits of his "actual" kingroup. He could identify all the persons within this group and accurately specify their genealogical connections. The second group, marked B, he considered to be merely distant relatives. The informant's father, however, gave a more complete picture, and knew that Group B were his "second" cousins (*mindon*), by means of a grandfather sibling link.

The young informant, aged about eighteen, was intelligent and outgoing. He was on very good terms with the members of Group B, who lived no more than one hundred yards from his house, and, in his generation alone, there had already been two marriages between persons of Group A and Group B. There was no personal reason why he should be ignorant of his kinship ties with Group B.

neighborhood contains a much wider range of specific kin ties than for younger ones, and their knowledge is not, by and large, transferable. When the younger men grow older they will know the ties which have been generated in their time, but not those of their fathers' and grandfathers' times.

Endogamy and Kingroup Integration

As teknonymy is the major mechanism by means of which the peculiar organizational flexibility of Balinese kingroups is maintained, so endogamy is the major mechanism by means of which their internal solidarity is maintained in the face of this flexibility. Where teknonymy erases ties, endogamy reinforces them; where teknonymy facilitates the adjustment of kinship structure to situational exigencies, endogamy acts to make that structure stand out within the context of the wider society. Marriage of closer relatives is what gives Balinese kingroups their integrative strength, and the degree to which endogamous rules are observed within any particular kingroup is directly correlated with its size and with the degree of corporate strength that group is able to display in village political, economic, and social life.

In general, the Balinese rule of endogamy can be stated in terms of a series of alternative marriage possibilities of declining preference, which fall onto a scale of increasing kin distance between the potential spouses. The most preferred marriage is with one's parallel patri-cousin, one's father's brother's daughter.[40] If one cannot or will not marry his father's brother's daughter, then he should marry a member of his own subdadia (or household cluster); if not a sub-dadia member, then a dadia member. And if not a dadia member, then at least a hamlet member or a member of the title-group in another hamlet.[41] The rule says that (outside of the prohibited circle of primary relatives), other things being equal, the closer the spouse the better, and there is a finely graduated continuum of "closeness." Between one's actual patrilateral parallel cousin and the range of candidates classed as "from the same origin-temple," there are many distinct steps. One's second or third patrilateral parallel cousins are also highly desirable. Next to these come those members of the dadia who are close relatives through one's mother (if she, too, was a dadia member originally), that is, those who are simultaneously cousins on one's father's side and on one's mother's side.[42]

The basic norm for endogamy is not so much a fixed requirement which, in practice, occasionally is ignored or evaded; rather it is a model and an ideal indicating the general direction in which approved conduct lies. That most marriages are not actually between parallel cousins but, rather, endogamous to village or dadia, and that a sizeable number are not endogamous at all, does not disprove the importance or the reality of the father's brother's daughter preference but merely indicates that here as elsewhere moral excellence is only sporadically achieved and not always desired. A rule for endogamy cannot be absolute, for unless the unit of in-marriage is very large, there is never an adequate ratio of marriageable women to men at the necessary times. And, it follows almost logically, given some sort of kingroups larger than the immediate family, that the rule will be stated in terms of a sliding scale.

How and when actual marriage practices follow these cultural directives can be explored through statistical studies. We have two sorts of quantitative data here. The first is a complete genealogy of the entire population of Tihingan covering four generations and 243 marriages. With this we are able to trace out the stepwise pattern of endogamous preferences within the kinship networks. Tables 3 and 7 are drawn on this material. Table 3 gives the broad outlines of the pattern: how seven percent of these marriages were with the father's brother's daughter, another seven percent were with further patrilateral parallel cousins, while a cumulative total of forty-nine percent were within the same dadia.

TABLE 3. ENDOGAMOUS MARRIAGES BY DEGREES OF DISTANCE FROM EGO (TIHINGAN, MALE COMMONERS)

Wife's Origin	Number of Marriages	% of Marriages	Cumulative %
Father's brother's daughter	18	7.4%	7.4%
Second or third patrilateral parallel cousin	17	7.0	14.4
Same dadia	84	34.5	48.9
Same village but different dadia	73	30.0	78.9
Outside village but same title	15	6.2	85.1
Outside village, different title	36	14.8	99.9
Total	243		

NOTE: This table is based on a count of men's marriages found in our genealogies of all living members of the village of Tihingan, going back three generations from the main informant, the sixty-year-old leader of the main dadia. These genealogies were extensively checked with a number of other people both in his and in other kin groups. Since the anchor point was living members of the village, some now dead lines may have been lost, though we explicitly probed for these. Likewise, some brief, unsuccessful marriages may have been omitted. The criteria for "dadia" were general public label as a dadia and the presence of a temple. The four main dadias of Tihingan were counted as "dadias," while members of other title-groups were considered not to be dadia members.

The second sort of statistical data is not genealogical but enables us to make comparisons between the three villages of Tihingan, Penasan, and Pau. This is a census of households, that is to say, of living married couples together with their titles. This census data of the three villages makes it possible for us to specify how marital choices within title-groups relate to the structure of the community.

The most important general point is that *the intensity to which title-group endogamy is practiced in any particular village is primarily related to the extent that kinship has become an important organizing principle in the village's social structure.*

Table 4 shows two aspects of this proposition.[43] First, title-group endogamy is directly correlated with the degree of kinship differentiation of the village—that is, *the greater the degree to which dadias have developed the greater the proportion of close-relative marriages.* Thus, line one shows that title-group endogamous marriages account for about forty-eight percent of all marriages in Tihingan, thirty-five percent in the intermediate village, Pau, and only twenty-four percent of the marriages in the least differentiated village, Penasan.

TABLE 4. RELATIONSHIP BETWEEN VILLAGE SOCIAL
ORGANIZATION TYPE AND DEGREE OF ENDOGAMY.
(Endogamy is measured by percent of marriages of household heads to women
of title-group of village.)

Wife's Origin	Villages Ranked by Degree of Kinship Differentiation		
	Tihingan (Greatest Kinship Differentiation)	Pau (Medium Kinship Differentiation)	Penasan (Least Kinship Differentiation)
1. Same local title-group (1a. Dadias only)	48.7 (52.7)	35.2 (44.4)	24.4 (29.8)
2. Same village but different title-group	29.7	59.2	51.9
3. Total village endogamy (1 plus 2)	78.4	94.4	76.3
4. Outside village	13.2	4.0	18.3
5. No wife	8.2	1.6	5.3
Total household heads	121	125	131

Second, *village endogamy is not directly related to the degree of kinship expansion of the community.* The high village endogamy (grouping kin and nonkin marriages: ninety-four percent) of Pau, is, for example, mainly attributable to the fact that it is socially self-sufficient, being land-rich, very rural, egalitarian, and, relatively speaking, rather more economically autonomous than the other two. Tihingan, the high-differentiation village, is economically centered on the craft of blacksmithing, and Penasan, the least differentiated village, is land-poor and rather heavily proletarianized, with many of its members holding unskilled jobs in the nearby town and serving as sharecroppers to other hamlets. All of these elements are of course interrelated; but, in general, village endogamy seems not to be highly responsive to differences in kinship differentiation as such. The marked preference of commoners for local marriage is fairly intense whether kinship institutions are highly developed or not, though it may be weakened by increased contacts with the outside world.

The argument could be made that a correlation between size of dadia and degree of endogamy is a statistical artifact, that the larger a kingroup is the greater is the possibility of finding a mate within it. This is, of course, partially true. There are two ways to explore the extent to which sheer size of an in-marrying group creates higher endogamy rates and the extent to which other forces are at work.

The first method is by simply holding size of dadia constant and making comparisons between dadias of similar size. This is the method of table 5, in which the dadias of the three villages are arranged side-by-side according to descending size. From an inspection of this table it is apparent that dadias in Tihingan have consistently higher endogamy rates than comparable dadias in the other villages.

If as in table 6, the dadias of the three villages are listed simply by descending size, they do not show a simple pattern of descending endogamy rates. Rather, those of Tihingan again are regularly out of place.

The second method for taking the size and the segmenting of marriage populations simultaneously into account is in the construction of an index that combines information on observed choice frequencies with probabilities calculated on the basis of the ratio of dadia members to total village members. This is the "Marital Choice Index" given in table 6. It answers the question: to what degree have the members of a particular dadia actually chosen to marry within it, over and above what they might have done had their choices been

TABLE 5. RELATIONSHIP BETWEEN SIZE OF DADIA AND DEGREE OF ENDOGAMY: THREE VILLAGES COMPARED (COMMONERS ONLY)

	Tihingan (Greatest Kinship Differentiation) Number of Households		Pau (Medium Kinship Differentiation) Number of Households		Penasan (Least Kinship Differentiation) Number of Households	
Dadia # 1						
Size	46		46		32	
% of endogamous marriages		60.8		63.0		43.7
Dadia # 2						
Size	25		21		12	
% of endogamous marriages		52.0		33.3		8.3
Dadia # 3						
Size	25		14		9	
% of endogamous marriages		44.0		14.3		11.1
Dadia # 4						
Size	12		9		4	
% of endogamous marriages		41.1		22.2		25.5
Others in village who are not in dadias						
Number	13		35		74	
% of title-group endogamous marriages		10.7		11.4		20.0
Total number of households in village	121		125		131	
Proportion of village in dadias		89.2		72.0		43.5

randomly distributed among the dadias of the village. It shows that three of the four Tihingan dadias do in fact overchoose their own dadia mates.

Not only is the amount of close-relative marriage closely related to the degree of kinship differentiation in the community as a whole, but the rate and range of endogamy is also correlated with the strength and size of the individual dadia. That is to say, *the larger and more prominent the local dadia the greater the degree of en-*

TABLE 6. RELATIONSHIP BETWEEN SIZE OF DADIA AND DEGREE
OF ENDOGAMY: THREE VILLAGES COMPARED

Dadia In order of absolute size. Title-group name in parenthesis.	Size (Households)	% Endogamous Marriages	Marital Choice Index*
Tihingan #1 (Pande)	46	60.8	.67
Pau #1 (Pasek Gelgel)	46	63.0	.46
Penasan #1 (Pasek Gelgel)	32	43.7	.48
Tihingan #2 (Pasek Kayusiem)	25	52.0	.52
Tihingan #3 (Kebun Tubuh)	25	44.0	.37
Pau #2 (Pemedilan)	21	33.3	.20
Pau #3 (Kebun Tubuh)	14	14.3	.07
Tihingan #4 (Pulasari)	12	41.1	.50
Penasan #2 (Kebun Tubuh)	12	8.3	.04
Pau #4 (Pasek Selain)	9	22.2	.20
Penasan #3 (Manikan)	9	11.1	.09
Penasan #4 (Daoh)	4	25.5	—

*MARITAL CHOICE INDEX: This index explores the patterns of marital choices
within a segmented bounded population. Ignoring all marriages to persons outside the population (here, commoners in a particular village), it answers the
question: do the members of the different segments (here, dadias) exhibit distinct patterns of choice, either for or against certain segments? The fact that
larger dadias present more marital possibilities both for their own members
and for persons from other dadias is taken into account by including in the
formula the proportion of households of each dadia to the total number of
households in the village.

The index goes from 1.00 (all choices by segment A are for segment B, or
all choices by segment A are within segment A—perfect endogamy) to 0.00
(no choice pattern at all exhibited) to −1.00 (absolute avoidance of all marriages between or within the segment). The figures in the table are, of course,
those for "self-selection," that is, kingroup endogamy. Penasan # 4 has not
been calculated because of the small N.

The formula used here is a revised version of one constructed by Millicent
Ayoub ("Parallel Cousin Marriage and Endogamy: A Study in Sociometry,"
Southwestern Journal of Anthropology 15 [1959]:266–75). She called it an
index of "preference," but in actuality it is based on tabulations of accomplished marriages. The relationship between action (the choices actually made
and acted upon) and "preferences" (which may range from emotional in-
clinations to institutionalized directives) cannot be assumed to be direct and
simple. It is for this reason we call it a "Marital Choice Index." The formula
is applicable only to bounded populations in which all or nearly all marriages
are contracted with persons from within the population itself, as is the case
with these Balinese villages.

Formula for Marital Choice Index:

$E_{ij} = R_i \cdot P$

Index $= O_{ij} - E_{ij} / R_i - E_{ij}$

E_{ij} is the expected frequency within the cell
O_{ij} is the observed frequency within the cell
R_i is the sum of observed frequencies in row
P is the number of households in dadia/number of
   households in village

dogamy it shows. This can be seen from a closer analysis of the dadia endogamous marriages in these same three villages (see tables 5 and 6).

Since endogamy, fusing as it does affinal and consanguineal ties, clearly intensifies ingroup solidarity, its correlation with the size and power of a dadia is perhaps not surprising. But it does reveal the dynamics of kinship expansion, the actual processes of bringing about the differentiation of kingroups and sub-kingroups out of the general community background, much more clearly. The progressive narrowing of the range of endogamy, a focusing of affinal connections within an increasingly contracted consanguineal field is the primary mechanism by means of which well-defined, corporate kingroups are produced in Bali.

A fully differentiated Balinese system can be seen as a set of endogamous groups placed within one another like so many Chinese boxes. The largest box consists of the community as the most weakly favored endogamous unit; the smaller boxes consist in turn of the dadia and the subdadia, more contracted and, in preferential terms, more strongly favored endogamous units. As a dadia grows in size, its members more and more tend to marry one another rather than nonmembers. Out of the general pattern of village endogamy develops a specialized pattern of common title- (or origin-) group endogamy, which makes of the group employing it, and to the degree to which it does employ it, a differentiated nucleus within the larger social cell— a discriminate, bounded subgroup with a definite internal solidarity set within general village life. When, and if, subdadias develop, they do so on the basis of a concentration of endogamous relationships within a yet narrower range. A somewhat closer look, by means of table 7, at the details of the endogamy pattern for all four generations of commoner men in Tihingan will perhaps clarify this argument somewhat.

The table shows this focusing endogamy pattern quite clearly. It gives the number of each type of marriage—first patri-cousin, second or third patri-cousin, common origin only, villager only, and from outside the village—contracted by members of each type of kingroup—those belonging to a subdadia, those belonging to a dadia but not to a subdadia, and those belonging to the village but not to any dadia or subdadia. The theoretically expected number of each type of marriage for each type of kin member, if kingroup membership and intensity of endogamy were related, is given in a parenthesis next to the observed number. Thus, the table is to be read "thirteen, rather than the six expected by chance, commoner male subdadia

TABLE 7. RELATIONSHIP BETWEEN DEGREE OF ENDOGAMY AND
KINSHIP DIFFERENTIATION; TIHINGAN COMMONERS

| Wife's Original Kinship Position | Husband's Kingroup Affiliation | | | | | | Totals |
| | Subdadia | | Dadia Only | | No Dadia Affiliation | | |
	No.	Expected	No.	Expected	No.	Expected	
First patri-cousin	13	(5.2)	5	(11.6)	0	(1.2)	18
Second or third patri-cousin	12	(4.9)	5	(11.0)	0	(1.1)	17
Same title-group only	22	(24.2)	61	(54.2)	1	(5.5)	84
Same village but different title-group	8	(21)	53	(47.1)	12	(4.8)	73
Outside village	15	(14.7)	33	(33)	3	(3.4)	51
Totals	70		157		16		243

X^2 significant above .01 level

members have contracted parallel cousin marriages; twelve, rather
than 4.9 have married their second or third patri-cousin; twenty-two
rather than 24.2, common-origin dadia members (that is, *not* including cousins); and so on.

The figures indicate, of course, that the tendency for close endogamy to be concentrated in the more highly kinship-organized parts
of the community and to broaden out in the less organized parts
is very strong. The subdadia has far more cousin marriages than
would be expected on a chance basis and far less village-only marriages, while nondadia people have far more village-only marriages
than would be expected and far fewer close-relative ones of any
sort, with the dadia-only people falling, as they should, in between
on each scale. That the marriage figures for persons of the same
village but different title-group are in each case almost exactly at
the chance level shows once more that the absolute degree of village
endogamy is fairly independent of kinship organization as such, and
is a function of other factors.

Endogamy and the differentiation and subdifferentiation of kingroups are, therefore, part of the same dynamic process. As a kingroup grows in size it becomes more self-contained, producing its
wives from among its "sisters," and as it becomes more self-contained
it becomes more solidary. Thus endogamy increases as the kingroups

themselves emerge, it expands in importance as the system expands. The ultimate of such development would be a fully in-married group where all affinal ties are also consanguineal ones, and in fact all paternal uncles are also fathers-in-law. But, like many ideals, such a complete achievement of endogamy is more practically viewed as an unreachable utopian goal to be striven for (or, perhaps, only cele-brated) than a state to be actually realized, because such a realiza-tion would almost completely undermine the equally valued ideal of local community solidarity. For if endogamy makes for intragroup solidarity it also tends to make for intergroup conflict, so that the more highly differentiated a village is in kinship groupings, the more difficult it is to keep kin allegiance and kin-based factionalization subordinate to the demands of local territorial organization. A rule of endogamy, so far as it is adhered to, uses affinal ties to cement relations within groups, in the same way a rule of exogamy uses such ties to establish and maintain relations between descent groups at the cost of possible conflicts of interest within them. This tension be-tween a press toward kingroup endogamy, kingroup solidarity, and kingroup autonomy on the one hand and village endogamy, village solidarity, and village autonomy on the other, forms—the more so the more developed the dadia organization—one of the basic dynamics of the Balinese political system on its lowest levels.

The Dadia and Political Leadership

How the pattern of kingroup differentiation within any hamlet is related to the struggle for social eminence can be seen more clearly through an examination of local political leadership in our three villages. By political leadership we mean here simply the position of power and influence, formal and informal, and the processes by which these statuses are filled. The prestige of title, wealth, and other personal attributes such as education, magico-spiritual force, or leadership abilities, are all factors of importance in bringing a par-ticular man to the fore. Nonetheless, in general, we found that in those villages where dadia organization was highly developed, politi-cal, economic, and stratificatory ascendancy were usually expressed in kinship terms.

As we have seen, any Balinese community consists, from the point of view of kinship, of several classes of household groups. First, there is the "unaffiliated mass," those households which have no kingroup membership above the houseyard or small houseyard cluster level; they usually consider themselves members of the hamlet only. Then there may be some who belong to incipient dadias, weakly corporate houseyard clusters approaching crystallization as fully differentiated descent groups. Next, there may be a class of households who belong to well-established dadias, with temples, dadia chiefs, and a relatively high degree of internal integration. Among these there may be those who belong to incipient subdadias vaguely emerging within the dadia. Finally there may be those who belong to a fully differentiated subdadia where intermarriage and group solidarity reach a peak.

This ordering of village members according to their affiliation to kingroups also represents, to a remarkable degree, an ordering of subordination and superordination, of obscurity and eminence, within the local community. If the hamlet contains a dadia, its members tend to form a dominant leadership group in the hamlet, and if within the leading dadia there is a subdadia, its members correspondingly tend to dominate their kingroup and hence their hamlet. As a matter of fact, within subdadias there are often large, dominant single-houseyard extended families in which are focused all the positions of power and influence in the hamlet. Again the Chinese box image is appropriate: it is the man inside the smallest box, the man who heads the main family of the main subdadia of the main dadia in the community, who is, other things being equal, most likely to be of local consequence. The unaffiliated man, the outsider, is considerably at a disadvantage in the political process, although he may form alliances with other nondadia members on a voluntary basis to balance the power of the dadia groups in local factional struggles, and they may find strength in such factors as personal leadership abilities, wealth, and so on. Art groups and work groups may also form a basis for factional formation among such unaffiliated people.

How dadia membership relates to village leadership can be shown in a statistical tabulation of the major village officers and their dadia affiliations. The two most powerful roles within a village are those of perbekel and klian subak. Both can be important because their domain extends far outside the hamlet within which their occupant lives. Not every village, of course, has a perbekel or a klian subak living there, but when it has one he is likely to be one of the most prominent villagers, partly because of the power the office confers on him and partly because he was chosen precisely on account of his leadership capacities. Aside from special personal competencies, such as literacy and sophistication in dealing with urban administrators, one very important attribute is often that of position within a large and powerful kingroup, especially a dadia. Lesser political statuses, whose domains are confined to the village itself, include the pengli-man, the assistant to the perbekel, appointed by him, the klian banjar or hamlet chiefs who are under the authority of the banjar council rather than its directors, but who nonetheless are persons of weight, and the priests in the village temples, the pemangku dalem, pemangku puseh, and pemangku bale agung.

In the villages of our study, these various village officials were more often dadia members than not. If the members of subdadias are singled out and set against all the other members of the villages (combining both ordinary dadia members with unaffiliated villagers) the relationship is even clearer. Table 9 uses material only from Tihingan and Penasan, the only two villages in our study with sub-dadias as well as dadias.

TABLE 8. DADIA MEMBERSHIP AND POLITICAL LEADERSHIP

	Village Officers		Remaining Villagers		
Dadia Affiliation	No.	Expected	No.	Expected	Totals
Dadia members	25	(19.6)	257	(262.4)	282
Nondadia members	6	(11.4)	158	(152.6)	164
Total	31		415		446

X^2 significant above .05
NOTE: This table is based on census material from four villages: Tihingan, Penasan, Pau, and Mengguna. The leaders (both present and retired) tabulated were perbekel, klian subak, klian banjar, pengliman, and pemangku desa.

TABLE 9. SUBDADIA MEMBERSHIP AND POLITICAL LEADERSHIP

	Village Officers		Remaining Villagers		
Subdadia Affiliation	No.	Expected	No.	Expected	Totals
Subdadia members	8	(2.1)	39	(44.9)	47
Non-subdadia members*	6	(11.9)	260	(254.1)	266
Total	14		299		313

X^2 significant above .01
*That is, "ordinary dadia members" plus unaffiliated villagers.
NOTE: This table is based on census material from the two villages with sub-dadia, Tihingan and Penasan. The leaders tabulated are the same ones as in table 8.

The three villages show interesting differences in the role that kinship plays in their political processes, differences which are related to the particular pattern of title distribution in each village, differences in wealth apportionment, the presence of gentry, and relative proximity to the town of Klungkung.

In Tihingan, as we have seen (see fig. 9 above), there are four large title-groups accounting for eighty-eight percent of the commoner population and five smaller ones. The four large ones have crystallized into dadias, and in recent years have further consolidated into two factions. The first and third largest dadias are allied over against the second and fourth largest, with the unaffiliated groups plus the gentry lending their support to the latter, smaller, faction.

As a result the hamlet is split quite evenly. There are usually four klian banjar, officers of the hamlet council, in Tihingan, and they have usually been chosen from each of the four dadias. The village temple priest, the pemangku puseh, had been a Pandé, but on his death the two factions disagreed so violently on appointing a successor that a somewhat inconvenient compromise was reached—the office is filled by the priest of each dadia temple in turn, rotating every few months. One prominent family in each of the four dadias owns a large blacksmith's forge for the making of gamelan instruments. The workers in these forges are almost exclusively the members of each dadia alone. As mentioned earlier, the manufacturing process requires an ability to recruit large numbers of workers for short periods of time, and it is easier to call on kinsmen than on nonrelatives. For this reason the unaffiliated members of the village play little or no part in the gamelan-making industry. There are very few marriages between members of the four dadia, and, in the present generation, none between the two factions.

Thus in this hamlet with a highly differentiated kinship system, kingroups form the focus of social organization, the four main blocs of common-origin, highly endogamous, kinsmen providing a simple and explicit framework for the internal structure of the hamlet. The influence of this structure extends even to national politics, for the first of Tihingan's factions belongs to one of the two major parties represented in Bali, the Socialist party, while the second faction is unanimously committed to the other party, the Nationalist. The gentry of Tihingan play only a secondary role in this situation. In the "Balinese time"—that is, before the advent of the Dutch—they may have had more influence on the hamlet, and in the first years of this century they did possess the perbekel office; today they are largely spectators. An exception to this passive role are the younger generation of men in the Brahmana house, who are semieducated government clerks and who take some leadership in the Nationalist faction.

The second village, Penasan, presents a rather different picture. Here there is only one title-group of any size, the Pasek Gelgel, and it has crystallized into a dadia, with a sharply marked subdadia within it. Two of the three smaller title-groups also have dadia temples and some degree of organization. The third, the Tangkaban, despite its fairly large representation has never attempted to form a dadia. The top dadia, the Pasek Gelgel, entirely dominates local life, with all important political offices held by members of this group, and in fact by one large extended family which controls the subdadia. Within this one family are the pengliman, the klian banjar, the klian subak, and also a regionally powerful politician, the head of the Socialist party for the entire Klungkung region. The remainder of the villagers are atomized, poor, and inactive. The political power of the pengliman is reinforced by his reputation as a man of extraordinary and dangerous psychic powers: in the annual dragon-and-witch ritual drama performed by the people of Penasan before their death-temple, he plays the part of Rangda the witch, goes into an intense trance, and in so doing has intimate connection with the supernatural. His son, the Socialist politician, while on the surface a most westernized and modern man, is a noted curer, deriving his healing powers through meditation in the village death-temple. Thus, in this case, three factors are found associated: political office and influence, strategic kinship location, and personal charisma.

There is, in Penasan, one small, ineffective dissident group that has the temerity to oppose this formidable combination of kinship position and magical power. This group is headed by a man, Pan Pugeg, reputed to be the illegitimate son of the head of the dominant dadia. Adopted at birth by a man of another title-group, Pan Pugeg has been trying recently to establish the new dadia in Penasan, the aforementioned Pura Ibu Daoh (see page 81) with his own title-group at the core, but augmented by members of several others. He has, in fact, attracted into it a set of five households that had been evicted from the Pasek Gelgel dadia, the dominant one, after a quarrel over a woman. With Pan Pugeg's legal advice, the evicted group sued to the high court in Klungkung for its portion of the dadia-owned land, and won. Some of this land it may have transferred to the new dadia of Pan Pugeg.

Despite these efforts to build an effective opposition, the hamlet affairs of Penasan are still run entirely by the ruling elite. Most decisions made in hamlet council unanimously follow whatever suggestions are put forth by the top men of Pasek Gelgel. Most task-group arrangements cut across dadia membership lines. As in Tihingan, modern voting patterns are a remarkably precise guide to the fundamental hamlet faction structure. The mass of the people of Penasan are Socialists, and the only exceptions are Pan Pugeg and his son, a teacher, who are Communist party members.

In the third village, Pau, kinship plays an even less prominent role. Although three title-groups, the Pasek Gelgel, Medilan, and Kebon Tubuh, have built dadia temples, kingroup ties are here fairly well subordinated to village loyalties. Perhaps this is due to the presence of a plurality of medium-sized title-groups which give an egalitarian quality to local political life and make the achievement of stable alliances difficult; perhaps it is because the rural, agrarian, and socially encapsulated nature of this hamlet causes it to place more emphasis on territorial unity. In any case kingroup ceremonies, activities, and allegiances are sharply played down in Pau, and village ones played up. Kinship continues to play a role, and local eminence and leadership are still correlated to some degree with dadia membership, but it is far from being the central organizing principle that it is in Tihingan. In fact, there seems to be an active and conscious effort to inhibit the influence of kinship in the way that Pau is subdivided into banjar for funerals and civil affairs. It has four banjar, whose members are drawn from all over the village community, with care taken that no two are absolutely adjacent neighbors and that no kinship group is concentrated within one banjar.

The case of the ambiguous Bendul dadia, discussed above, is interesting from the point of view of political processes. One small title-group containing only three households, the Bendul was in 1958 making tremendous efforts to establish itself as a recognized dadia. The three Bendul men were wealthy by Balinese standards (among them they have twenty-nine plots of rice land, and therefore at least twenty sharecroppers under their influence). One was a klian subak, a position which gives him considerable opportunities to grant or withhold favors. His brother was a local political party leader. The third, their cousin, was the priest in the village death-temple. The dadia which they were in the process of organizing was a composite one, containing people of four different title-groups. The largest of these, the Badeg, is fairly wealthy, and is closely intermarried with the influential Bendul trio. In the early days of our study, when we asked the inhabitants of Pau to list their dadias, they always headed the list with this composite one, calling it after its leading, but numerically fewest, members, the Bendul.

Thus, in both Penasan and in Pau during the period of study there were emerging new dadias of composite membership. In Penasan, it was a result of efforts on the part of a dissident minority to consolidate their efforts and to gain social status through the possession of a dadia temple. In Pau, on the other hand, eminence had preceded the building of the temple, and its actual construction was the capstone of several generations of effort.

Rivalry Between Dadias: Marriage by Capture

In those villages where kinship is an unusually prominent principle of social organization, the competition for prestige between dadias reaches a high pitch of intensity. This rivalry may be fought out, as we have shown, in terms of striving for dominance in hamlet affairs. It may also be fought out on an economic level. Wealth, however, is not displayed through consumer goods such as clothes or housing but by lavish temple ornamentation and festivals, or tooth-filing and cremation ritual celebrations. But the master symbol of the relative prestige of every kingroup lies in the title itself, to some extent in the deferential behavior of other villagers toward the members of the title-group, and most particularly in the placement of extra-kingroup marriages.

The fact that the commoner title system is not an explicit and fully agreed upon hierarchy of titles does not diminish the ferocity of the contest. A particular commoner title has quite different relative rank in different villages, entirely dependent on the strength and local prestige of the titleholders in each particular hamlet. (Some groups, such as the Pasek Gelgel, for reasons of recent history, namely, their retainer position to certain nineteenth-century kings, are dominant in their hamlets more frequently than other titles, but numerous cases can be found where persons bearing these same titles have a markedly subordinate local position.)

In spite of this lack of consensus, Balinese all believe that there is no equality among titles, and, usually, every title-group secretly regards itself as, in fact, higher than all the others. The discrepancy is reflected in the inconsistent versions of origin myths for each title-group. Different sources give entirely different stories to account for each title. For instance, bearers of the title "Kebon Tubuh" claim to be descendants of a nobleman named Gusti Kebon Tubuh who was declassed because he rebelled unsuccessfully against an unjust king. Others privately say that Gusti Kebon Tubuh was declassed because he was caught stealing in the king's garden and tied there as punishment; as they say, you can see from the title itself—*kebun* means garden, *tubuh* means body. Similarly, bearers of the title "Pulasari" trace their origin to nobility; but their detractors claim that the name comes from *pules*, to sleep, and *ari*, day—the Pulasari ancestor was so-named because he was lazy and slept all day.

The title-group conflict becomes overt, and at times has a violent climax, whenever there is an attempt at marriage between two competing dadias. A marriage of a kinswoman to a competing group is considered an implicit acknowledgment of the inferiority of her kingroup to the one into which she is marrying. For this reason, unions which are exogamous to kingroup are often marked by intrigue, kidnapping, and prolonged intergroup hostility.

Where marriage takes place within the dadia the process is a straightforward and quite undramatic one. Usually such a marriage is arranged by the parents of the couple, who may, particularly in the case of a cousin marriage, have been discussing the possibility of such a tie since the betrothed were children. The marriage is announced to the hamlet by the father of the girl. He beats the hamlet slit gong to call everyone together and informs them that he is agreed to the girl being taken as wife by his kinsman's son. The couple themselves are usually in favor of the marriage, in many cases have been sleeping together for some time, and in any case, should the marriage not work out, are free to divorce. In keeping with the general non-legalistic, and secular Balinese approach to marriage, the only ceremony is the *masakapan*, a brief and simple ritual performed in the husband's houseyard temple, in which the woman is presented to her husband's ancestors and accepted by them as a member of their kingroup. Occasionally, a custom of temporary matrilocal residence in which the groom lives and works for six months or so in his father-in-law's household as a kind of bride payment (the custom is called *nungoning* or *madig*) is followed, but this is quite rare today. All in all, kingroup endogamous marriage is, at least for the commoners, a very simple, subdued, almost wholly intramural affair in which the larger public community participates in only a routine, marginal, but half-interested manner at best. It is a concern of the kingroup, not the hamlet.

With kingroup exogamous marriages, however, it is quite otherwise. These always involve some form of real or sham "wife capture,"
called *ngerorod*. The woman steals out of her houseyard at night to
join her lover, or she is snatched up against her will on the road, or
the groom's friends bring her to him under a ruse, and so on, and
the two go into hiding, usually outside the village and often some
distance away. On discovering their loss, the woman's family and kingroup rise up in arms, strike the kingroup slit gong to alarm the
populace, and launch a mass search for the missing couple. When the
couple is found, often after several days, the girl is asked by the village chief if she wishes to stay with the man, if she has gone with him
willingly. If she is willing to marry her "abductor," then that part of
the hamlet not directly involved, anxious to keep the conflict from
erupting into the open, turns its efforts to convincing the girl's parents to give in and let the marriage take place. Usually, after a greater
or lesser number of protestations, insinuations and threats, they do,
and the wife's father beats the slit gong as a sign of his grudging
agreement.[44] If they do not, then the marriage will probably still take
place, unless the girl decides to come home to appease her parents,
but a very tense situation between the two groups will have been
created. If the girl is an unwilling captive, or, less often, if relations
between the two groups are simply too hostile to allow the marriage
to continue, her family and kinsmen may attempt to free her by force,
and pitched battles sometimes still occur in such marriage conflicts.
In a modified reflection of the gentry pattern, a woman marrying
exogamously is said to be "thrown away" by her family and kingroup. She can no longer worship her paternal ancestors at the dadia
temple (a right which ordinarily she never entirely loses), and in
serious conflict cases no one in her family will have any kind of
social intercourse with her. The social exclusion often ceases after
awhile and normal relations between her and her family are restored;
but the ritual exclusion is permanent.

Thus, there are actually various degrees of hostility generated by
various forms of "wife capture" or exogamous marriage. In a simple
elopement, where the girl is willing and the relation between the kingroups is not unusually tense, the whole alarm, flight, discovery, and
ultimate unwilling acquiescence pattern is simply a sham. The parents would perhaps prefer to have their daughter marry within the
group, but they are willing to accept the situation. Their attitude is
related to the degree to which their group has crystallized out as an
important corporate unit, so that a small, unaffiliated houseyard fam-

ily may actually be secretly rather glad to have their daughter taken by a large, important dadia. Most kidnapping marriages, which are still exceedingly frequent today, are of this sort, being but sound and fury. Nevertheless, in all such exogamous marriages the forms of expressed outrage must be gone through, for even if endogamy is of relatively small importance in fact it cannot, for the sake of family pride, be admitted to be so in theory. The wife-capture pattern, even when it is sham, serves as an expression of the view that the marriage is, although acceptable on realistic grounds, strictly speaking "illegitimate" or "wrong," because the husband's group is not really superior in title terms.

In many cases of wife capture significant tensions develop and the outrage is not wholly a matter of form. Particularly when the marriage occurs between two strong, locally competitive groups, or where the girl was intended for someone inside an important dadia, or when there has been a past history of conflict over such matters between the groups, there may arise genuine hostility and open struggle. Such marriages often lead to an institutionalized avoidance and mutual sulking relationship between the two families involved, called *puik*, in which all social intercourse is broken off, personal bitterness intensified, and the girl excluded from any relationships, even informal ones, with her family of orientation. Usually such puik relationships involve only the immediate houseyards and houseyard clusters of the girl and boy, but sometimes they can spread to the whole of both kingroups. Some, perhaps most, of these puik relationships dissolve in time, after the bitter words on both sides are forgotten or the irreconcilable protagonists die off, and good relationships are restored; but many last a lifetime and are inherited by descendants. Any community with a highly differentiated kinship system is likely to be marked by a number of these formal sulking-hostility relationships, and most of them are the scars of past marriage conflicts.

In general, any kingroup exogamous marriage where large dadias are concerned gives rise to aggressive feelings, for the value of keeping kinswomen in is felt more keenly in these villages, and although the majority of such conflicts are soon resolved more or less amicably, the persistence of real or sham hostility around out-group marriage is an indication of the reality of the preference for endogamy among members of established kingroups. Endogamy, kingroup differentiation, competition for local ascendancy between such differentiated kingroups, and the "wife-capture" pattern are thus of a piece; and the intensity of the hostility that cross-kingroup marriages tend to stimulate in any given village is a reflex, once more, of the degree to which the kinship system has become differentiated there.

Structural Tensions Between Dadia and Village and Their Resolution

But when kinship differentiation has a divisive impact upon local territorial unity, how is this divisiveness checked so as to maintain that unity? How are the fissioning tendencies and factional conflicts that a narrowing endogamy pattern stimulates moderated and contained within the broader framework of local territorial organization? In most villages this central integrative problem is primarily met by the concurrent application of two firmly held general rules of procedure which outline the way in which work groups must be organized and must operate while performing actual social tasks within the community. These two rules, essentially recipes for the avoidance of group conflict, outline the general form which social integration is required to take within the hamlet or village and, in so doing, reveal some of the most fundamental Balinese social values.

The first of the two rules sets forth a hierarchy of precedence which places the rights of the hamlet first, those of the dadia second, those of the subdadia third, and those of the unaffiliated household fourth. How this works in practice can be illustrated in the matter of harvesting. One of the main sources of income for any sort of organized group in Balinese villages, kin-based or otherwise, is the harvest share. The group, as a collective work unit, harvests the rice crop of the fields of its members, or of non-members who contract with it to do so, the one-tenth or so "wage" share of the harvest going not to the individual laborer but into the group's treasury. The rice can then be sold and the money used to renovate a temple, hold a feast, hire an entertainment, and so on. In most villages, however, the hamlet council as a corporate group has primary harvest rights on the fields of all of its members. If the hamlet has decided in the public meeting to harvest this season, no other group may do so, all must join in the community effort on the pain of expulsion and exile. If, however, the hamlet decides that it is not in immediate need of income, then the dadias usually have next rights. Each dadia requires, also on pain of expulsion, that its members allow their fields to be harvested by the group as a whole and to participate in the work. People not belonging to dadias are, of course, free to make their own arrangements, either contracting with the dadias or other local organizations or banding together to form a temporary harvesting group of their own. If, in turn, the dadias do not need to harvest, the rights fall to the subdadia groups in the same fashion; and if the subdadias do not harvest, then any individual or group in the community is free to make any arrangements which seem suitable.

The same sort of precedence order applies throughout village life: hamlet before dadia, dadia before subdadia, subdadia before un-affiliated households. There are variations between villages on the exact phrasing and explicitness of this rule of precedence. The hamlet is always first and basic, but secondary ranking is flexible; for example, kin-based units may be secondary to such units as dance clubs or special temple groups. In some hamlets (or more exactly, in some of the desa adats—see above, chapter 1), there is a fixed rotation scheme for harvesting, with the hamlet harvesting, for instance, one year of three, dadias the second year, and subdadias with non-kin-based groups the third. In yet others, there is no explicit rule but rather merely a general unexpressed consensus that the hamlet has primacy when it asserts it.

For all the internal solidarity a kingroup may achieve, it can never, at least in theory, gain precedence over the hamlet of which it is but a part. When kingroup loyalties conflict with hamlet ones, kingroup loyalties *must* give way; on this the Balinese are unanimous. The hamlet is the context out of which the kingroups emerge and as such has primacy over them. Unlike a lineage system, where higher order units are but derivative compounds of lower order ones, it is the more, not the less, comprehensive groups—the hamlet rather than the dadia, the dadia rather than the subdadia—which are the more fundamental units.

If one is excluded from the subdadia, one at least remains a member of a dadia. If one is ejected from the dadia, one still has a place in the hamlet. But if a person is ostracized from the hamlet, even someone who had a dominant position in the kinship system, that person is a complete outcaste, with no effective social group membership at all. Ostracism from the hamlet is the Balinese equivalent of capital punishment. Thus, in Tihingan, during the period of fieldwork, there was a man who had refused to accept hamlet responsibility and office out of rage against another villager who had stolen his wife. The man was supported in his position by his kin-group, but only until the hamlet meeting expelled him from the hamlet in punishment. At this point his kin abandoned him, refusing to speak to him or to have anything else to do with him, as did all the other hamlet citizens. The man was forced to leave the hamlet and to become a dependent of the king, traditional protector of such exiles. However, a woman of the same village, ejected for adultery from her dadia, was not excluded from the hamlet and took refuge in the household of the local Brahmana priest as his servant. She was snubbed the rest of her life by her kingroup but not by the entire hamlet.

It is better, the Balinese say, to be wrong with the many than right by yourself. The hamlet is our only support in the face of sickness, poverty or other calamity; with it we can live, without it we die. Despite the strength and immediacy of narrow kingroup ties over wider ones, and of kingroup loyalties over community ones in everyday life, it is always the broader, more comprehensive group which must be given precedence in a case of direct conflict of interest between them, because it forms the basis without which the less comprehensive groups could not exist, the bottom layer in a house of cards upon which the more delicately situated upper layers rest.

The second of the two procedural rules is what we have called the seka principle, after the general Balinese term for "an organized group of any sort." As we stated, the seka principle demands that for functional purposes any group must be viewed as having one and only one basis of organization. That is to say, in operation any group must be viewed as being internally undifferentiated, as being but a collection of households brought together in terms of one classifying feature only. Thus, when the hamlet harvests, repairs public buildings, organizes a dance performance, or whatever, no subdivision in kinship (or caste, territorial, or irrigation society) terms is allowed. Each household is, in this context, exactly like every other—a hamlet member pure and simple—no closer by any ties to one than to the next. And if suborganization is needed, into work groups, for instance, deliberate effort is made to scatter people randomly so that all other allegiances crosscut one another: lines dividing the hamlet into sections are carefully drawn so as to bisect important kin-based residential clusters, or else such section membership is determined in a nonterritorial manner so as to distribute close relatives into different groups. "The hamlet," runs a Balinese proverb, "knows no kinship."

On the dadia level the same principle operates. If the dadia is harvesting, or holding a ceremony, or forging a gong, subdadia ties are completely ignored. All, whether subdadia members or not,

whether actually local in birth or not, are regarded as identical—
they are all dadia members, a view made easier of course by the
relative lack of explicit genealogical structure in Balinese kingroups.
And so on with the subdadia, and, as is noted, all Balinese organizations. "One principle of organization at a time," could be said to
be the basic structural rule in Balinese society.

The general principle involved is further reflected in the pattern of
temporary ritual impurity (*sebel*) after a death in the vicinity. When
anyone in a hamlet dies, no citizen may enter the village temples for
three days; if one of those days of impurity happens to be a festival
day for the temple, the festival is not held. However, members of
the dadia or houseyard cluster of the dead man may not enter either
the village temples or their own kin temple for a much longer period
—for most commoners, forty-two days, but the time varies with
status, being shorter for higher groups. In some villages, only the
houseyard group of the dead man keeps this longer taboo period.

The seka principle protects the integrity of a social group against
its parts, insures its autonomy as a functional unit in its own terms
rather than as a mere derivative of its components; more specifically
it keeps the highly solidary kingroup tail from wagging the less
tightly organized hamlet dog. Balinese social integration, in general,
consists not so much of a building up of larger units out of smaller
ones, a pyramiding of elemental building blocks into composite
structures, but rather of a set of semi-independent, crosscutting
social planes each one complete in itself within its own prescribed
realm of action. Combined with the hierarchy of precedence principle,
which gives the groups organized on a broader basis primacy over
those organized on a narrower one, this provides a framework within
which the conflicts inherent in endogamous kin differentiation can,
in the majority of cases, be fairly effectively handled and the opposed
tendencies toward kingroup and community autonomy balanced off
against one another.

4

Kinship in the Public Domain
The Gentry Dadia

The Dadia as the Basic Unit
of the Classical Balinese State

The differences in the political game as it is played by the gentry and by the commoners—the divergent arenas, goals and prizes, strategies and tactics—are reflected in variations in their respective kinship organizations. The political position of the Balinese gentry has of course changed during the last sixty years with the introduction of a modern administration with distinctly bounded districts, and impersonal civil offices which tie together the entire island of Bali. Today, increasingly, individuals rather than dynasties compete for power, influence, and prestige, and the contest is more and more in terms of abilities rather than ascribed status, and based on popular support rather than assumed elite position. Nonetheless, many of the characteristics of the nineteenth-century Balinese polity remain, despite their nominal replacement with modern forms, and much of what is distinctive of the gentry kinship system also persists.

To appreciate the functional significance of the special peculiarities of the gentry variant of Balinese kinship, it is necessary to place it in its proper political context of the last century.[45] At the time of the advent of the Dutch in South Bali in 1906–8, there was no unitary state, nor even a determinate number of bounded lesser states, but rather a highly complex series of competing, nonterritorial, interpenetrating spheres of influence, each centered on a particular "king," "prince," or "lord." Each king was engaged in a constant effort to expand or defend the reach of his control, not so much in terms of the acquisition of new territory, but of men's allegiances. These allegiances were of various types, but they were always personal and specific. At all the various levels, between the peasants, stewards of the lords, the lords, and the paramount lords or princes, each such tie involved the recognition of the superiority of the lord, the acceptance of ritual duties at the lord's ceremonies and festivals (which amounted to a corvee on labor and a tax on produce), and participation in his wars. Although the competition among the numerous princes often enough broke into war, it was mainly carried forward in the forms of intrigue, of marriage politics, assassinations, coup d'etats, and the like.

Commoners, who made up some ninety percent of the population, were essentially passive spectators of the drama of politics played out by the gentry. They provided the great casts of extras for the ritual extravaganzas, the cremations, coronations, temple sanctifications, and so on, of the nobility. They also made the regalia, built the temples and palaces, and performed much of the dances, dramas, and music. But above all, the commoners were the audience for the gentry's productions.

The political struggle among the aristocracy for dominance in nineteenth-century Bali was, of course, based on such essentials as economic resources and personal leadership qualities, but the vocabulary of the contest was always drawn from that peculiar Balinese fusion of kinship and ranking systems, the dadia system. The competing political units were the numerous noble dadias and subdadias, even at the topmost levels. The term "dadia" is, strictly speaking, applicable only to commoner kingroups and their temples, and any member of the Balinese gentry would be deeply offended by our use of the term for royal and noble houses. However, since in structural terms, the large corporate kingroups of the gentry are almost identical with the Balinese dadia, we have adopted this usage.[46]

The principalities of Gianyar, Badung, and so on, with which the Dutch negotiated, were not bounded territories with reigning monarchs but precarious pyramids of traditional personal allegiances and alliances, ties which were in significant part defined by descent and affinity. The peak of each pyramidal polity was a sprawling royal dadia, which embraced a large number of subdadias, or "houses," all recognizing the king in the inner core of the kingroup as their lord, and all intricately ranked in descending steps around him. The lower slopes of the pyramids were made up of other, unrelated gentry dadias, each one a lesser pyramid of allegiances in itself, which allied themselves to the ruling dadia in one fashion or another. At the base of each pyramid, of course, were the commoners, who were parcelled out among the various ruling gentry. Subjects were said to be "owned" (*druwé*) by their lord, and should the lord die or be conquered, his subjects were then the property of the lord's heir or conquerer. Actually the subjects were "owned" not by the individual lords but by whole dadias and subdadias.[47]

The king or lord occupied his status by virtue of his central kinship position within the core line of the dadia. More precisely, he was steward of the dadia's title, political power, subjects, temples, and wealth. His brothers and cousins, who moved out of the core houseyard as they came of age, served as the lord's lieutenants, advisors, representatives, and so on. They were also potential rivals for his seat, but such rivalry had to be supported by a claim to legitimate occupation of the core position in the dadia.

The internal organization of such a reigning dadia was very complex in comparison with its smaller commoner counterparts, yet it was, nevertheless, governed by the same major premise of the primacy of the whole dadia over any of its parts, and the course of its development was likewise one of progressive differentiation out of its background in the larger community. *For the gentry, however, the community was, and still is, not the small local settlement but the entire, regionally-dispersed, gentry population.* There are a good many gentry who have no dadia affiliation, gentry whose kingroup has shrunk in numbers and political power, down to little more than the contents of a single impoverished houseyard. And, on the other hand, there are histories of the emergence of a powerful royal dadia out of such inauspicious beginnings, with a rapid expansion in numbers, leadership capacities, wealth, and political sagacity.

The Growth of a Royal Dadia: An Example

A highly simplified account of the rise of the royal dadia of Gianyar may give a general idea of the relationship between political processes and dadia development. This is the royal line of the present (1957–58) head of the government in the Gianyar principality, the Kepala Dewan Perwakilan Rakyat (Chairman of the Council of Representatives of the People), and of his brother, Anak Agung Gde Agung, a leader in the former Indonesian Socialist party and onetime Foreign Minister. This history was pieced together from informants in Klungkung and Pliatan, both of which are royal houses in direct competition with Gianyar, who give a slightly less exalted version than that which would be obtained from the Gianyar nobility themselves. All of the versions agree, however, that the Gianyar dadia is a relatively new one, going no further back than the eighteenth century. They also agree that the founding ancestor of the line was a young man, named Dewa Manggis, who started out virtually alone, with no large kingroup to support him but whose charismatic leadership qualities (his body gave off light in the dark, in one version) were soon recognized by the existing political powers. The Gianyar history claims that he was the legitimate son of the Raja of Klungkung, highest-ranking king in Bali, and that his mother was a Klungkung princess, although the written Klungkung chronicles do not mention him. The Pliatan informant, however, asserted that Dewa Manggis was the illegitimate son of the Klungkung Raja, whose mother was a village woman, briefly made love to by the Raja during a hunting trip. He grew up, apparently, in the court of Badung (another rival royal house, near the present-day town of Den Pasar), but eventually established a home of his own in the village of Pahang, in the Gianyar region, halfway between Klungkung and Badung. Such stories of obscure origins, illegitimacy, foster parenthood, and so on, are often found in gentry dadia histories; they perform the obvious function of providing an acceptable claim to royal status while at the same time explaining the mysterious emergence of the dadia out of nowhere.

Dewa Manggis had a son, who was also named Dewa Manggis. (One of the difficulties in determining Balinese history, factual as well as mythical, is that the occupants of the core line position in many dadias all have the same name. In this case there were at least eight kings named Dewa Manggis, and the historical accounts often collapse the generations into one another.) Dewa Manggis II was also poor and wanting in kinsmen, and so he became a sentana, an heir through marriage, to a gentry family in the village of Beng, in Gianyar. This move did not mean, however, that he relinquished his claim to descent from the Klungkung kings and to his high title of Dewa. At that time, the most powerful royal house in the Gianyar region was that of Sukawati, and it was this dadia, entrenched and many-branched, which Dewa Manggis and his descendants had to challenge. Even today the house of Sukawati with its subdadias of Pliaten, Ubud and others, is a strong rival of the Gianyar royalty. The Dewa Manggis dynasty began as dependents of Sukawati but within several generations had built up a network of dependents and subjects of its own. Its methods were those of peaceful, relentless, subtle political maneuvering, first by marrying its women into the many Sukawati subdadias, then by distributing its men in villages around the region to set up branch lines in widely separated places, and third, by taking its wives from carefully selected lesser gentry and more wealthy commoner dadias. As the house acquired wealth, it was able to appoint commoner stewards to administer it, and to scatter its subjects in hamlets through the region, who kept it informed of all the political maneuvers of its rivals.

Dewa Manggis IV moved into an abandoned Brahmana palace in the village of Gianyar, set up his court there, and is counted as the first true prince in the line. He died in 1820. He and his brother had many wives and children, and the steady accretion of power through marriage politics and the strategic placement of cadet-line houses continued. A serious split between two brothers vying for the Sukawati crown, which broke out into a fraternal war, provided a nice opportunity for Dewa Manggis to slip in between, making one large wing of the Sukawati dadia his ally and permanently crippling the other.

The seventh Dewa Manggis, who by this time had accumulated a very large body of kinsmen and affines, reigned at the pinnacle of the dadia's success, between 1867 and about 1885. With the aid of an extremely astute commoner, Made Tjedok, this most famous Dewa Manggis (who is always identified as "the Dewa Manggis who died at Satria") reduced the houses of Sukawati, Pliatan, Ubud, and so on, to dependency, and even expanded into villages which had been under the control of Klungkung. His power is indicated by the fact that he seems to have been the first paramount lord in the region to be able to institute a direct tax on rice land, payable in kind at every harvest, a tax which was not mediated or shared by his stewards and underlings. His downfall came when Pliatan and Klungkung allied to trick him into leaving his palace and making a royal visit to Klungkung, where he was captured and imprisoned in the village of Satria, where he died five years later, in 1891. This was the beginning of the decline of the house of Gianyar and, ultimately, the end of the classic Balinese state. The fertile region of Gianyar was then a political vacuum which Pliatan by herself was not strong enough to hold, and the royal houses in nearby areas began to move in on Dewa Manggis' former homes, lands, and subjects, by force and by marriage. In the end Pliatan maneuvered to bring the sons of Dewa Manggis back from exile and put them on the throne. But the threats from the edges of the region, from Klungkung, Bangli,

Bandung, and Tabanan, continued. In a desperate move, in 1899, the son of Dewa Manggis requested the Dutch army to intervene, a step which proved finally fatal to all the kings of Bali.

This chronicle of the rise of the Gianyar dynasty illustrates the manner and rapidity in which a small, possibly low-status gentry house could rise to prominence. Within seven generatons it had grown from what was apparently an obscure isolated family, a mere house-yard cluster, with few close kinsmen and little property, into a large and extended, but tightly integrated, dadia. The rise to power was legitimized by a claim to superior social status, that is to say, to a higher title. Hence the stories of the origin and wanderings of the first Dewa Manggis. Possession of the title alone, however, does not bring eminence, since there are a good many persons with the title "Dewa" scattered all over Bali who have no political position whatsoever.

The rapidity of the dadia's growth is in part explained by the fertility of the line but mainly by the ability of its leaders to keep the branches loyal to the core line, and the shrewdness in geographical location of the branch houses. The first Dewa Manggis had only one son, but all of the others after him had several, each of whom established a lesser court in a different village. Figure 13 gives a simplified genealogy, showing the males in the core line, the seven Dewa Manggis, and its various branch houses, identified only by the village in which they are located.

The branch houses, which were scattered over a region roughly ten miles in radius, maintained ceremonial, kinship, and marital ties with the core-line house. In time, most such branches developed a large enough body of members to have some corporate standing of their own and to establish their own lesser core and branch lines. But despite the passage of generations and the endemic rivalries and strains among the branch houses, the political and ritual unity of the whole Gianyar dadia was maintained. To the outer world it was a single politically prominent dynasty, represented by the incumbent of the core position and faithfully supported by its subsidiary segments.

The integration of such a royal dadia, set as it was in a political environment which fostered factioning, treason, and secession, is clearly a difficult process. The cultural concept of a single ritual origin for even the most remotely related houses provides a rationale for keeping stragglers within the fold. But despite the religious commitment to worship at the origin-temple and despite the demanding

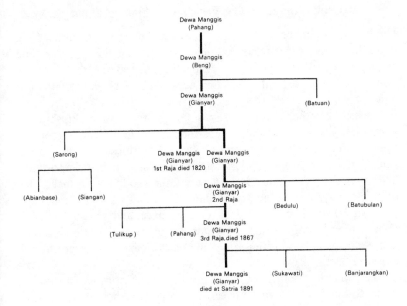

Fig. 13. The rise of the House of Gianyar

ceremonial activities entailed by such a temple affiliation, which in themselves brought about considerable mutual interaction and dependence, this ritual framework is insufficient. It is always perfectly acceptable to substitute ceremonies at the subdadia temple in place of those at the dadia temple itself.

Two main institutions operate to keep the dispersing branch houses from severing themselves from the original dadia and allying themselves with a political competitor. The first is a system of reckoning descent which accounts for all offshoots of the dadia and provides a precisely ranked locus for each one in relation to all the others, in terms of its degree of structural distance from the core line. The second is that of preferential endogamous marriage, as among the commoners, but with certain additional complications arising from the simultaneous practice of hypergamy. Even endogamous marriages among the Balinese gentry are expected to be at the same time hypergamous, because of the internal ranking system of the dadia. All exogamous marriages are regularly hypergamous also, and this fact has far-reaching implications for the political integration of the kingroup. We will explore these two institutions below.

Gentry Descent: The Principle of Sinking Status

Unlike the commoners, the gentry view the internal partition of the dadia in terms of a (real or fictionalized) genealogical history. The history sets forth the points of branching off and the rank distinctions among the several subdadias according to a cultural premise which we have called "the principle of sinking status." To be sure, this principle is not characteristic of the gentry view of kinship organization alone, for commoners, too, think in its terms, for instance, in considering the early origins of their titles. But, among the gentry, the principle of sinking status is raised to first importance and is applied systematically to a very large group of kinsmen. This principle plays, in the gentry variant of Balinese kinship, the same functional role in defining lines of allegiance and potential fission points among kinsmen that the principles of equivalence of brothers and segmentary opposition play in an African-type "segmentary" kinship system.

The principle operates by the simple device of ascribing a lowered status to any brother who moves out of the core houseyard relative to the one brother who can remain in it and inherit the father's core position. This means that over time those lines descendant from brothers who have, as the Balinese put it, "gone out of the palace earlier" are the lowest in status, while those descendant from a generation of brothers who "left" more recently are higher. The most recent ones to leave, that is, the brothers of the present reigning monarch, are highest of all of his kinsmen in status. Thus an "old family" which claims descent from the full brother of an early king is much lower than the one which traces descent from the full brother of a later one, and *it is in fact closeness to the presently reigning king which, so far as kinship is concerned, determines status.* As each king is succeeded by his eldest son who remains in the core houseyard, the palace, all the peripheral noble houses deriving from previous kings automatically drop a notch in status, the empty notch at the top being filled by the new king's full brothers as they move out of the palace to found new noble houses of their own.

This image of descent is pictured in Figure 14, which shows, in model form, the genealogical relationships and relative status of a core royal house and four contemporary peripheral noble houses. In this diagram, the brother of the reigning monarch, "D," has, next to the king himself, the highest status, while the incumbents of noble house "A" have the lowest, for they are merely descendants of the

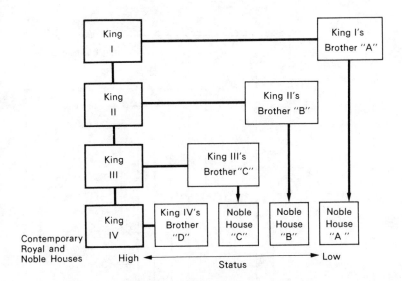

Fig. 14. Gentry descent: the principle of sinking status

brother of the earliest king. In former times, noble house "A" may have had considerable power, but its descendants have now sunk to a near commoner level, being distinguished from the masses merely by their title, which supports their claim to superiority within their immediate village.

For example, in the Gianyar dynasty charted above (fig. 13), the genealogical lines indicate not only kinship but also the bases of invidious status distinctions between the several branches. The highest-ranking branch houses are those established most recently, those located in the village of Sukawati and Banjarangkan. Next below them in rank come Tulikup and Pahang, then Bedulu and Batubulan, Abianbase and Siangan, and the lowest status house is one established earliest, at Batuan.

An example which we can give in more detail is that of the royal house of Tabanan. Figure 15 gives, in schematic form, the kinship connections of a number of the royal and noble houses existing in 1906 in the Tabanan region. This diagram is an adaptation of one shown to us in the noble house of Den Bantas, a low-ranking branch in a village near Tabanan. It has been necessary to simplify this genealogy to a certain degree for purposes of descriptive clarity. Only a few of the noble houses that the royal line of Tabanan has generated in its six-hundred-year history are shown here. Altogether,

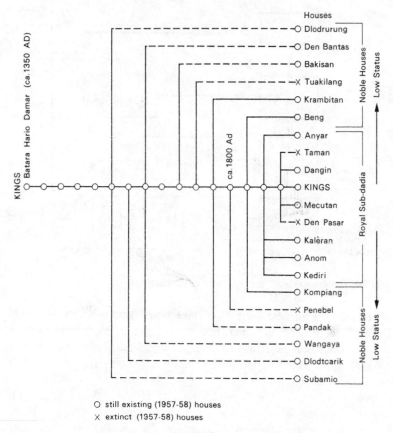

O still existing (1957-58) houses
X extinct (1957-58) houses

Fig. 15. Genealogy of the royal houses of Tabanan to 1906

probably more than forty such houses have been created, of which slightly more than half have died out, been destroyed in war, or migrated (exiled). The houses shown, some of which are extinct, are chosen for illustrative purposes only, though they do include all of the more important Tabanan houses today.

The living members of the houses named across the bottom of the diagram all regard themselves as descendants from a single original ancestor, Batara Hario (Arya) Damar, a semimythical Javanese general from the great East-Java kingdom of Madjapahit, who came as colonial conqueror to Bali around the middle of the fourteenth century.[48] In ritual recognition of their common descent, the members all congregate, twice a year or more, for worship at their mutual origin-temple, the Tabanan *batur dalam*, which is located within the castle of the preeminent prince. In addition to this ritual association, they also form the traditional ruling group in the Tabanan area. With the prince, the Cokorda, at the peak, the heads of the various houses held various subsidiary ruling positions, as his lieutenants and representatives. Despite the fact that today there may be as many as a thousand living members of the group (although in the nineteenth century, before the present population explosion, there were no doubt considerably fewer), it can be seen as a single dadia, comparable in structure to the commoner dadia.

Such a royal dadia is different from a commoner dadia, both by its larger size and more elaborate subdifferentiation, and also, more importantly, by the wide differences in status between subunits of the group. Houses such as Den Bantas, Wongaya, or Pandak are but minor branches, hardly thought of in the same category with the major houses of the dadia, Kaleran, Den Pasar, Mecutan, Anyar, Anom, Dangin, Kediri, and Taman. This last group of houses, whose living heads are cousins and brothers, the immediate relatives of the king, represents the ruling subdadia, the real locus of power.

Only this small cluster of houses in the royal subdadia maintains fully documented genealogies which actually connect them to the core line. The gentry houses of lower status, usually, can supply concrete genealogical information back only a few generations, and above that there may be an empty gap over which they leap to the founder of their line, some brother of some prince, who is actually more or less anonymous, known mainly by the name of the house he founded. Thus the founder of the noble house of Subamio was named Kiyayi Madja Utara Subamio, the founder of the noble house of Wangayu was Kiyayi Wangayu, and so on. There is considerable room in this sort of system for fictional manipulations, and at least some of the Tabanan gentry houses were, according to available evidence, not actually related to the core line at all but were migrants from elsewhere.

The core line itself is not immune to manipulations of various sorts. While the form of the diagram suggests straight line of fathers and sons succeeding one another, in reality there were considerable variations, with brothers succeeding brothers (peaceably or by fraternal murder), and it is possible that outsiders too may have wormed their way into the throne by a sentana marriage, or by more devious means. The line, thus, represents the sequence of incumbents of the position however they in fact got there, and the crux of the claim of gentry houses to high status is that they are descended from a former holder of the royal title.

It is the core line which is the firm spine for the system, the point of reference for every issue. Each branch, in turn, establishes a core line of its own, and its branches likewise step down in status. The process of hiving off while at the same time retaining membership in the royal dadia—of subdifferentiation, that is—is not without limits. There is always some point at which the lesser subbranches of lesser branches off the core line are no longer admitted to full dadia membership. Where this point comes, apparently, is relative to the current power and prestige of the royal core line itself, to, that is, the degree of pragmatic need that the royal core line has for the services of its least eminent and poorest members. In any case, many peripheral low-ranking gentry houses themselves have subbranches, the members of which worship at the origin-temple within the gentry house, but are not expected to attend the ceremonies at the royal dadia temple of the king. In such a case the lowly branch relatives are represented at the king's dadia temple by their slightly higher kinsmen.

This stress on the core line is reflected in nomenclature, that is, in the conferring of status titles and, among a set of gentry siblings, of birth-order titles. With the exception of the less elevated marginal families, where living patterns approach those of peasantry, the gentry do not employ teknonymy. Rather, in daily intercourse each individual is addressed by his title. He is also referred to by this title, plus his birth-order title, plus his personal name.[49] Thus, for example, if a man's title is Gusti, he is always addressed as "Gusti." In reference, if he is a second child, and his birth-order is Made, and if his personal name is Oka, then he is referred to as "Gusti Made Oka."

The core status is given special recognition by the birth-order title system among a set of siblings, as employed by the gentry. Among commoners, the firstborn child, the fifth, the ninth, and so on are all called Wajan. Among the gentry, however, this repetition is avoided, and the firstborn is singled out by a special title, Putu or Gdé, and only one child is given this title.[50] This fits with the circumstance that it is the firstborn who is most likely to succeed to the core position.

This system of status titles, as opposed to birth-order titles, also reflects the stress on the core line, for the incumbent of that role always has a slightly higher title than the peripheral members of his house. The prince himself always bears a unique title which distinguishes him from everyone else. In the Tabanan royal family, the prince's title is Cokorda, while his brothers and sisters are Gusti

Ngurah. In Klungkung, the prince is Dewa Agung, while his immediate family are all Cokorda. Since there is, in Tabanan, only one
Cokorda, and in Klungkung, only one Dewa Agung, the address and
reference terms are the same and the prince's personal identity is
entirely submerged in his role. The dynastic chronicles are full of
confusing sequences of such personally anonymous regents, for example, the row of Dewa Manggis in Gianyar, whose title-names are
virtually identical. The core line is thus marked out as a title-line, not
as a sequence of individuals.

Likewise, in the noble houses of Tabanan, the incumbent of the
core position usually has the title of Gusti Ngurah (which has,
roughly, the meaning of "pure Gusti") while most of his lesser brothers, cousins, and further kin, are called I Gusti or even just plain
Gusti. Again, the core line of the branch house and the status-steps
down and away from it are delineated by title distinctions.

In addition to title, there are a number of other symbolic modes
of recognizing slight distinctions in rank among the various houses
within the royal dadia. Aside from the complexities of marriage practices and of architectural discriminations, both of which will be gone
into in detail further on, there are the matters of eating and of address
between close kinsmen.

To eat with someone else from the same dish signifies precise
equality, and only a very narrow circle of kinsmen are eligible to do
this. This means only those within a single subdadia, those who are,
roughly speaking, the descendants of a single great-grandfather. On
formal occasions each person's meal is served separately, but on less
formal occasions the food is set in the center of the group on large
platters, and each person takes what he wants. Those who are permitted to *saling carik* (also termed *paredan*), to "eat together," may
serve themselves some of this common food with their right hands,
then eat it, also with their right, and reach again for more with their
right hand. But those who are more distantly related must take the
second helping with their left hands. If there are even greater status
differences, that is, if the diners are from different dadias, or are
widely different in age, they ought not even to be eating together. In
the latter situations of marked status differences there is a second
pattern called *ngelungsur*, in which those of lower status wait till the
higher have finished eating, and then receive the leftovers. The
ngelungsur pattern obtains also among close kinsmen of different
generations, that is, father and son, or even among siblings of great
difference in age. It also always obtains among the various branches

of a large dadia. This pattern of status-structured eating always provides a precisely discriminating set of rank indicators within the dadia.

The same can be said of informal modes of address among the members of a large royal dadia. Since they all consider themselves kinsmen, they use kin terms (generally together with the appropriate title or the more general honorific title "*ratu*"). The kin terms employed are elevated variants of the common terms for "father," "mother," "grandparent," "older brother" and "older sister," but the specific application of the term varies with the relative status of the persons speaking, not their kinship connection. Here is a concrete example from one of the Tabanan houses, from a young man in Jero Kompiang, the house of Kompiang. He addresses all the men, women, and children of the royal subdadia (the houses of Mecutan, Dangin, and so on, down to Kediri) and of Krambitan (which has a special status) as "ratu." The members of the house of Beng are superior to him in status, so he calls all the men "father" and "grandfather" even though they may be his same age. The boys in Beng he calls by their title and name, but as soon as they marry and have a child, no matter how much younger they are than he, he changes his address to "father." For the remaining noble houses, which he considers to be on his own level, such as Dlodrurung and Subamio, he uses kin terms, this time according to the relative age of the person—thus, to older men, "father," to men slightly older than he, "older brother," and to younger men, their title and name. Balinese commoners do not employ kin terms in this extensive fashion but restrict their use to immediate kinsmen.

This pattern of sinking status—the image of a high-status core line with branches of graduated ranks, each shifting down a peg in status with every generation—is the cultural conception by means of which the gentry perceive their relationships with great numbers of kinsmen. It is an ideal pattern, and any Balinese can point out exceptions to it, noble houses which are "higher in rank than they should be." Jero Subamio, for instance, in the Tabanan group, has an actual social rank nearly as high as Beng, and it is permitted to employ a number of cremation customs which are symbolic of royal status that its genealogical superiors are not. This was explained by Tabanan informants as a consequence of a special deed of loyalty which was once performed by a Subamio ancestor to the Tabanan king, who then rewarded him by raising his rank. Such exceptions in ranking according to the prescriptions of the cultural conception of sinking status merely underline the central governing importance of the conception in Balinese social life.

The Politics of Marriage

The discriminations of rank within a group of gentry siblings and their descendants are made even more precise by bringing into account the relative rank of their various mothers. Polygamy was, and is, the usual practice among well-to-do gentry families, and it was an absolute necessity for a royal dadia with expansionist ambitions. As a consequence, virtually every king had a large number of sons by different mothers. The genealogies of gentry houses nearly always specify the title and origin of the mothers of the men in the core and branch lines.

There was always one highest-status wife, one who was given the special term *padmi* or *prami*, and whose eldest son, the *putra mahkoto*, was expected to succeed the king or lord in the core position in the dadia. The padmi had to come from a family of as high a rank as the king himself, and was therefore usually chosen from another unrelated royal house or from the immediate royal family itself, that is, from among the king's patrilateral parallel cousins or nieces.

All of the other gentry wives of the king, of which there could be hundreds, were termed *penawing*. A wife who was a commoner was called a selir. The offspring of the penawing and the selirs were collectively termed the *ulun pada* and were all destined to leave the core houseyard, the castle, and to have a status lower than the children of the padmi. A commoner woman who married into the gentry received a title, Mekel or Jero. A woman of gentry status kept her original title, perhaps raised a notch or two. Thus the penawing themselves were not all of the same rank, and the differences in their titles were further accentuated by differences in the personal wealth which they may have brought with them from their own fathers.

These considerations of the relative status of the mothers of gentry men are called upon frequently in mythic traditions which purport to explain discrepancies between one's present-day actual prestige level and one's presumed position according to patrilateral descent. An example here is from the house of Krambitan, a royal subdadia of Tabanan which is located some fifteen miles west of the court town. It appears on figure 15 in a rather low position, but as a matter of fact it is of highest rank, equal to any of the houses in the royal subdadia. It has even received wives from among the daughters of the king of Tabanan, which could only be permissible if it had nearly the same status as the king. We received two slightly different explanations of Krambitan's anomalous position, but the disparity between them in itself gives a suggestion about the sources of flexibility in the whole system.

In the first version, told us by the present lord of Krambitan, the kings of Tabanan, Badung, and Krambitan were three half-brothers. Krambitan was the youngest, but he was highest in status because his mother was the padmi, while the mothers of the others were merely lower gentry. He was expected to succeed his father on the Tabanan throne, but he was too restless to stay at home, and liked to go off on hunting trips. He left his older but lower-ranking brother at home in the castle to run the country and, despite many invitations, could never be persuaded to return home and rule, because of his reluctance to take responsibility. He finally set up his own much smaller domain in its present location, "because it was so beautiful there." The other older brother also broke off to establish the kingdom of Bandung, near modern Den Pasar. Thus the lord of Krambitan claims to have higher original status than the present kings of Tabanan and Badung, both of whom in 1906 were much more powerful than he.

The second version states that the king of Tabanan had had no children by the padmi after many years of marriage, and finally he made a solemn oath to make the next son born to him the king, even if it were the son of one of his commoner wives. Soon after that, such a son was born. But it also happened that a few years later the padmi gave birth to a son. The king kept his oath, and when the highest-ranking son was grown he was sent away. He started off for Java but was dissuaded from going so far by a Brahmana priest; he finally settled in the then uninhabited region of Krambitan.

These tales are probably tailored cover-ups for a bitter conflict between two brothers. Stories of fratricide in such succession battles are not uncommon. But the present pacific versions are much more suitable for the current political situation in which the king of Tabanan and the lord of Krambitan are close friends and allies. Neither version explains, however, how Krambitan maintained its high status over the generations. One explanation might be its geographical location, in a fertile valley located right on the border between Tabanan and its rival, Jembrana. Its rich land provided wealth, and its position as a buffer state guaranteed its autonomy against Tabanan, who could afford neither to risk Krambitan's displeasure nor to replace him with a less powerful lord in that militarily vulnerable spot.

Another example of the way in which these status differences among the mothers of a group of siblings are called upon to account for present-day distinctions among descent groups, comes from a Brahmana civil servant's explanation of the relationships between the four main Brahmana title-groups. He stated that all Brahmanas are descended from one great holy man, Pedanda Sakti Wauwerauh, who came from the Javanese kingdom of Majapahit. The four groups are descendants of four of his sons, Kemanuh, Manuaba, Keniten, and Mas. The first two are generally considered higher, said our informant, because they were the older brothers, but the third, Keniten, is actually higher because his mother was the daughter of a Javanese king. The informant was, as might be expected, a Keniten, and other informants gave different versions, placing the Kemanuh branch clearly at the top because its ancestress was a Brahmana girl.

Thus the marriages of earlier generations, insofar as they produced offspring, are significant as aspects of the system of descent, especially in the crucial matter of determining rank among siblings and hence among descent groups. They serve, along with primogeniture, to indicate and validate the points of hiving off the core line and the process of stepping down in status. Marriages in a present generation, on the other hand, have a different, but even greater, function in denoting and even determining the political attainments and prestige levels of the present-day dadias, through their functions in consolidating wealth, promoting alliances between different dadias, or strengthening ties with retainers and subjects.

Types of Gentry Marriage

There are four main types of legitimate gentry marriages: (1) those which are endogamous to the subdadia; (2) those which are exogamous to the subdadia but still between members of the same dadia; (3) those exogamous unions which are between unrelated gentry dadias of the same rank; and (4) those exogamous unions in which commoner women are brought into the gentry dadia. Each of these has different social or political implications.

The first type, the strictly endogamous marriage, that is, with the father's brother's daughter, has an obvious integrating function for the subdadia. Such a union serves to pull back together two lines which are threatening to draw away from one another, to keep the allegiance of the men of the cadet lines for the core-line man. It is also the safest marriage from the point of view of status, for any other marriage automatically asserts that the girl's family has a lower position than the boy's.

Father's brother's daughter marriages are extremely common today in gentry circles. While we do not have a large enough sample to establish percentages comparable to the commoner rates, we can give one example, the marriages of the Tabanan royal subdadia—that is, "noble house"—of Beng. In its older generation, whose members are past their fifties today, out of eleven girls born into the subdadia, four married their patrilateral parallel cousins. Of the eighteen women who married men of that generation, four (the same ones of course) were their father's brothers' daughters. In the younger generation, not all of whom are old enough to marry, there are nine adult girls, of whom four have married the preferred cousin; on the other side, of the women who have married men of the house, four out of five are their father's brother's daughters.

The second type of legitimate gentry marriage is that which is exogamous to the subdadia but still between members of the same dadia. Since a gentry dadia is usually extremely large, comprising many houses of widely different ranks, such unions are fraught with prestige considerations. Among the Tabanan houses there was a sharply defined rank order, set by the relative distance of their lines of descent from the core line of Tabanan kings. It was customary for certain houses to supply wives regularly to certain other houses slightly superior to them. Thus, in Tabanan, the subdadia houses of Kediri and Beng regularly supplied wives to Kaleran, the ranking house next to the prince in power, and even came to regard this as their unwritten privilege, to the point that any marriage outside of these established channels gave rise to acrimonious dispute.

There were also a number of intradadia marriages which were not exactly illegitimate, but which went against the grain of the rank order. That is, occasionally a man of a slightly lower house took a wife from a house above him. For instance, wives were regularly given to the houses of Krambitan and Kediri from among the king's own sisters, and these were considered to be stepping downwards. These marriages were arranged legitimately but the negotiations were protracted and delicate. There were also cases reported to us of elopements within the dadia in which the girl was of slightly higher status than the man. For example, we were told that a man from the house of Anom had once "stolen" one of the Tabanan king's sisters, without royal permission. The couple were actually second cousins, and thus very close in rank, but the king was nevertheless insulted, and there ensued a marked and protracted coolness between the core house and the house of Anom. Such elopements, however, were regarded by other members of the dadia as essentially legitimate, despite their rebellious aspect.

The third type of legitimate marriage is that between members of unrelated gentry dadias. If the marriage is negotiated amicably, it means either that a clear status distinction is recognized and accepted by both parties, that is, that the man's family is recognized as higher, or that the two families are considered to be roughly at the same rank level. The latter type of marriage, especially, was characteristic of the kings and princes, as the occupants of the summits of their dadia. The kings of Tabanan usually took as their official primary wives girls from allied kingdoms, for example, from the royal houses of Badung and Mengwi. By winning a wife from an important competitor's family, the king or prince accomplished simultaneously an assertion that his prestige is equal to if not higher than that of his rival, and a reaffirmation of his and his rival's mutual alliance vis-a-vis other kingdoms. Below the level of the king or prince, such exogamous unions with unrelated gentry of distant regions were rarely, if ever, contracted, apparently because they represented a political act in the forwarding of "foreign affairs" of the kingdom, a concern which was the prerogative of the king or prince alone.

Today, of course, under a different political system, gentry marriages have lost their diplomatic functions and retain only their status-indicating ones. Nonetheless, the lower branches in a very large gentry dadia such as Tabanan continue to be almost completely endogamous. For lesser gentry, however, those who have no real affiliation with a dadia, the choice is usually between marrying a close cousin and, since further relatives may be lacking, someone from an unrelated gentry family. These latter exogamous marriages are difficult to negotiate, even when the relative rank is quite clear, as for instance when a Brahmana man takes a Satria wife, and are often presented as elopements or wife-stealing in order to avoid lengthy negotiations.

The fourth kind of legitimate gentry marriage is that with a commoner woman. In the nineteenth century, to bring a village woman into the royal harem was a simple way to reward a prominent commoner dadia for its support and to guarantee its continued loyalty. The woman who marries a noble receives a special title (Mekel, or

Jero, among others) and usually takes a new and more elegant personal name. Her kinsmen are then said to be *pewargian* or *wargi* to the noble house, and their tie to it grows even stronger with the birth of her children. Gentry children of a commoner woman usually keep close ties with their maternal relatives, visiting them often throughout their lives, and the wargi attend every important festivity at the gentry house, contributing both labor and produce. A further reason for a noble lord to acquire commoner wives is that such wives often brought with them a piece of their father's land, as a dowry. This land remained, however, in the woman's name, and if she was divorced she kept it. On her death her personal land passed on only to her own children. Such marriages to village women were clearly advantageous in the past of the gentry both politically and economically, and this explains why, at least until this century, the largest proportion of their wives were commoners.

We have some fragmentary data on the wives of the prince of Tabanan, the one who ruled in the 1870s; that is to say, we know the origins of those wives who became mothers of his children, thus omitting what was probably a significant number of other, childless, wives. The paramount wife came from the royal house of Mengwi, a kingdom which was shortly thereafter conquered by Tabanan and Badung as allies. One wife came from the Krambitan royal house, two others came from very low village-gentry families, and four others were commoners. In the following generation, the sons of the king brought in at least eight village and one low gentry women.

Another example on which we have almost complete data comes from the noble house of Beng. In the first generation for which we have records, the grandparental generation for today's (1957–58) young adults, there were two brothers. The brother who remained in the core position within the house took as his primary wife a girl from the house of Subamio, and five women from the village. His brother had seven wives, all of whom were commoners. In the next generation, the son who moved into the core position took his primary wife from the royal house of Kediri, and two other wives from among his father's brother's daughters. His brothers had among them eight wives, four of whom were gentry, four commoners. In the other wing of the family there were seven wives, of whom five were commoners. The youngest generation, which today is still in its twenties and thirties, appears to choose even a smaller proportion of village women: of five marriages so far, only one is with a commoner. This apparent shift toward greater endogamy among the gentry may be a response to the new political conditions, in which affiliations with village families no longer provide much strategic advantage.

One of the inevitable results of a system of hypergamy systematically carried out must be the accumulation in the topmost families of a number of unmarriageable girls, unmarriageable because there are not enough men of high enough status for them to marry. This was indeed the case in every Balinese gentry house of any stature. Of the seven sisters of the prince of Tabanan who ruled in the 1870s, two were spinsters. Of his nine daughters, six never married. Of his ten granddaughters, three were spinsters. In the present-day house of Beng the same situation prevails. In the older generation, out of eleven women, six are spinsters; in the younger generation, one out of nine is.

There were always a few rebellious women who chose neither to marry the approved suitor nor to remain single, but who ran off with commoner husbands. This was a totally unlawful act, and in pre-colonial times could be punished by death, if the culprits were caught. Usually, however, such nonconformists managed to escape to another kingdom. Today it is possible for the couple to remain in the same region, but the girl is always entirely ostracized by her kinsmen. Such illegitimate marriages do occur with some frequency. Of the ten granddaughters of the king, two ran off with commoners, and in the house of Beng, of the nine women in the youngest generation, two have married commoners. In the village of Tihingan, there were at least two contemporary cases of girls from the local gentry houses marrying commoners. In the Tihingan cases, the couples continued to live in the village, and, after some years had passed, relationships had become more comfortable between the girl and her gentry family, but she was utterly excluded from any participation in their temple rituals, and hence from any protection from their gods.

To summarize, the patterns and dynamics of gentry marital choices are essentially the same as those of the commoners. For those members of both strata who are part of powerful or would-be powerful dadia, the strategic considerations are much the same. On the one hand, the aim to keep the dadia integrated, to draw back again dispersing branch lines, means that the girls of the dadia should be married off endogamously to the men of the dadia. If the subdadia is gaining or attempting to maintain its political salience, these endogamic pressures are even greater, for such in-group alliances serve to accentuate the boundaries of the subdadia. Moreover, the status implications of any exogamous marriage are such that it is better to keep the dadia girls within the dadia if no highly advantageous, sharply upward marriage is proposed.

On the other hand, since a powerful dadia needs to insure that it constantly grows in size, it becomes strategically wise to bring in as many women as possible as wives. Since the political operations of gentry dadia were much more extensive than those of the commoners, this exogamic choice is much more meaningful. Further, the more frequent practice of polygamy, itself a function of wealth, makes possible, for the gentry, a much higher ratio of externally born wives. An examination of the local origins of commoner wives in the Tabanan dadia gives a strong impression that they were apparently quite systematically drawn from scattered, politically strategic villages.

The Spatialization of Kinship

In describing the commoner variant of Balinese kinship we found it necessary to start with diagrams of the layout of the houseyard with its temple and pavilions, and to anchor our discussion of the dadia on its geographical locus in the dadia temple. This intimate connection between physical space and social groupings is a general characteristic of Bali, although the connection is never simple or direct. The dadia temple represents the place of origin as well as the generic source of the family line, and the mere existence of a tangible dadia temple is a strong, but not a necessary, incentive to the maintenance of a dadia organization. The fact that, in marrying, women sever their ties with their ancestral temples and become full and unqualified members of the dadia of their residence, further strengthens the link between physical space and the form of kinship groupings.

At the gentry level the spatial aspects of kinship structure are even more pronounced than among the commoners. Each gentry subdadia is identified with its core houseyard, which in itself is a specific site with a name of its own. The name of the core houseyard may indicate its location (Puri Kaleran is "northern palace," Jero Dlodcarik is "noble house south of the rice fields"), or it may be the same as the hamlet within which it stands (Jero Pandak, Jero Tuakilang, Puri Gde Tabanan), or the name may be specifically its own (Puri Anyar is "new palace," Puri Mecutan is "blow-pipe palace," and Jero Beng has, apparently, no literal meaning at all).

Each one of these noble houses considers itself to be a part of a royal dadia at the central peak of which is a prince living in the royal core houseyard, or palace. Each one, likewise, has its own lesser subsidiary branches, in various houseyards both nearby and in distant villages. All of these tertiary branches consider themselves members of both the subdadia and the dadia, but to be represented first by the noble incumbent of the subdadia core houseyard, and second by the prince himself as head of the entire dadia.

The spatial distribution of all of these houses corresponds remarkably closely to their kinship and status positions in regard to the core. That is, the nearest collaterals of the prince, those of the highest status, are usually located within the central capital settlement itself. Those kin units which are politically and socially peripheral, the lower noble houses, are scattered around the countryside. In Tabanan, referring back to figure 15, the houses of Anyar, Taman, Dangin, Den Pasar, Kaleran, Anom, Kompiang, and Beng are or were all situated within the town of Tabanan itself, their walls all nearly touching the royal compound. The lesser houses of Dlodrurung, Den Bantas Bakisan, Pandak, Wangaya, Dlodcarik, among others, are all located in various villages outside of Tabanan town. There are some interesting exceptions to this pattern: the two low gentry houses of Dlodrurung and Wangaya are today situated within the town limits of Tabanan, but it has only been the urban expansion of the last fifty years which has engulfed their hamlets, formerly separated from Tabanan by rice fields. The house of Subamio, on the other hand, genealogically low in status, received at some time in the historic past a special honor from the king, and in consequence today enjoys both a high status and a location which are anomalous. The other exceptions, the houses of Kediri and Krambitan, are examples of another process at work: that of stationing very high noble houses at some distance from the court as secondary rulers.

From the appearance of this spatial distribution, it seems that there must have been a regular tendency to move the inhabitants out of those houseyards in the immediate proximity of the court into the hinterlands, as they sank in status, and, every few generations, to refill those proximate houseyards with newly emerging royal houses. This need not have been a formal or an invariable process of eviction and replacement, for there was apparently enough houseland space in the environs of the court for new houseyards to be erected if need be, and, with high death rates, there was also always a number of lines which died out of themselves, whose locations could be reassigned to new houses. Nevertheless, many sites must have had a sequence of different subdadia lines occupying them in turn, in order to have produced the present arrangement, this spatial objectification of social distance. It probably came about primarily by royal fiat, for the Balinese princes had a general policy of keeping all their highest kinsmen (and most probable rivals) in houseyards in their immediate proximity, and of choosing mainly those lower-ranking noble houses which were well outside the royal subdadia for transfer to outlying village posts on the troubled edges of the domain.

Succession and Inheritance

The mechanism which brought about the primary displacement, the movement of all but one of the sons out of the core houseyard, was the set of gentry rules for succession and inheritance. In nineteenth-century Bali, there could be only one mature man living in a gentry core houseyard. Even today, although this residential pattern no longer obtains, due to changes in political roles and pressures of population, only one son can succeed the father. This is so whether he is the king or prince at the head of a royal dadia, or the lord at the head of a subdadia, or merely a minor member of the gentry with a modest houseyard full of dependents. This son takes his father's place as incumbent of the core-line position, and, if that office is one of a subdadia or a dadia, he inherits the ritual obligations toward the family temple, the political leadership of the group, and a good deal of the kingroup's wealth. The economic burden on the occupant of the core position is much more severe for gentry than for commoners, who divide the load more evenly among all the members of the dadia.

The rule for division of a gentry estate follows, first, recognition of the principle of core versus peripheral statuses and, second, distinction between children of mothers of different social origins. The man who is the oldest son of the primary wife is normally the one to succeed the father. Because of the heavy financial obligations of the post, he is entitled to receive the largest portion of the estate, sometimes as much as two-thirds of the total. The other brothers divide the remainder according to the status of their mothers. There are actually no precise arithmetical fractions which are legally binding but rather a general consensus on the relative weights placed on office and descent, and each inheritance settlement is slightly different from all others. The terms of division are reached in familial council meeting, and, in cases of dispute, more distant relatives may be called in. It was also possible to take an inheritance dispute to higher authorities, to a Brahmana pedanda, for instance, or to a high lord or king, and, today, to the government court, but such a step was, and is, avoided as much as possible.

A few examples of estate division may make the general pattern clear. The first is an actual case, a settlement that took place at the end of the nineteenth century, in the noble house of Kompiang, in Tabanan. There were five brothers and ten pieces of property. The oldest son of the prami, the primary wife, was dull-witted and incompetent, but nevertheless he was given the core position, with a younger brother, also a son of the prami, at his side as the de facto ruler. When this younger brother died, the prami adopted one of the sons of a lesser wife, and placed him in the role of assistant to her oldest son. The division of the father's estate took place after this time. The oldest son of the prami, the titular head of the house, received five of the ten pieces of land. His assistant, the son of the lesser wife who had been adopted by the prami, received two and one-half portions, while the remaining three lower-status sons divided the remnant equally.

The other examples are hypothetical cases furnished us by informants in illustration of the inheritance principles. If there are only two sons, one the son of the prami, the second the son of a penawing, a lesser wife, the division is simply two to one. If there are three sons, one of the prami, the other two penawing offspring, then four parts go to the prami's son and one part to each of the others. If there are two sons by the primary wife, they sometimes can get equal portions; thus if there are two prami's sons and two penawing's sons, the higher-status sons each get two portions of land, while the lower-status ones each receive only one.

In the nineteenth century this mode of succession and inheritance operated to keep the lion's share of the subdadia property in the core-line household, thus giving each noble house the concentrations of resources necessary for it to maintain a leading political position in regard to lesser gentry and commoners. As each generation moved up, only one brother became wealthy and powerful, while the other became relatively poor and dependent. The brother in the core position was thus able to gain and retain the allegiance of his other brothers, half-brothers, and cousins through shrewd gifts or loans to them. The commoner subjects of the noble house were under the authority of the core post, and their services could be transferred by him to one of the branch houses, contingent on its continued loyalty.

A consequence of such a disproportionate division of the estate was that rivalry between brothers for the core position could be very intense. While the oldest son was formally entitled to the post, he could be passed up for another son if he were clearly incompetent or if he should die before his own children reached maturity. If one of the other brothers took power, he was often then able to retain the post for his own children. One of the most serious challengers to the throne of Tabanan in the first half of the nineteenth century was one of the prince's own half-brothers, who established a realm for himself in a mountainous region, Penebel, and from that base descended on the Tabanan domain, murdering the prince and many of his retainers, and seizing the throne by force. However, he was unable to keep his hold on it in the end, for the lesser Tabanan nobles passively refused to recognize him, and finally forced him out, in favor of a more legitimate heir. Another example of intrafamilial violence appears in the family chronicle of the house of Beng (see Appendix B), wherein one of the lesser wives of the lord of Beng conspired to turn the anger of the lord against his heir, his oldest son, to the point that the lord murdered his potential heir and thus made room for another son, that of the treacherous lesser wife.

Daughters, if they marry, lose all legal claim to inherit from their fathers, but if they do not marry and continue to live in the parental houseyard, they are entitled to receive half as much as their brothers of equivalent status. In many cases, whether they marry or not, daughters can receive from their fathers a large piece of property as a gift, which they may take with them to their husband's home, thus obviating the inheritance rule.

A complicating factor in a good many succession and inheritance transactions is the sentana custom, the practice of bringing in a substitute heir from outside the immediate family when true sons are lacking, to succeed in the core-line position. This imported man may enter the subdadia as a son-in-law, relinquishing his rights and status in his natal family, or he may be directly adopted. As in the case of commoners, the substitute heir is sought first from the nearest families, from among the brother's sons in the case of son-in-law sentana, or from the daughter's sons in the case of adoption. But at times the heir had to be sought farther afield. Among the group of noble subdadias in Tabanan, there were regular, more or less informally established, lines along which both types of sentanas—adoptions and sons-in-law—moved. A house which customarily provided brides to another would also provide sentana sons-in-law, if needed. The recipient house was slightly higher in rank. Thus Beng regularly provided wives and possibly also sentana sons-in-law to Kediri, while

Kediri in turn sent wives and sons-in-law to Kaleran. Needless to say, there were a good many violent inheritance disputes which arose from misunderstandings involved in bringing in an outside man as heir in a wealthy line.

Residence: Palaces and Houses

The residence patterns of the gentry were, and are, strongly shaped by this custom of selecting one man to fill the core-line status, to inherit the greater portion of the familial property, and to live within the core houseyard. The one noble man living within the core houseyard, however, was by no means alone. He was surrounded by his wives and concubines, who could number in the hundreds, their children, and his "mothers," the surviving wives and concubines of his father and grandfather. In addition, large numbers of commoner retainers, male as well as female, lived within the walls of the royal compound. Also, the immediately related houses, those of the lord's brothers, uncles, and sons, were all in the immediate neighborhood, sometimes pressing so close to the walls of the royal compound as to seem almost part of it.

As a first example of Balinese gentry residence patterns, here is the palace of the king of Klungkung, Dewa Agung Gde, as it existed around 1905, just before its sacking by the Dutch. Figure 16 is a sketch of the palace layout as given us by a grandson of Dewa Agung Gde, a man who had been a child at the time, and shows the functions of the courtyards, their inhabitants, and so on.

The basic layout of the palace was one of a cluster of rectangular courtyards connected by large ornate gateways, within which were set various pavilions and small windowless houses, much like those of the commoners but much more lavishly decorated. Since, however, the palace served not only as a residence but also as the place where the political activities of the king—his great state ceremonies and festivities, his royal audiences, his tax-collecting, and so on—were carried on, there were a number of courtyards which were not strictly domestic in function. In one of these, at the extreme northeast corner of the palace compound, the most sacred corner, north of the temple of the royal subdadia, was a high pavilion where three pedandas met, as proxy for the king, to judge the legal cases brought him, cases which were largely disputes between different gentry houses, and capital crimes. Below this pavilion was a sacred garden, where flowers to be used in offerings were grown. The judges' pavilion and the garden were peculiar to the palace of Klungkung, but

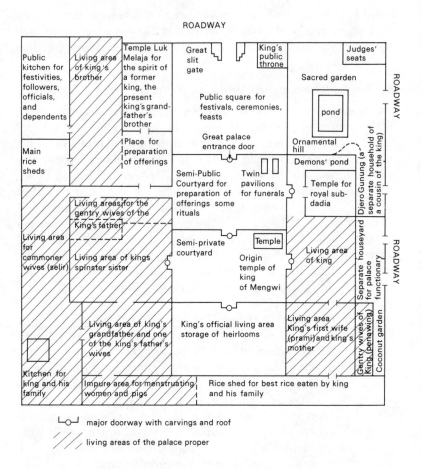

Fig. 16. The palace of the king of Klungkung (Dewa Agung Gde, died 1908)

the other features described below were more or less characteristic of any of the Balinese royal palaces.

Down through the center of the entire courtyard ran three public courtyards, each more exclusive than the next. The first was entered through a huge, finely carved, "split" gateway, while the second had as it opening a splendid ornate door, called the *Pemedal Agung*, the "great exit," which was the door proper of the palace itself. The common throng was permitted to go into only the first courtyard or square, while more important people or those helping with offerings were allowed to enter the second, and only persons of the highest status or functionaries of the palace were free to pass through into the third. Beyond it was a fourth courtyard which was reserved for the king himself to live in, although he probably actually slept there only on high ritual occasions.

In 1905, the king's ordinary living quarters were in another courtyard, to one side of these public areas, next to the subdadia temple. His wives lived in various other courtyards together with their children, visiting the king only at his request. The primary wife, the prami, lived in a large adjacent courtyard with her mother-in-law, the king's mother. The lesser wives of gentry descent, the penawing, had another place, while the wives of commoner descent, the selir, were in a courtyard on the far southwest side of the entire compound, the side of lowest status and least sacredness. At the time described, the king's father was dead, but his grandfather, formerly king himself, still lived, in yet another courtyard, cared for by one of his daughters-in-law—not the mother of the reigning king but one of her co-wives. There were also three more of these co-wives, foster mothers of the reigning king, who were allotted space to live in. The other wives of the previous king, those of lesser gentry status, and the commoner ones, had all been moved to another home after his decease. There were two kitchens in the palace, reflecting its dual function as center for state activities and as domestic establishment for the king's family. The large kitchen, facing onto the main road, and backed by large storehouses of rice, served all the public festivities, the many visiting dignitaries, and the daily needs of all the numerous servants, stewards, and dependents of the royal household. The smaller kitchen, with a smaller shed filled with the finest quality rice, was for the king, his wives, children, sister, grandfather, "mothers," and so on. It was located in the living quarters of the commoner wives, who prepared the food for the rest of the household.

In 1905, in a slightly separate courtyard, next to a secondary temple, lived a brother of the king named Dewa Agung Sumarabawa, with his family. This brother had nearly as high a title as the king and was eligible to rule should the regent have proved incompetent or died without issue. In 1908, when the king of Klungkung led his family and followers in the magnificently tragic suicidal surrender march into the guns of the invading Dutch soldiers, this brother accompanied him into death. But years later when the Dutch reinstalled the monarchy, there were no direct descendants of Dewa Agung Gde surviving, so that one of the sons of Sumarabawa, his brother, took the throne. This pattern of keeping at least one equally high-ranking brother within, or almost within, the household of the king, always ready to take over the reins in need, seems to have been quite common. He could share some of the duties of the throne, and in any case, as the king's most eligible rival, was in this way kept in firm control. In some cases the brother of the king moved out to a lesser palace immediately north of the king's residence, where he served as a deputy monarch. This had been the case in an earlier generation in Klungkung, and also in Tabanan, where in both cases the head of Puri Kaleran ("Northern Palace") was popularly called "the second king." (See the Beng family chronicle in Appendix B.)

The other brothers and uncles of the king all had houses of their own, most of which were located within a few hundred yards of the palace, within the town of Klungkung. Along the eastern wall of the palace were three small houseyards, each separate, as indicated by the fact that these lesser houseyards had doors of their own. One was occupied by a cousin of the king, while the other two were held by two brothers, low-level gentry, who were the main stewards to the king, one for financial affairs internal to the king's household and the other concerned with external matters, such as supervising cultivation of the king's rice fields.

The lower nobles' houses all followed, on a reduced scale, much the same pattern as that given for the palace of Klungkung. Like the palace, the lesser houses all had basically the same layout as that of the commoner houseyards, as shown in Chapter 2, with a houseyard temple in the northeast corner, kitchen in the southwest corner, and rice-storage sheds usually in the southeast corner. However, the gentry houseyards differed from those of commoners in being much more extensive and in having greater internal subdivision into component courtyards, with the higher the status the more numerous the courtyards and the larger proportion of vacant public and semi-public areas for the holding of shows and ceremonies.

Gentry with political position, and also those Brahamana houses which had a pedanda priest, followed the same rule as the Klungkung king, of having only one mature male living in the core compound. However, the cohesiveness and mutual interdependence of larger gentry dadias and subdadias meant that their houseyards tended to be placed near one another in an urbanlike contiguity.

In the twentieth century several significant changes have occurred in the residence patterns of the gentry, which have intensified even further their tendency to cluster densely together. The custom of reserving the entire core houseyard compound for the one male who occupies the core position no longer holds today, mostly because the gentry dadia is no longer a significant political unit, and political office no longer goes to the core representative of the whole dadia or subdadia. Increasingly there are efforts to assure all the sons, regardless of rank, an equal share in the estate, and rather than most of them being established in houseyards of their own outside the parental yard, they are each allowed to take a corner of it for themselves and their family. The spacious ceremonial courtyards, formerly vacant, are now being filled up with living pavilions, kitchens, rice sheds, and all the apparatus of domestic life. Today, most gentry compounds, while still great in extent, are crowded with people, living in densities resembling those of a Middle Eastern city. These shifts resulting from changes in the Balinese political structure were further encouraged by the pressures of the rapidly growing population during the last thirty years.

An example of a modern gentry compound, its layout and inhabitants, is Jero Beng, the "house of Beng," a prominent gentry house in Tabanan. Within a walled area no larger than two hundred feet on each side, are crowded some thirty-six adults, twenty children, and several servants. Despite many modern alterations, notably the filling up of the former public areas with domestic structures, and the establishment of a drygoods store on the roadside, it is possible to reconstruct a picture of the more courtly arrangements which must have obtained in the nineteenth century, when only one man, the lord of Beng, lived there with his wives and dependents. By examining the placement of unusually ornate double doorways, of elaborately carved pavilions, and the names still used to refer to each courtyard, it becomes clear that the basic pattern is a simplified version of that which underlay the form of the palace of Klungkung. There is, in the forefront, a large open square, which is still empty, for public festivities and ceremonies. Behind it, through a great carved gateway is the first courtyard, semipublic, where the great decorated pavilion for laying out the deceased for cremation stands, and where more private ceremonies are held. Finally, in the rear, entered by another elaborate gate is the innermost courtyard, where the lord of the house of Beng was expected to live, and where still today is a beautifully painted and carved pavilion, set much higher than any other in the compound, where the lord slept. Today, an old man, oldest son of the highest-ranking wife of the former lord of Beng, sleeps there.

In those days, there was probably only one temple where the household of the lord worshipped as well as the rest of the subdadia of Beng.

Today, however, with the multiplication of households within the compound walls, several subsidiary temples have been added and, with each of them, a pavilion for ceremonies and numerous other living structures. Figure 17 shows the layout and contents of the house of Beng as it exists today. The kinship relationships of the contemporary living adults are charted in figure 18, with household identification numbers keyed to their spatial arrangement within the courtyards of figure 17. There are today in the house of Beng thirteen households, and the older members of these are all siblings and cousins. The households are divided socially into two sets, which are referred to as the "eastern" and "western" sides of the family, according to the rough placement of their respective courtyards within the compound. The eastern branch are the children and grandchildren of the former lord of Beng who died in 1920. He had been a Penggawa (lord) under the old prince of Tabanan before 1908, and after that time had been appointed by the Dutch as a Penggawa (the term had been reinterpreted to mean "subdistrict officer") in a nearby part of the Tabanan regency. As lord of Beng, he held the core status for the subdadia, and his successor, under traditional circumstances, would have been chosen from among his sons, with first priority to those born of his prami, or primary wife. Today, however, since political office is no longer assigned according to kinship location, this core status no longer has its former significance outside the family. Nonetheless, the six sons of the lord inherited his paramount status within the family, his wealth, and a disproportionate share of the physical space within the compound, as compared with the inferior or western side of the family, who are crowded into three small courtyards in the rear of the complex and who are noticeably poorer than their cousins.

All of the people on both sides of the family consider themselves to be full-fledged members of the house of Beng. The great front gate stands for their living together in a single "house," for even though there are smaller gaps in the walls through which short-cut entrance may be made, they always refer to themselves as being *semeton,* "one doorway." They all also worship collectively at the great temple in front, the Beng subdadia temple.

Nonetheless, there are lines of segmentation within the group. Of course, the smallest, and fundamental, fraction is the household, and,

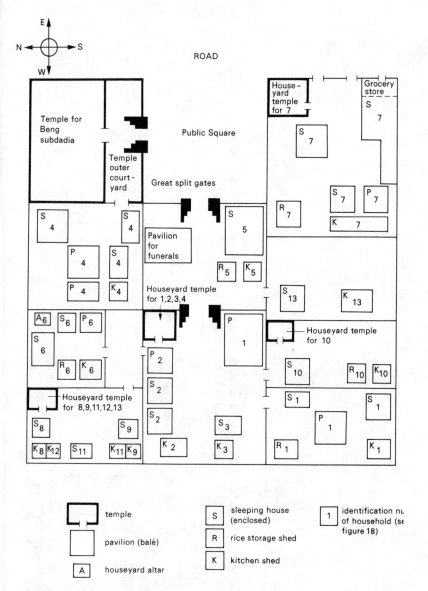

Fig. 17. A modern gentry compound, showing courtyard layout, temples, living structures, and component households

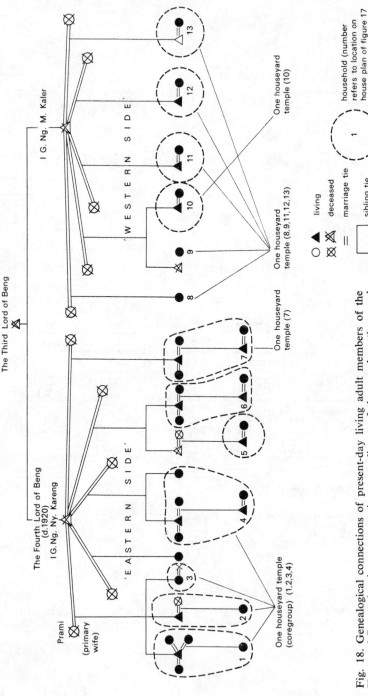

Fig. 18. Genealogical connections of present-day living adult members of the House of Beng, showing segmentation according to fathers and mothers and organization into households and temple groups.

as with the commoners, the subdadia is essentially an association of member households. A household is identified by its having a separate kitchen, that is, a separate economic existence, and as being capable of carrying full ritual obligations. Most of these households are composed of one nuclear family, or the two families of a father and one son. (It happens that in Beng today, there has been only one man who has had two sons, and one of these sons married outside of Jero Beng entirely, becoming a sentana, substitute heir, in another subdadia.)

In addition to the division into households, there are several other ways in which the occupants of the compound are segmented. In terms of genealogy, the most significant fission point after the paternal tie is the maternal. The children of the lord of Beng are aligned according to their mothers. The lord had had numerous wives, of whom five produced children who lived to adulthood. With the prevailing high infant mortality, there are very few full siblings among the progeny of the lord of Beng; most are half-brothers and half-sisters. Those who are full siblings tend to be much closer, as can be seen by the way they are grouped into worshipping congregations of the small subordinate temples which are the rough equivalent of the commoners' houseyard temple.

Worship at one of these temples seems to be in large part a matter of personal inclination and adjustment to circumstances. Households 1, 2, and 3 are the children of the prami, the primary wife, and therefore are entitled to occupy the core status in the subdadia. They have the central courtyard. However, in keeping with modern practice, when the estate of the lord of Beng was divided among his sons, the primacy of the children of the prami was ignored and the property distributed almost equally among all of them. The heads of households 1 and 2 are full brothers, and they share the rather considerable ritual responsibilities of the core status between them. Household 3 consists merely of their widowed sister, who had been married to a man from the western side of the family, but returned to her brothers' courtyard at his decease. Household 4 shares the same "houseyard" temple with 1, 2, and 3. Households 5 and 6, on the other hand, do not bother with keeping up a subsidiary temple and perform all their ritual duties directly in the great subdadia temple. Household 7, headed by a somewhat younger man, more vigorous, modern, and better educated, is prominent both in government and politics, and is also active in numerous business ventures. He is quite wealthy and maintains a separate "houseyard" temple for himself and his married son who runs a modern grocery store built into the front wall of the compound. The members of the western side, likewise, group themselves for daily ritual observance into two smaller sets, with two subsidiary temples.

5

Do the Balinese Have a Kinship System?

Once upon a time, the one thing that was certain in anthropology was that every people possessed something called "a kinship system," which could be identified, described, analyzed, and even according to its nomenclature, classified. Iroquois, and a large number of other matrilineal peoples, had Iroquois systems; Hawaiians, and other Oceanic groups, had Hawaiian ones; Americans, Frenchmen, and Eskimos had Eskimo ones. In some societies, ours for example, "the kinship system" didn't count for much; its operations—then called functions—were confined to narrowly domestic contexts, the self-absorbed concerns of the isolated nuclear family, stranded somewhere on a suburban island. But in others, including most tribal ones, it counted for almost everything, and extended monographs on the life of black Africans, Beduin nomads, American Indians, Australian Aborigines, or Pacific Islanders consisted largely of analyses of how they got married, decided where to live, classified relatives, formed descent groups, inherited property, organized households, raised children, and worshipped ancestors. It was an extraordinary period, out of which came some of the most creative work on social organization ever done—brilliantly executed anatomies of the institutional structure of exotic communities which led on to our first real understandings of how such communities worked. But, like Bloomfieldian linguistics, "culture circles," or the Newtonian world, it was based on simplicities which couldn't last; and what once seemed so indubitable—that kinship forms a definable object of study to be found in a readily recognizable form everywhere, a contained universe of internally organized relationships awaiting only an anthropologist to explore it—now seems very much less so.

What has happened is that the consensus, never terribly well spelled-out in the first place, as to what a kinship system in fact is—what it is that is being studied—has dissolved. There are, by now, at least three main views of the matter current (and to which we want to add here a somewhat off-center fourth): what we may call "the affective," "the normative," and "the cognitive."

The "affective" view, perhaps most closely associated with the name of Malinowski, who held a rather pure version of it, takes the emotional relationships within the immediate family—husband-wife, parent-child, sibling-sibling—as paradigmatic, and then regards all other social uses of kinship conceptions as extensions of these. "The kinship system," in the wider sense (descent group, extrafamilial use of kin terms, exogamy rules, or whatever), is regarded as a series of projections onto the wider social stage of an attenuated form of the "family feeling" that appears, in pristine form, in the immediate contexts of domestic life. Beyond the bounds of the family, properly speaking, kinship conceptions, institutions, terms, relationships are, in a sense, metaphorical: the transfer of ideas, and most especially sentiments, built up through interaction with one's father, mother, daughter, son, brother, sister, wife, or husband to settings—political, economic, ritual—where they do not literally apply but yet can serve to weld individuals together.

The "normative" view, associated mainly with the British school of social anthropologists following after Radcliffe-Brown, sees the basis of "the kinship system" less in the passions of the immediate family—though the importance of these is not denied—than in the need for societies to be governed by collectively accepted moral and jural rules if they are not to degenerate into Hobbsean war. Kinship is regarded as a mechanism in terms of which, in many societies, and especially in tribal ones, the rights and duties of specifically denominated social actors are defined and enforced, and so the social order is kept intact and humming. There is a French version of this approach, stemming from Durkheim and developed, in a somewhat special form, in Lévi-Strauss's earlier work, in which the stress is laid on the formation of wider alliances and solidarities through the operation of kinship institutions, most especially marriage. But the basic notion is the same: "the kinship system" is a system of moral and jural norms, more or less comprehensively applied—a constitution, an etiquette, an ethical code.

The "cognitive" view is the most recent, at least in its developed form, having been worked out to some degree of refinement over the past two decades by the "new ethnography" movement in the United

States. It sees "the kinship system" as essentially a psychological, even an intellectual, phenomenon, an internalized categorical scheme in terms of which a given social actor, *Ego*, perceives other social actors, *Alters*, as standing in a certain formal relationship to himself. Kinship terminologies, in particular, mark out from the universe of logically possible "consanguinity-and-affinity" type relationships (the so-called "etic grid"), that subset of such relationships locally recognized to have social importance (the so-called "emic system"), much the way the phonemic system of a given language marks particular sounds, or clusters of sound, out of the universal background of phonetic possibility as meaningful units. And in so doing, they, and the conceptions surrounding them, provide individuals with a "cognitive map," in terms of which they can shape their behavior toward significant others according to the locations of those others on that map. Where kinship is regarded as central in the general culture, as in so much of the world outside of Europe and North America, the system of categories thus defined—a several-dimensioned mathematical space with discriminate regions in it—provides a general, in-the-head guide to who is who in one's encountered world, a mental representation of social form.

It is not our view that any of these approaches is simply wrong, that they necessarily contradict one another, or that they are totally discontinuous with our own. Each has serious inadequacies, incessantly rehearsed by the partisans of the others; but each has also had its larger and smaller triumphs and has contributed to our understanding of how social life is ordered. What we would like to suggest, however, and what the Balinese material we have presented seems to us to support, is that to start with the notion that there is an isolable, internally integrated system of, "sentiments," "norms," "categories," to which the adjective "kinship" can be unambiguously appended is not the most profitable way to go about the matter. When one sets out to study "kinship" and ends up talking as much as we have found ourselves doing about status rivalry, political combat, and, especially, religious style, the idea begins to dawn that whatever system there is in all this (and we hope we have shown there is a great deal) is not likely to be formulable in terms of the sentiments, the norms, or the categories pertaining to "consanguinity and affinity"—notions as foreign to the Balinese *"kawitan* and *dadia"* idiom as those are to ours.

It seems better, then, to speak, as we have, of "kinship in Bali," much as one would speak of, say, "witchcraft in Bali" or "dance in Bali," and to begin with the recognition that there are—probably in every society, certainly in this one—certain symbols whose most immediate role it is to give meaning to the relationships of people domestically involved in one another's lives.[51] There is no particular harm and a certain indexical advantage in calling such symbols "kinship symbols," so long as it is remembered that the activities that can fall under "domestically involved in one another's lives," is an open class. Sexuality, the division of labor in the household, procreation, nurturance, and socialization, the diffuse solidarities of growing up together, the passage of personal property and office, the memories of predecessors and the anticipations of successors, patterned visiting and mutual-help relations, collective worship, and a great number of other matters may (or may not) be included. Some—sexuality, procreation, socialization, division of labor—may be more central to the broad and vaguely outlined notion of "domestic life" than others. In some places some rather strange things may be included—trading partnership, for example; in others, some rather surprising ones excluded—coresidence, for example. But the fact that everywhere people neither grow up nor, save marginally, live psychically alone, free of the phenomenological presence of primordial others, gives to the notion, and with it the notion of kinship symbols, a quite general, if unrigorous, applicability.[52]

Thus defined, kinship (or "kinshiplike") symbols and the conceptions they embody, are clearly not confined in any society solely to domestic concerns; but, inextricably woven in with other sorts of symbols relating to other sorts of concerns, they play a role in a variety of social contexts. What we call culture is everywhere an organization, to some degree comprehensive, to some degree systematic, of symbols and clusters of symbols centered in a whole host of quite different, even discontinuous, aspects of social life—a web of disparate conceptions meaningfully arranged. The whole notion of "a kinship system" as an isolable structure of sentiments, norms, or categorical distinctions is misleading because it assumes, or seems to assume, that the ordering principles of a society are partitionable into natural kinds only adventitiously connected. The integration of any society is limited, but to the extent that it exists it does not consist in the agglomeration of autonomous parts.

If one takes this view—that it is kinship symbols and their social employment we should be interested in—several corollaries follow.

First, as already stressed, kinship symbolization varies in importance—in the scope of its application, in the force of its impact, and, of course, in "what it says," its content—from society to society, and even from place to place and group to group within one society.[53] Despite numerous arguments to the contrary, the symbols drawn from familial—or as we prefer to say "domestic"—contexts are, a priori, no more "basic," "elementary," "fundamental," and so on than symbolism drawn from, say, the sense of time passage (in seasonal change, in aging), the perception of sexual dimorphism, the awareness of death, or from such pervasive realms of human concern as religion, politics, art, agriculture, trade, or moral judgment. Indeed, sharp lines between such different sorts of symbolism are often impossible to draw—What is a dadia? Is it a lineage? A caste? A cult? A faction?—precisely because of the extensive interconnections among them. The degree to which symbolism reasonably identified as having something to do with the creation of a viable domestic life plays a significant role in commerce, worship, or government is an empirical matter, as is the degree to which the symbolism associated with such matters penetrates the domestic realm. There is no privileged zone in culture from which the others necessarily derive, and society is neither the family expanded nor the polity generalized.

Second, like all cultural symbols, kinship symbols form what one of us has called elsewhere both "models-of" reality and "models-for" the construction of it; both represent the way things are conceived in fact to be and provide guides to feeling, thought, and behavior such that things will in fact be more or less that way.[54] On the other hand, any set of kinship symbols pictures how things "really" are—emotionally, morally, practically—between, say, husband and wife, father and son, brother and sister, uncle and nephew, daughter-in-law and mother-in-law, heir and ancestor, core houseyard and peripheral one, and so on—what the shape, the tone, the nature of domestic life is. And, on the other, it provides "information," rather in the way a genotype provides information for the organization of biological process, as to the ways such people, or classes of people, should think about, feel, and treat with one another to construct a domestic life with such a shape, tone, and nature. Kinship symbols, or clusters of them, are images at once of the facts of domestic life and templates for the creation of that life. And to the degree they find application outside the domestic realm, the situation is the same: they portray a way of doing things, whether approaching gods or commanding subjects, and give direction for the doing of them.

And third, what are usually referred to as kinship institutions—the family, the household, the descent group, bridewealth, marriage and divorce customs, child-rearing practices, property and inheritance rules, or whatever—represent the social establishment of these "models-of, models-for," the casting into social structure of the cultural conceptions defining and regulating domestic life. It is these institutions and social structures, or some of them, which may come to play a wider role in society, serving as does the dadia, for example, as an agricultural work group, a celebrant of caste honor, a religious congregation, or a building block of the state. It is through them and their operation that the symbols of domestic order and propriety—the conceptions governing the way people most comprehensively involved in one another's personal life ought to conduct themselves—penetrate the other institutions of society: in Bali, the temple system, the hamlet, the irrigation society, the caste system, the kingdom, or nowadays, when dadias so often align themselves as a body with one or another national political movement, the republic.[55] Whatever may be the case in West Africa, or Australia, Balinese society is in no way dominated by the institutions of kinship.

If, looking back upon our analysis, one were to attempt to list such ideas of order implicit in Balinese kinship institutions and symbolized in the vocabulary and practices of domestic life, there would be, perhaps, nine main ones:

1. A sharp distinction between the public and the private domains of social action.

2. The concept of "origin-point," and the attendant distinctions between core and peripheral houseyards, founding and way-station temples, main and cadet lines.

3. Virilocal residence, unigenitural succession, and patrifiliative inheritance.

4. The anonymity pattern: naming by repeating, generalized, and impersonal role designations (among the commoners, teknonyms, among the gentry, "office names") which enforce a systematic genealogical amnesia.

5. The title system, and the attendant scuffle for prestige.

6. Preferential endogamy and the differentiation of less inclusive groups out of more inclusive ones.

7. The *seka* principle: the equality of members in the context of the group of which they are members; the irrelevance of that membership with respect to other groups to which they may belong; and the legal precedence of originative groups over derivative ones.

8. The houseyard, to houseyard cluster, to on-public-ground temple system with the worship of ancestors promoted to gods and the assertion of kinship as a political force.

9. The polar tension between kinship and community.

As the interconnections among these ordering principles are multiple, oblique, and intricately tangled, forming them into a web rather than a series, the sequence in which they are here arranged for summary is largely arbitrary, designed only to evoke as exactly as possible the manner in which they add up to a way of seeing which is also a style of relating, an approach to treating people that expresses a view of what life in society is all about.

1. A sharp distinction between the public and the private domains of social action. The Balinese sense of contrast between personal life (including, but not exhausted by, domestic life) and the multiple civic worlds of hamlet, temple, irrigation society, and so on, is in fact a reflex of the unusual degree to which the latter are defined in the culture as legal, moral, and metaphysical entities. As the *awig-awig* constitution for the village of Aan given in Appendix C demonstrates, with its detailed regulations for everything from the disposition of trees on village land to the penalties imposed for swearing during a temple festival (and its total silence on anything having to do with marriage, divorce, adultery, inheritance, succession, adoption, and the like), such seemingly abstract structures as the hamlet, the "custom village," and the temple congregation are very concrete realities in the minds of the Balinese. Were similar "constitutions" to be presented for irrigation societies, kingdoms, or even voluntary organizations, the effect of an intense sense for the tangible actuality of what to us are but institutional arrangements and social customs would be equally strong. Whatever the Balinese are, they are not philosophical individualists: groups are as real as people. Perhaps, pervaded, as the more formidable of these groups are, with the awesomeness of the divine, they are in fact somewhat more real.

So far as kinship is concerned, this emphatic boundary between what goes on in sitting rooms and kitchens and what goes on in streets, fields, and civil arenas makes of the movement of a domestic temple out from behind houseyard walls into the broader realm of village space a most consequential act. When a family sanggah becomes a kingroup dadia it becomes "affected with the public interest," a force of no mean proportions in Bali, where social exclusion is equivalent to capital punishment. Sorted now with the council pavilion, the village temples, the graveyard, the Rangda witch-mask, the slit-gong tower, the communal granary, the market, the banyan tree, and, in the old days, the cockpit (in the present, the school, the cooperative, the coffee shop, and that newer cockpit, the perbekel office), it functions in the world they define. What was a family ritual becomes a civic cult; what was a private communion becomes a public celebration.

2. *The concept of "origin point," and the attendant distinctions between core and peripheral houseyards, founding and way-station temples, main and cadet lines.* What lineage does in many societies and cognation does in others, the notion of "origin-point"—*kawitan, kemulan*—does in Bali. The master image by which people and groups who regard themselves as ancestrally related to one another conceive the nature of that relation is neither the downward branching tree of the typical descent system nor the symmetrically spreading network of the typical bilateral one, but that of a primal cell and its spontaneously generated replicas. The present has emerged from the past by the continuous reproduction of exemplary forms, social archetypes repeatedly reincarnated, not by the transmission of rights and essences across forking lines of procreation nor by the steady radiation of claims and liabilities through collateral connections.

This image (pattern, paradigm, notion), which is fundamental to the entire culture, not just to kinship, generates, or perhaps better, translates into, specific conceptions of a cluster of secondary houseyards centered on a primary houseyard from which they have emerged (and if the process has gone far enough, of tertiary houseyards centered on secondary ones, and so on); of certain temples as being facsimiles of certain others (which may, in turn, be facsimiles of yet others), and thus local stopping places for gods whose main destination is elsewhere—the coreyard temple, the "title-group" origin-temple some place on the island, the great, all-Bali founding temple at Besakih; and, among the gentry, of noble houses having "gone out" of the royal house in a particular sequence that, inversely, determines their status relative to it and to one another—a process which can also have secondary and tertiary ramifications. For all its indefiniteness and generality, the "origin-point" ("birthsite," "core," "archetype"—the sense of commencement, of place, of precedence, and of exemplar are equally involved) and "replica" ("way station," "emergent," "surrogate") conception ties the various aspects of Balinese "kinship" symbolism together as firmly as notions of clan, blood, affinity, or pedigree do elsewhere.

3. Virilocal residence, unigenitural succession, and patrifiliative inheritance. The specific mechanisms by means of which Balinese domestic units are created and maintained are such that in the normal course of things they would cause the society's "kinship system" to be classified as "patrilineal." Inheritance—of property, titles, group membership, and so on—is from father to child. When a woman marries she moves out of her natal household into that of her husband, which often enough is included in a houseyard with various of his close agnatic kin—his father, his brothers, his patri-cousins, and so on. If she is marrying exogamously, outside her local title-group, she will leave her own group and be ritually incorporated into her husband's. If she is marrying endogamously, she is already in it (indeed, if she is marrying a first cousin she may not even be leaving her natal houseyard). But in any case, she is symbolically moving into her husband's ambit, not he into hers. And, finally, succession to office, whether merely to the maintainer of the core houseyard and temple or to kingship or priesthood, is unigenitural—mostly ultimo- among commoners, mostly primo- among gentry. Described this way, the way the *Ethnographic Atlas* would describe it, the system sounds almost African.

But it is not almost African. If it is almost anything, it is almost Polynesian; and if one were to classify it in the classical terms— something we do not think it profitable to do—"bilateral" would be as hospitable a pigeonhole as "patrilineal." Not only is there no real sense of a descent line in Bali (even the gentry "core line" is more a status map than a clan charter), but the combination of classificatory parallel cousin marriage and the "substitute heir" pattern, where a "male" line runs through a female connection (and a male lives uxorilocally), leads to a conception of kinship connection in which ties through men in no way dominate—cognitively, affectively, morally—ties through women, nor indeed those running through irregular sequences of either. Looked at in terms of how, deep down in the temper of things, it is organized, rather than in terms of the surface features it happens to display, the Balinese "web of kinship" resembles more the kindred-utrolateral kingroup pattern of much of the rest of Southeast Asia and Oceania (and, most especially, the explicit, all-out "bilateralism" of Java) than it does the segmentary rigorism of the Tiv or the Talensi. Virilocality, unigeniture, and patrifiliation shape the immediate composition of households, houseyards, and courtyards, and they provide the main criteria for the allocation of dadia membership and the succession to certain political and religious positions; but they do not place the stamp of "patrilineality"— Middleton and Tait's "lineage ideology"—on the general quality of relationships either within the domestic domain or outside of it. They are devices, not doctrines.

4. *The anonymity pattern: naming by repeating, generalized, and impersonal role designations (among the commoners, teknonyms, among the gentry, "office names") which enforce a systematic genealogical amnesia.* The counterdevice that keeps patrifiliation and virilocality from blossoming into a full-fledged version of the sort of descent-obsessed weltanschauung that in a simpler day would have been referred to as "patriarchy," are, primarily, teknonymy and coreline genealogizing, though, in fact, a wide range of customs—from a strikingly egalitarian view of the relations between the sexes to a systematically androgynous origin myth (it concerns a sinking-status core line composed first of self-propagating bisexual gods, then incestuous identical-twin culture hero and heroine ur-rulers, and then parallel-cousin-married kings and queens)—conduce to the same end.

In actively repressing the memory of ascendant generations disappeared into the anonymizing world of gods and focusing attention instead upon oncoming ones recently emerged into particularity from it, teknonymy short-circuits any tendency to construct a catalog of identifiable ancestors in favor of a continuous celebration of regenesis. Like Balinese temples—and Balinese kings—Balinese parents replicate themselves and view genealogy (if that is even the appropriate word to apply in such a context) not as something which produced them but something they produce. The focus is on the perpetual re-creation of an established pattern, the maintenance—to use again Gregory Bateson's luminous phrase—of a steady state. And in that sort of intellectual and emotional atmosphere, one in which time is less a stream of events flowing causally from past toward future than a permanent backdrop to a repeating drama, a sense of lineality is very hard to maintain.

The core-line approach to the legitimation of dynasties and the determination of status relationships within them embodies essentially the same underlying conception in a somewhat different surface form. The replication in the core line, and for that matter in the "sinking" cadet lines that emerge out of it, of an impersonal "office name"— Dewa Manggis, Gusti Ngurah, Anak Agung, Dewa Agung, or whatever—projects again the image of a fixed pattern endlessly recreated. The core-line, cadet-line conceptualization is less a record, even a fictitious record, of the hereditary transmission of legitimacy down a chain of men (and the actual links can also be through a woman "regarded as" a male in the "substitute heir" pattern), than yet another statement, here in terms of the status relationships among royal and noble houses, of the general principle that closeness to an origin point—a Javanese culture bringer, a royal palace, a reigning king—is closeness to godliness and, thus, to the springs of power, authority, splendor, and excellence.

5. *The title system and the attendant scuffle for prestige.* If the Balinese are not obsessed with descent, they certainly are with prestige. What matters to a man—or to a woman—is public repute: the social deference it brings, the sumptuary rights it confers, the self-esteem it engenders, the cultural assertion it makes possible. Who one is—or, as the Balinese put it, where one "sits"—is what counts; and who one is, notable or nonentity, or where one sits, high or low, "inside" or "outside," is most succinctly indexed by title. Wealth and power make the stratificatory world go round in Bali as they do elsewhere; but they do so in terms of a developed and settled vocabulary of status, a hierarchy of formal rank that, in Balinese eyes, transcends them both.

Dadias, commoner or gentry, are formed out of title-groups—that is, groups of people bearing the same title, and therefore presumptively related. Among commoners, sudras, this occurs within the boundaries of the local community, most particularly the hamlet; among gentry, triwangsas, it is the region, the stretch of landscape through which the group is, or wishes to be, of consequence, that is relevant. But in either case, the crystallization of dadias (or sub-dadias), a process itself in part dependent upon the realities of wealth and power, though not merely on those, leads to an unending competitive struggle among them, a struggle that expresses itself most immediately in ritual and the machinery of ritual. It is the elegance of the dadia temple and the scale of the ceremonies held within it that not only signalize, but in fact establish, the relative status of the title-group whose dadia it represents with respect to rival others.

In the sudra case, where the contenders are local, this status competition proceeds largely in terms of the size, strength, and inner cohesiveness of the dadia as a corporate body, and title prestige is in great part a resultant of the outcome of that competition. In the triwangsa case, titles are more explicitly ranked vis-a-vis one another in their own terms, a priori, and competition takes place within a more determinate, less pliable symbolic structure. But, in either case, the claim to moral, artistic, spiritual, and metaphysical superiority (states largely synonymical in Bali) of one title-group over others, a claim stated mainly in ritual terms, is what "kinship in the public domain" comes finally down to. The grander the group, the grander the temple; the grander the temple, the grander the ceremony; the grander the ceremony, the grander the group—and so on, to aesthetic and liturgical heights that have astounded the world.

6. *Preferential endogamy and the differentiation of less inclusive groups out of more inclusive ones.* By doubling consanguineal ties upon themselves as affinal ones—and indeed blurring altogether the sharpness of the distinction between the two—endogamy provides the hamlet, the dadia, the subdadia, the houseyard cluster, or even on occasion the houseyard, with an inward-drawing cohesive force. From one point of view, a kind of demographic one that the Balinese themselves at least implicitly employ, the structure of a local community consists of a set of marriage-outlined regions, subregions, and sub-subregions in an encompassing marital field. The degree to which the encompassing field—which for commoners is the hamlet, for gentry the regional title-group—is internally differentiated is a function of the degree to which dadias and subdadias have developed within it; and the degree to which dadias and subdadias have developed within it is in turn a function of the degree to which the habit of kin-marrying has flourished. The whole thing is circular, a chicken-and-egg affair, and endogamy is both unequally sought and variably achieved. But it is, for all that, a major mechanism for marking out and solidifying smaller and more narrowly focused groups within the boundaries of similar, more broadly focused larger ones.

It is, thus, the larger ones that, conceptually at least, are basic. Though hamlet endogamy is, in a sense, residual to dadia endogamy, and dadia endogamy residual to subdadia (and all three to parallel-cousin marriage as such), hamlets are not conceived to consist of dadia or dadias of subdadias. And indeed they do not. Even in the most highly kinship differentiated hamlets (a few one-dadia cases aside), a significant number of houseyards belong to no dadia, and the membership of no dadia (or, at least, none that we have encountered) is divided without remainder into subdadias. The hamlet —or, among the gentry, the regional title-group—is the originating field out of which dadias to some extent crystallize as subfields, and the dadia is the originating field out of which, to some extent, subdadias crystallize as sub-subfields. The pura puseh, the village "navel" temple, is the "core," the "birthsite," the "archetype"—the origin point; the pura dadia, the kingroup temple, is the "way station," the "emergent," the "surrogate"—the replica. Similarly, with the dadia and subdadia temples and, in the few cases where the situation obtains, with the subdadia and the sub-subdadia temples.

Whether the hamlet is the largest kinship group, a kind of endogamous clan, or the subdadia the smallest political one, a kind of miniature village (or they are both religious cults of varying scope), is a problem meaningful only to Western eyes. To Balinese eyes, what is important in this Chinese box pattern of groups within groups within groups, is not what species of group they are—they are all sekas. What is important is that the outer groups are the matrix within which the inner ones arise. Big sekas are not built up out of little ones; little ones emerge from the womb of big ones.

7. *The seka principle: the equality of members in the context of the group of which they are members; the irrelevance of that membership with respect to other groups to which they may belong; and the legal precedence of originative groups over derivative ones.* The view that all organized groups are in some fundamental way similar, whatever the particular end or ends—hunting coconut squirrels or hymning gods—to which they are devoted, has some general corollaries affecting the way kingroups, or what pass for kingroups, operate in Bali.

In the first place, within the dadia no member has any different status than any other. There are dadia "heads," usually elected, almost always rotated, but they are mere stewards, not chiefs with special prerogatives or powers. There are also dadia priests, to conduct the temple ceremonies, but they too are but functionaries, their authority confined to their ritual tasks. Within the dadia, the moral slogan, "same level, same feeling," governs the relationships of members, and rights and duties are apportioned with strict equality, deliberately blind to differences of general condition.

Second, dadia membership is not recognized as a fact to be taken into account in the operations of any other group—hamlet, irrigation society, voluntary organization, or whatever. The dadia functions in the public domain *only* as a corporate entity, a collective actor vis-a-vis these other collective actors—a conversation of sekas. So far as the individual is concerned, dadia membership is not a directly negotiable property at all outside the bounds of the dadia as such: in the context of the banjar or subak it has simply no reality. Even within the dadia itself, subdadia membership has no relevance aside from the role of the subdadia as a unit. Members of subdadias and "general" members without such subdadia allegiance are totally on a par. Next to "same level, same feeling," "one basis of organization at a time" is a leading principle of Balinese social structure overall and of kingroup structure in particular.

And, finally, groups considered to have arisen within others—dadias within the hamlet, subdadias within dadias—are viewed as further back in a precedence queue than those within which they are included. The hamlet, as a corporate body, a seka, takes precedence over the dadia, the dadia over the subdadia, the subdadia over the unorganized houseyard, and loyalties to the former therefore outrank loyalties to the latter. The Chinese box pattern of group relationship is also an ascending order of legal priority ("legal" in the sense of *adat*—that is, moral, religious, customary, and jural all at once), with the outer, more broadly focused groups at the top. Taken together, within-group equality, cross-group segregation, and between-group hierarchy prevent the baroque exuberance of Balinese social organization from drowning in its own complexity.

8. *The houseyard, to houseyard cluster, to on-public-ground temple system with the worship of ancestors promoted to gods and the assertion of kinship as a political force.* Though from the point of view of the framework within which they emerge—the hamlet or the regional title-group—dadias may be said to arise by differentiation, from the point of view of the dadias themselves, they may equally well be said to arise by expansion, or even by aggrandizement. The growth of a dadia, driven centrally by the lust for status, but also by the material and political interests that status serves and signalizes, is in one sense an attack on hamlet or royal-house hegemony, a claim to at least a part of their power, a share of their wealth, and an approximation of their prestige. As a group of kinsmen, or supposed such, move from the houseyard and houseyard cluster stage of things to the dadia stage, they are making an assertion that they are significant collectively and corporately rather than merely singly and personally, that they represent a force to be reckoned with on the local or regional scene. In the same way, the expansion of a subdadia within a dadia amounts to a claim to recognition for a subgroup of more closely connected kinsmen, or supposed such, as a significant entity within the dadia. The promotion of domestic cults to the status of civic ones, and of household assemblages to the status of unitary sekas, is more than a peacock gesture: it is an announcement of a

determination to exert the power of kinship symbolism in the group-dominated arenas of public life.

The external signs and immediate mechanisms of this ambition are again mostly religious: the building of an extra-houseyard temple rivaling, and at times even exceeding, the ornate elegance of the village temples; the conducting of ceremonies in that temple of such a scale and such a richness as to approach, and at times even surpass, those of the village as a whole; and the elevation of title-group ancestors ("origin-point" culture heroes) to the level of true gods, often by identifying, in the usual model and replica fashion, the one as versions of the other. Dadia formation is, in the very nature of the case, a threat to the moral, religious, and legal primacy of the hamlet (or the state), as subdadia formation is a threat to that of the dadia (or the dynasty)—a threat normally contained, but more than occasionally only narrowly. In a village with "high kinship differentiation," such as Tihingan, the domination of the whole by what are theoretically mere underparts of it can be quite marked, as can the domination of those parts in turn by its parts. Kingroups, civic cults, and microcastes, dadias are also political factions.

9. *The polar tension between kinship and community.* The relationship between hamlet (or state) and dadia is, therefore, essentially also a competitive one, a competition between the symbolism of settlement and citizenship and that of filiation and origin-point. The competition, as all competition in Bali, is at once religious, stratificatory, aesthetic, and political, and it amounts to a struggle between the principle that the fundamental bond among men is coresidence, sociality, and the principle that the fundamental bond is sameness of natural kind, genus. From the former emerges the notion of the desa adat ("custom village," to give a literalistic gloss for what is actually neither a village nor a body of custom but a metaphysical idea) as an expanse of sacred space within whose bounds the fates of all residents are supernaturally intertwined. (A similar notion—*negara adat*—exists with respect to the realm of the state.) From the latter emerges the notion that Balinese are divided into a multiplicity of separate "peoples" (*wangsa*) whose right arrangement in terms of rank is crucial to the spiritual well-being of the world and everyone in it. *Homo hierarchicus* and *Homo aequalis* are engaged in Bali in war without end.

The forms the war takes are manifold, and its importance and intensity vary from place to place and from time to time. In some villages, the main threats to hamlet hegemony come from voluntary organizations; others are divided by gentry-commoner, landlord-landtenant, craftsmen-peasant oppositions. But everywhere that dadias have crystallized out at all, and embryonically even where they haven't, loyalties formulated in terms of kinship symbols and loyalties formulated in terms of those of community or polity form opposing poles of group attraction. The intensely factional character of Balinese life, apparent from the time of the dynastic struggles of the nineteenth century to the popular massacres of 1965, is but the clearest evidence that the famous "organic" quality of Balinese culture is a delicate and tremulous thing—a result more of the complex balancing of autonomous forces barely contained within restraining structures than of any pervasive and unquestioning submission of sectarian interests to diffuse wholes. And of the autonomous forces that agitate Bali, none is more dynamic than those summed up in the concept of the dadia; of the restraining structures, none more resilient than those summed up in the concept of banjar.

The search for the dadia thus ends not with a single answer but a multiple one; and one which only gives rise to more questions and a continued search.

In one sense the dadia surely is a "kingroup" of some kind, even if a rather peculiar one. Its members regard themselves as agnatically related, even if they can't say exactly how and don't really want to know. They worship their ancestors, even if these are transformed into faceless and generalized Indic gods. They marry one another, at least to some degree, and complain, at least ritualistically, when this does not occur. And they invoke the symbols of domestic life, at least metaphorically, in the service of group solidarity. But in other senses it is as surely a religious cult, celebrating a vision of divinity as the generative archetype of the phenomenal world, the avatar of avatars of avatars that terminates in oneself; a microcaste, claiming, defending, and demonstrating an established position in an ascriptive hierarchy of corporate status groups; and a political faction, advancing the practical interests of its members in the general scramble for wealth and power. Were one to write an anthropological treatise on Balinese religion, Balinese stratification, or Balinese political organization—or for that matter, on Balinese economic life or Balinese art—the dadia would play as essential, if perhaps not as prominent a role, descriptively and analytically, as it has in this one on kinship. Along with the temple, the hamlet, the desa adat, the state, the priesthood, and the irrigation society, it is one of the master institutions of Balinese public life.

Thus does the analysis of "kinship" disappear into the general analysis of Balinese culture. Rather than an autonomous system of affectively toned and logically organized social relationships dominating or dominated by other differently toned and differently organized autonomous systems, political, economic or whatever, "kinship" turns out to be a variety of social idiom, a way of talking about and understanding, and thus of shaping, some aspects of social life. All the great theaters of collective experience—the household, the community, the workplace, the temple, the market, the palace, the farm, the battlefield, the law court, the playing field . . . the theater—generate conceptions of how things are and how one must therefore act, which, expressed in the symbolism such experience fashions, combine diversely with one another to provide what one can only call, as Wittgenstein has, a form of life. So far as the Balinese form of life is concerned, symbolism arising out of the experience of living as a child, spouse, parent, and elder in a small, walled yard of pavilions, kitchens, granaries, toilets, and altars with a dozen or so familial others does not determine the whole. But neither, as we trust we have shown, does it leave it untouched.

Appendix A

Balinese Kinship Terminology

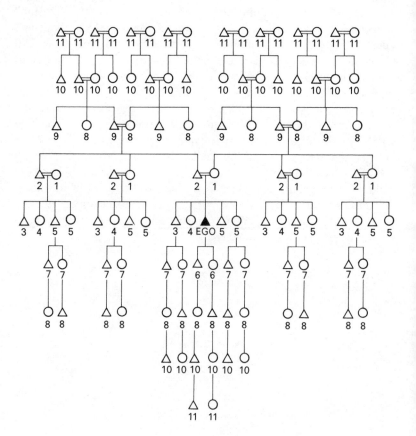

CONSANGUINEAL KIN TERMS

Number on chart	Term of Reference	Term of Address	Meaning
1	*mèmèn (ibu, biyang)*	*mèmé (bu, biyang)*	Mo, MoSi, FaSi, FaBrWi, MoBrWi
2	*nanang (bapan, ajin)*	*nang (pan, aji)*	Fa, FaBr, MoBr MoSiHu, FaSiHu
3	*belin*	*beli*	OBr, PaSibSo older than ego, PaPaSibChSo older than ego
4	*mbok (mok)*	*mbok (mok)*	OSi PaSibDa older than ego PaPaSibChDa older than ego
5	*adin*	(no address term)	YSib PaSibCh younger than ego PaPaSibChCh younger than ego
6	*pianak*	(no term of address)	Ch
7	*keponakan*	(no term of address)	SibCh, PaSibChCh, PaPaSibChChCh
8	*cucun (dadong, niyang, mbah)*	*cucu (cu, dong, niyang, mbah)*	FaMo, ChCh, MoMo FaMoSi, MoMoSi FaFaSi, MoFaSi PaSibChCh, PaPaSibChChCh
9	*kaki (pekak, kiyang, kakiyang)*	*kaki (ki, kak, pekak, kiyang)*	FaFa, FaFaBr, MoFa MoFaBr, FaMoBr, MoMoBr
10	*kumpi*	*kumpi*	PaPaPa, ChChCh
11	*kelab*	*kelab*	PaPaPaPa, ChChChCh

AFFINAL KIN TERMS

	kurenan	(no term of address)	Sp
	nanang matua (bapan matua, ajin matua)	*nang (pan, aji)*	SpFa
	mèmèn matua (ibu matua, biyang matua)	*mèmé (ibu, biyang)*	SpMo
	mantun	(no term of address)	ChSp
	ipah	*beli, mbok*, if older; by own name if younger	BrWi, SiHu, WiSib, HuSib
	warang	(no term of address)	ChSpPa

NOTE ON ALTERNATE USAGE

1. Use of the alternative terms indicated above in parentheses is dependent primarily on status position of the family. For instance, *nanang* is the term for father in most commoner (*sudra*) families, *bapan* is found in high *sudra* families of Pasek or Pande title, while *aji* is used by aristocrats (*triwangsa*).

2. Cousins can be distinguished, if necessary, from own siblings (in reference only, not in address) with the use of several terms: *misan*, meaning parent's sibling's child; or *mindon*, meaning parent's parent's sibling's child's child. Specification of more distant cousins is also possible: *mindon pindo*, meaning one's parent's *mindon's* children; and *mindon ping telu*, meaning one's parent's mindon pindo's children. These are both exceedingly rare.

Cousins can also be distinguished according to whether they are patrilateral parallel cousins (*misan kapurusa*, "cousin in the direct male line") or all other cousins (*misan ulian luh*, "cousin through females").

3. Parent's siblings also can be differentiated, if necessary, from own parents in reference, by stating that so-and-so is one's *nanang tulèn*, meaning real parent. In address, uncles and aunts are differentiated from parents by the use of their name after the kin term, for example, Nang Nyoman Darsana, or simply Nang Nyoman (if the man has not yet had a child.) The same mechanisms can be used to distinguish cousins from siblings in address.

4. Similarly, sex can be indicated, if need be, in reference terms such as those for child, younger sibling, sibling's child, great grandparent, great grandchild, which do not indicate sex, by the addition of the words *muani* (male) or *luh* (female).

5. There are some regional variations in the terminological structure for the parent's sibling group. In the Klungkung area, the following forms are frequently found: parent's older sibling is referred to as *wan*, and addressed as *wa*, while parent's younger brother is called *nanang* and addressed as *nang*, and parent's younger sister is called *mèmèn*, addressed as *mèmé*. A second alternative system is found in Tabanan, possibly elsewhere; parent's older sibling is referred to as *reraman*, while if this is the parent's older sister she is addressed as *mèmé*; however, the parent's older brother is addressed as *rerama*. In this second system, parent's younger brother is referred to as *bapan*, addressed as *bapa*, and parent's younger sister is *mèmèn*, addressed as *mèmé*.

6. Balinese kin terminology is described in Jane Belo, "A Study of a Balinese Family," *The American Anthropologist* 38, no. 1 (1936), and V. E. Korn, *Het Adatrecht van Bali*, 2d ed. (The Hague, 1932), pp 465ff.

Appendix B

The Family History of the House of Beng

(From a manuscript in Indonesian, by I Gusti Ngurah Oka, of Jero Beng, Tabanan, dated 17–11–1946)

In the Balinese caka year 1615 [A.D. 1693] the Cokorda [the prince of Tabanan] died. This was I Gusti Ngurah Ktut Celuk, the eighteenth Singasana, son of the fourteenth Cokorda, Sirarya I Gusti Ngurah Sekar, Singasana the fourteenth. After his death the penggawas and perbekels [noble officials of the court, the former usually being heads of noble subdadias, the latter low gentry or commoners] from the Tabanan court were all killed by the king of Penebel, who was also a son of the fourteenth Singasana and who wanted to make himself king of Tabanan. But after the king of Penebel had moved into the palace in Tabanan, none of the penggawas or perbekels came before him. So he summoned a certain perbekel, a perbekel of the royal domestic staff [*perbekel sedjeroning kori*] named I Gagus Limpar. When he appeared, the king asked, "Hai, Gagus Limpar, you know all about conditions here, why don't the penggawas and perbekels come to my presence? How do they think I can rule my country? Do they consider me unfit to govern?" Gagus Limpar then answered with a sign of obeisance [*sembah*]: "Yes, your Highness, but before I say anything I ask your forgiveness, and I will tell you what I know from his deceased highness, the Raja Singasana the eighteenth. Yes My Noble Highness, according to the wishes and will of his deceased Highness, if someone takes his throne from outside the immediate family of Puri Gde [the king's household] the country will not be safe. That was the message he left us." After he heard these words from Gagus Limpar, the king could not withhold his anger, and he turned his head to hide it. When Gagus Limpar saw this, he felt the danger of death upon him, and he asked leave to return to his home. After he arrived, some slaves of the Cokorda came after him, fully armed. Gagus Limpar requested time to clean himself up because he knew that he was about to be killed. After this was accomplished, the Cokorda became more angry thinking about the news he had heard. So he quietly returned to Penebel, bringing with him all the riches from the Puri Gde, and there his fury increased even more, and he planned to destroy all the penggawas and perbekels of Tabanan. Then he ordered every penggawa to come to Penebel, but every penggawa who set off for Penebel never arrived there, because the Cokorda had the roads guarded and his men captured and killed the penggawas. So then the news spread around, and all the penggawas stopped to think.

Then the command came to the penggawas of Jero Beng and of Jero Buruan. But the Penggawa didn't want to go to him in Penebel because he knew what the Cokorda of Penebel intended to do. The news went around, and some of his subjects from the villages of Suda and Pejaten, and some from the caste of Pungakan came, about forty people, to ask about this danger that threatened Jero Beng and its people, and to think of a way to resist the fire that threatened to burn it up. If their lord wanted to resist, they were all willing to go with him to fight. But the penggawa answered softly, "Hai, friends and relatives, I am convinced that we should not fight, because it would be of no use, and because I feel that we have done no wrong, that this is all because of the rage of our Cokorda. So I feel that it would be better to surrender to him rather than commit a grave error against our ancestors, and in order to stay in the right, to choose the noblest path. We will surrender within two days. That is all, now you can all go." So then he talked it over with his mother: "Hai, beloved mother, since I have a wife, Ni Pesak, who is pregnant, whom I recently sent back to her home in the village of Suda, because when she gave birth here, the babies were always born dead, should I not send for her to come and die with us?" His mother answered, "Hai, my child of noble heart, I believe that you should leave her there, because we are to be destroyed for no fault. It would be better if there were someone on the family line of Jero Beng, and if we are reincarnated, there will be a place—a body—to come to. Also it would be better if there were someone to make *bubur pirata* [offering to the dead] and to affirm our righteousness before everyone. Now it would be better to get together our property to leave to this unborn child." When he heard this advice, he quickly got together all his wealth to take to the village of Suda. Suddenly he heard a sound of a voice shouting that was none other than the troops of the Cokorda of Penebel coming to destroy the Jeros that he considered at fault. So the penggawas all came out, and in front of the door of Jero Beng they were attacked and killed. The thatched roof of the gate fell on the body of the penggawa and a fire from an unknown source caught it, and the body turned to ashes.*

After that Jero Beng became an empty field which was used for the grazing of cattle. Now the story begins about Ni Pesak [whose name indicates that she was a commoner], who was left in the village of Suda, pregnant. She gave birth to a boy whom she named I Gusti Wayan Beng, and she was taken care of by her relatives in the village of Suda. After she had been cared for there for several months, I Gusti Made Kukuh in Jero Dlodrurung heard that she was there. Then I Gusti Made Kukuh wanted to find I Gusti Wayan Beng, and so he went to Suda to bring him home to Jero Dlodrurung, so that he could know the situation in Puri Gde and Puri Kaleran [the palace of the Cokorda of Tabanan and of his lieutenant] and because of his love for his kinsman, the descendant of Jero Beng who was left all alone. This was the second generation [meaning the second generation away from the core line of Tabanan, for his father, the murdered penggawa of Jero Beng, was apparently one of the sons of the Cokorda of Tabanan]. So he went with his uncles to find him, and when I Gusti Made Kukuh requested to have I Gusti Wayan Beng brought to Jero Dlodrurung in Tabanan, his uncles agreed. He grew up to be a young man there.

Now the story turns to a young girl, Ni Gusti Aju, from Jero Subamia Klodan [the southern section of Jero Subamio]. She wanted to go to Dlodrurung, and her father asked her, "Where are you going with all those people?" She answered, "I am going to Dlodrurung to get some mangga fruits." Her father answered, "Hai, my child, don't go there, because I am afraid someone will capture you there." The

---

*In the manuscript the passages regarding the destruction of Jero Beng by the Cokorda of Penebel have been altered slightly for the sake of clarity. In the manuscript the penggawa of Jero Beng usually appears as the "Penggawa Jero Beng Kanginan/Kawan." Kanginan means west and Kawan means east, referring to a division within the subdadia, probably between two sets of cousins. This same type of division appears today in many subdadias. In the manuscript as written in 1946 there apparently were two penggawas, the penggawa of the eastern half and the penggawa of the western half of Jero Beng, and at the time of the battle both were slain, and the bodies of both were magically burnt immediately. However, as the manuscript appeared in 1958, all references to the second penggawa had been crossed out. It seems reasonable to infer that this story is not an accurate historical account, and that it may have been altered at various times even before being written down in 1946, with the selection of a version with two penggawas or one depending on whether in the specific contemporary structure of Jero Beng there was a dual split or a single entity.

daughter then answered with a smile, "Who would dare to capture me?" And she went right on to Dlodrurung. But she didn't know that I Gusti Made Kukuh saw her come, and he called I Gusti Wayan Beng, and said, "You can take that girl, and you won't be at fault. She is a girl from Jero Subamio Klodan, an aristocrat." When he heard what I Gusti Made Kukuh, said, he looked at Ni Gusti Aju from Jero Subamio Klodan and he captured her and he hid her in the house of I Gusti Made Kukuh in Dlodrurung. Soon after that the sound of the slit-gong in Jero Subamio could be heard, a sign that there had been a theft from Jero Subamio. So I Gusti Made Kukuh went quickly to Puri Kaleran to tell them what had happened. And immediately the prince of Puri Kaleran went to Puri Gde to tell his kinsman, Singgasana the twenty-first [the prince of Tabanan]. "Hai, younger brother, Cokorda, I Gusti Made Kukuh tells me that I Gusti Wayan Beng has taken the child of our uncle in Jero Subamio Klodan. Let us go to them because our kinsman is the only one left [in Jero Beng's line]. If we don't help him he will be in trouble." So the two of them went to the Great Southern Gate [of the palace of the prince of Tabanan], and they saw hundreds of people going to Dlodrurung, armed, to the home of I Gusti Made Kukuh, and they had already torn down the walls of the house. So the lord went to Dlodrurung, to tell the people from Jero Subamio to come to him at the Great Southern Gate. Because their prince called them, the crowd from Jero Subamio came to him, and they did not dare do anything wrong. After they came before him, the lord said, "Hai, older brothers, uncles, and kinsmen: you all are trying to seize my younger brother, I Gusti Wayan. What would you think if you knew that he was a descendant of Jero Beng. If you think now that this marriage is not proper, let them be divorced; but if you think it is proper, since both of them are descended from aristocrats, just go home again, and tell everyone, and help make Jero Beng live, because now there is only one member of it left." After they heard what his highness had said, the group from Jero Subamio was silent and said nothing, but instead, bowed their heads and asked leave to go home. So then the lord from Puri Kaleran went to Dlodrurung, to the home of I Gusti Made Kukuh, and invited the couple to come to live in Puri Kaleran. The Cokorda had remained behind in the palace, waiting for the lord of Puri Kaleran, and when he returned, the lord said, "I have gone for I Gusti Wayan Beng and brought him to Puri Kaleran." "Very good," said the Cokorda of Puri Gde. So after the couple arrived in Puri Kaleran, the lord gave them a wedding according to traditional custom. They stayed for six months in Puri Kaleran, and then the lord told them he was going to rebuild their house in Jero Beng, and also give them some subjects [*panjak*] from the villages of Beng and

Punjuk, who would follow their orders, and who would build their houses for them. At that time Jero Subamio gave them no help. And Jero Beng had a wall which was made of coconut leaves only. Not long after they had moved to the new Jero Beng, Ni Gusti Ayu from Jero Subamio was pregnant and gave birth to a son named I Gusti Ngurah Made. When the time came near for his third-month ceremony, the people of Jero Subamio began to love them, and they took care of performing this ceremony and festival for the couple. As time went on, they were given some more subjects from the villages of Pendak Gde, Suda, Jadi, and others by the lord of Puri Kaleran.

During all the time that I Gusti Wayan Beng (1) [these numbers after each name have been inserted for the purpose of identification during the following complicated genealogical history] was penggawa, he was very careful in all his work and the two kings loved him. He had three children:

> I Gusti Ngurah Made (2)
> I Gusti Ngurah Nyoman (3)
> Ni Sagung Wayan (4)

And after they were all adult, I Gusti Ngurah Nyoman was moved, and a house built for him, on the east side of the road, where the old Jero Beng Kanginan had been. I Gusti Ngurah Made was the heir. When his father grew old, then I Gusti Ngurah Made was appointed to take his place as the penggawa of Jero Beng.

During all the time that I Gusti Ngurah Made carried out his work, he was considered very competent and he was loved by the people. Besides he was trusted more and more by the prince, because he was so wise in his judgments, and also good at sending letters to other principalities, and within his own domain. He was often sent to other principalities as the representative of the prince, together with the lord of Jero Anjar Krambitan. At that time the Cokorda of Puri Gde trusted I Gusti Made Ngurah of Jero Putu. I Gusti Made Ngurah had the desire to build a house of bricks like that of Puri Gde, because he felt that he was loved by, and also put to shame by, the prince. He planned to destroy the two penggawas of Beng and seize their wealth for his own. But as a result of his evil character he himself was destroyed by the people of the kingdom of Tabanan.

I Gusti Ngurah Made (2) had a lingga built which is now in the Bale Singesari [in the subdadia temple] and also had built a *wilmana* [?] in Sarenkauh [perhaps one of the courtyards of the compound] and had a *wayang wong* [opera] performed in the village of Belelang, Kediri. But during all the time he was a penggawa, he never had any children. So he adopted a boy from Jero Kompiang named I Gusti Ngurah Rai, to be made his sentana, his heir, in Jero Beng. After he did that he had thirty-five children. So I Gusti Ngurah Rai, the one who had been named his successor, was returned to Jero Kompiang, and given a kris [sacred dagger] named I Bagia and land in the village of Jadi. Later he was married to a girl from Puri Kaleran named Ni Sagung Putu.

The wives of I Gusti Ngurah Made who gave birth to children for Jero Beng were:

> Ni Sagung Rai (2a), girl from Puri Kediri
> Ni Jero Sisi (2b), from the village of Beraban
> Ni Jero Karang (2c), from the village of Wanasari
> Ni Jero Kaler (2d), from the village of Sekartaji

They had these children:

> I Gusti Ngurah Putu Purwa (5)
> I Gusti Ngurah Rai (6)
> Ni Sagung Gde (7)
> Ni Sagung Alit (8)
> I Gusti Ngurah Made Sisi (9)
> I Gusti Ngurah Nyoman Karang (10)
> I Gusti Ngurah Made Kaler (11)

I Gusti Ngurah Putu Purwa (5) had these wives who bore him children:

> Ni Sagung Made Sekar (5a) from Puri Kediri
> Ni Jero Serangang (5b) from the village of Wanasari

His children were:

> Ni Sagung Gde (12), who married into Puri Kaleran (her husband was later stabbed to death by a man from Jero Kawan) [see below]
> Ni Sagung Rai (13)
> Ni Sagung Oka (14), who married into Puri Kaleran
> Ni Sagung Ktut (15), who ran away to Buleleng

I Gusti Ngurah Rai (6) had this wife:

> Ni Jero Saren (6a), from Banjar Anyar Pasekan,

and this child:

> Ni Sagung Nengah (16), who married into Puri Kediri Klod

Ni Sagung Gde (7) married into Jero Anom.

Ni Sagung Alit (8) stayed in Jero Beng and was very good at *kidung* stories and at singing *kekawin*, and became head of the household of Jero Beng.

I Gusti Ngurah Made Sisi (9) was sent to heaven [killed] by an Ida Bagus from Sandan, Wanasari, at the command of his own father. A memorial altar (*pelinggih*) was set up for him in the [subdadia] temple on the west side next to the Muncak Kedatan.

This is how it happened that I Gusti Ngurah Made Sisi (9) was sent to heaven. He was very good at talking and he was loved by all the people. So Ni Sagung Rai (2a), his father's wife, was very jealous

and envious of him because she knew that her own sons, I Gusti
Ngurah Purwa (5) and I Gusti Ngurah Rai (6), were very different
from him in their behavior, even though they were older. Seeing
this, she became even more envious toward her stepson. When his
father saw the situation, he did not take the side of the boy at all,
but was afraid and ashamed before his wife. Because of this he just
left the boy alone, and didn't give him anything, so I Gusti Ngurah
Made Sisi (9) had an idea [to make some money] to borrow a cow
from a commoner subject, and the subject was pleased to let him
keep the profit. After awhile, because she was watching him, his
stepmother found out about this action and reported it to her husband, his father. The father thought that this was bad for his people,
and at the request of his wife had the boy sent away from Jero Beng.
So, because his father was afraid of his wife, the son, I Gusti Ngurah
Made Sisi (9), was sent to the village of Antesari, and during all of
the time that he was in Antesari his father paid no attention to him.
So then he thought that since he was not at all in the wrong he would
go back to Tabanan. He went to the house of Men Gunung [a commoner woman] on the north side of Tabanan. In the morning Ni
Sagung Rai (2a) heard the news that I Gusti Ngurah Made Sisi was
back in Tabanan, and her fury rose, and she went directly to her
husband and asked, "Who told I Gusti Ngurah Made Sisi that he
could come back?" Her husband answered, "I don't know who told
him to come home." Then she said: "If it's going to be like that, if he
doesn't respect his father's orders, it would be better just to kill this
boy. It will mean the loss of only one person." When he heard this,
he quickly answered briefly, "You speak rightly," and hurriedly went
to Puri Kaleran to tell the lord of Kaleran to tell him what had
happened. The lord of Puri Kaleran was very much against the boy
being killed, but he couldn't dissuade the lord of Beng. Se he went
directly to Puri Gde to tell the Cokorda, and the Cokorda was also
against it, and was very sorry for the boy besides. Soon after that
the people from Jero Subamio came to Jero Beng to ask for the son
to come and live with them. Because he was still firm in his intention,
he paid no attention to them and said that whatever happens, the boy
must be killed. So then the lord of Beng was called before the two
kings [Puri Gde and Puri Kaleran] to talk about his son. They asked
that he not be killed, and the lord of Kaleran said that he himself
would take him in. But the answer was brief: if the son lives, the
father will die. That was the answer. Everyone who was there could
do nothing, and they had to let him do as he wished. So then he took
his leave and when he arrived in Jero Beng, he immediately sent for
people to take his son to Jero Subamio [evidently the graveyard was
near there, or else it was a ruse]. When it was almost time for him to

be taken to the graveyard, all the people of Jero Beng, young and old, except those who had hate and jealousy for him, went with him to the graveyard. When they got there and saw what was going to happen they were all very sad. At that time I Gusti Ngurah Nyoman Karang (10) and I Gusti Ngurah Made Kaler (11) [the two half-brothers who were the fathers of the older men living today in Jero Beng] were still children. I Gusti Ngurah Made Sisi (9), seeing the situation and hearing the weeping and sobbing which was like the waves of the sea, called his brother, I Gusti Ngurah Nyoman Karang (10) and said to him: "Hai, younger brother, don't cry. I believe that what I am doing is the most honorable thing to do, because I have not done wrong. The one who brought me into the world wants to send me back to where I came from, and there is nothing more honorable to do than what I am doing. But I foresee that in the future you will become the head of Jero Beng, even though the others, those who are older than you, are still alive, so that you will make them realize the evil that they have done me." After I Gusti Ngurah Made Sisi (9) died, that night his father finally realized what he had done, because he had been influenced by a devil, and he wept thinking about his son who was so clever, and who had never done anything wrong. So he went to the graveyard and lay down on the new grave, and wept bitterly. Beware of women, lest we become their servants!

I Gusti Ngurah Nyoman (3) [brother of the lord of Beng who killed his son] was constantly sickly, so he moved his house [believing that the spirits of the houseyard were causing his sickness] from Jero Beng Kanginan to the place where I Gusti Made Ngurah from Jero Putu had formerly lived, and the place was given a new name, Jero Beng Kawan.

He had two sons named:

I Gusti Ngurah Rai (17)

I Gusti Ngurah Ktut (18)

But the two sons were both insane. I Gusti Ngurah Rai (17) went with the lord of Kaleran to the kingdom of Bandung as emissaries from the Cokorda of Puri Gde, to make a treaty with the three kingdoms, Tabanan, Badung, and Gianyar in the temple of Nambangan in Badung. At the end of these talks the lord of Puri Kaleran and his followers went to take a rest. But there, Rai's sickness overcame him again, and he stabbed the lord from Puri Kaleran to death. And then I Gusti Ngurah Rai (17) was killed on the spot by the people of Badung, and all his kinsmen, too, the whole group from Jero Beng Kawan, thirty-five people, were killed because of what Rai had done. [See below.]

I Gusti Ngurah Made (2), the lord of Beng, had grown old, and gone to heaven. After he died, his place as the third punggawa of Jero Beng was taken by his son, I Gusti Ngurah Nyoman Karang (10), who became the fourth.

He became punggawa at a time when he was still young, because his two half-brothers, who were older than he, and whose mother was the *padmi* [who were the eligible successors] were considered to be unable to carry on the work of lord. He was given much trust by the two kings, and he carried out all his duties, and was loved by them. He often went to pray to Batara in the temple of Dangin Bringen in the village of Beraban, and he went to every yearly ceremony [*odalan*], as long as nothing hindered him. He went to give honor to Batara, and besides he had no children as yet to be his descendants.

So one day at the yearly ceremony in the temple of Dangin Bringen, he went to worship as usual, and when it was over, a priest [pemangku] called to him, and said, "Hai, it is lucky you have not yet gone home. I am the Batara for whom this ceremony was held. Look at the sign in my hand and look up into the sky where you will see my name." [The priest was in trance, and the god was speaking through his mouth.] And he did what the Batara ordered and he saw the sign of the Cakra Teja, that is, the name of the Batara.

Appendix C

Basic Regulations for the Village of Aan
[Awig-awig wikrama desa adat Aan]

Introduction to the text

The *perbekelan* ("government village") of Aan contains ten *banjar*, or hamlets. These are distributed under four *penglimans* (assistants to the perbekel) in the following manner:

Penglimanan	*Banjars included*
Sengkiding	Sengkiding
Babakan	Babakan
	Carik Dalam
Aan	Pasek
	Gensir
	Gambang
Peken	Peken
	Selat
	Pempatan
	Sala

These in turn are divided into two *desa adat*, (literally, "custom village"), one named "desa adat Aan," for which we present a translation of the *awig-awig* or "basic regulations," and the other, *desa adat Sengkiding*, which includes only the hamlet of Sengkiding. All the remaining nine banjar belong to the desa adat Aan.

The penglimanan of Sengkiding is quite separate from the others and is only included in the perbekelan for administrative reasons. As a desa adat, it has its own set of civic temples (*Kahyangan Tiga*), and, as a banjar, its kingroups (dadia) do not include members from any other banjar. This is also true of the gentry, even the Brahmana, who live in Sengkiding.

The simple, sharply bounded, character of Sengkiding, where governmental, religious, and communal units coincide, contrasts sharply with the much more typical desa adat of Aan and its nine banjars. In the first place, the division of the whole desa adat into three sections (described in section 6, part 3 of the awig-awig), for the support of the various civic temples of the village does not correspond in any way with the banjar groupings. These three sections of the congregation are called *Pusèh, Dalam* and *Bukit*. None of the banjars have a civic temple which is exclusively its own, though each banjar has a small altar next to its meeting pavilion (*balé banjar*), where offerings are placed at each monthly meeting. Beside a meeting hall, each banjar has a large slit-gong (*kulkul*) to call the group together. The banjar as a group attends all life-cycle festivals of its members, tooth-filings, third-month birthdays, weddings, funerals (but not cremations), and the like. It is also the group for the *nyepi* ("day of silence") ceremony and for nightly guard duty, and each banjar has a treasury of its own. The desa adat has a separate treasury, and each of its temples has rice land of its own.

However, none of these banjars represents a continuous bounded territory. The two penglimanans of Babakan and Aan are actually one large community with members of its five banjars living scattered among each other. The penglimanan of Peken forms another community with its banjars intermixed within its boundaries. The Peken penglimanan is made up entirely of commoners, some of whom live in the Peken settlement but belong to a banjar in Babakan or Aan; but the reverse is not true, for there are many gentry in Babakan and Aan, and apparently these two "villages" are of higher status.

There is one banjar which has the highest status of all. This is the one called Pasek. It includes all the Pasek Gelgel in the desa adat, wherever they may live, plus the higher-ranking Brahmana and the upper Satria. The other banjars have gentry too. The perbekel of Aan is also the head of the Pasek Gelgel dadia, which is large and powerful, and a general leader for the Pasek Gelgel of the region.

The desa adat has, in addition to its temples, another unifying feature, a set of costumes for the witch-and-dragon ritual drama, the Rangda and Barong. At the time of fieldwork, the desa adat had just finished making a new Barong, and the rituals involved in its sanctification included a grand march to the sea, everyone dressed in their finest clothes, to purify the dragon costume.

Cremations are performed with the penglimanan group taking on primary responsibility, this group then being called the *patus*. Burial, however, is carried out by the banjar group.

The Text
Awig-awig wikrama desa adat Aan

Section 1

To begin, we give the rules for the ceremonies in the temples of the village [*désa*] which we take from the [book of] *Déwa Tatua*, which have been set for the village people and [also] for the king. For this reason it has been established that the leaders of the village must preserve the old ways. As we say, "the old ways are safest." We must act according to religion, in order to bring about the well-being [safety, welfare, *rahayu*] of the village. Take good care of these rules.

Section 2

This is the meaning of the three *wikrama: Siwa, Darma, Tirtha*
a. *wikrama* means good actions
b. *Darma* means God
c. *Siwa* means sacred heirlooms [the temples, etc.]
d. *Tirtha* means cleansing with holy water, meaning that all offerings must be purified with holy water of all impurities. Those things which are called impurities in the offerings are as follows:
   1. If the materials for the offerings were bought from a menstruating woman.
   2. If a chicken flew over the offerings or over the materials for them.
   3. If the offering was stepped over by a dog or a person.
   4. If people argued or if they were wearing salve while preparing the offerings.
   5. If a child nibbled on them, or if hair fell in them.

All these things cause ritual impurity. This is why we ask for holy water to cleanse the offerings. After the offerings are sprinkled with holy water, only then may they be presented to the gods. If all the offerings are not cleansed with holy water which has been blessed by a holy man [*pandita*, i.e., usually a Brahmana priest, or *Pedanda*] they will not be received by the gods or devils [*déwa muang buta*]. It is as if you were purposefully inviting the witches [*léyak*] to come, asking for unending sickness to come to the one who is having the offerings made, asking for trouble and for fights. This is why our religion is called the Religion of Holy Water [*agama tirta*].

Section 3

These are the rules for behavior of the members of the village council [*wikrama desa*], the supporters of the Six Great Temples of Bali [*Sad Kahyangan*] and the Three Temples [*Kahyangan Tiga*] of the village of Aan, *distrik* Bandjarangkan, *Negara* [kingdom] Klungkung.

a. That which is called the *krama désa (pemaksan)* is the village council which originally laid down the basic rules for secular and religious life. These rules were set down by the village council, and also observed by the king who ruled over the village of Aan. Because of this they have been followed since ancient times, as stated above in section two, and they have been agreed upon by the village as a group together. Their contents and meaning [sense] is as follows.

b. According to the old customs, these are the people who are permitted to be members of the village council.

1. Those who are occupying village houseland.
2. Widowers who occupy village houseland.
3. Widowers who have young children who occupy village houseland.
4. And those who are married are permitted to join in the calendrical rituals, to keep the *nyepi* ["day of silence"], and also to be members of the village council.
5. A man gives up his obligations to the village council when his oldest son marries. [The oldest son then replaces him. In many villages, e.g., Tihingan, he is not permitted to retire until his youngest son marries.]
6. If a man gives up his obligations to the village council, and is replaced by his heir [son or adopted son, or substitute heir], and if, afterwards, they quarrel and he disinherits his heir, then they must leave the village council and be fined 4,900 *kèpèng* plus his share of the cost of any village buildings which have been erected during his period of absence. [Because the older man has been dodging his obligations.] These rules hold for all members of the village council.
7. If a married couple from outside the village lives in the village longer than a month, they must enter the village council.
   a) If they don't want to join the village council they must be expelled from the village.
   b) And the man who has sheltered them and so is responsible for their entering the village council is fined 4,900 *kèpèng* because he is just the same as the man who won't fit in.
8. All the property of the village, such as temples, temple farmland, houseland, is owned by the village council collectively as was set down by the original village council.

a) Houseland has been from the beginning the property of the village council and may not be sold. This must be prevented by the villagers.

b) No member of the village council may own two pieces of houseland, extra pieces must be given to someone who has not yet received one.

    1) The giving of village houseland should be announced before the entire village council at a village meeting [*paruman*] and given to whoever asks for it.

c) All plants [trees, etc.] on the land must be paid for by the new holder of the land at a price fixed in terms of the size of the trees.

    1) If these trees are not bought, they must be chopped down by the previous owner.

    2) Whatever trees are not cut down at this time, become, after the previous owner has left the land, the property of the new owner.

    3) If in the future these trees and land revert to the village, the trees become the property of the village council and the former owner may make no claim for them.

d) A member of the village council who has been granted a piece of houseland is obligated to build a kitchen and a house within six months. If he is late in meeting this obligation, someone else may request this piece of land, move onto it, and build a house.

e) Village houseland may not be converted into dry farmland. If a piece of houseland is empty, it may only be used for a place to live. If in the future a piece of village land is empty and someone requests this unused land, it may be divided in two [i.e., need not be given out as a unit].

Section 4

It is fitting that the members of the village council choose leaders. The village officials to be appointed are the following.

Klians

a.1. The village leaders [*klians*] are chosen by village members for their cleverness in speaking and their knowledge of the correct way of doing things and ability to carry out the ceremonies in the traditional manner, including the ceremonies for gods, for demons, and the temple festivals [*odalan*], and all the other village ceremonies, all done in a way such as to bring well-being [*rahayu*] to the village. They must be of honest character and reliable in behavior. They are to be chosen by village agreement. Also, they are to be led by the *Klian Pengliman* or by the head of the adat [*penghulu ketua adat*]. [i.e., there is to be a head klian].

2. If a man refuses to be chosen klian, upon whom the village group has already unanimously agreed, he is fined 2,500 kèpèng per man [i.e., each such person]. The length of service of the klian shall be five years. After that time he may resign, and a new election is held. If a klian quits before this time of his own will, without fault, he is fined 1,700 kèpèng, each such man.

3. Also, if a man from the village nominated by a village member(s) as klian has a defect, such as deafness, insanity, lameness, chronic illness, or illiteracy, the man (men) who nominated him must be fined 500 kèpèng apiece, because the one so nominated is not eligible under the rules as stated above.

4. The village klian must make a report, for each village activity (work), explaining the income and expenses of the village. He must do this at the time of the village meeting. He is also responsible for producing the materials needed for temple ceremonies. If he is slow in buying these things [i.e., because he has spent the money for it on personal things, etc.; i.e., if he is corrupt], it is fitting that the village condemn him and that his property be seized to the amount of his debt and that he be fired as klian.

Penyarikans

b.1. The *Penyarikans* are obligated to write down everything that is discussed [at the desa meeting], such as the work to be done, and who must do it, the fines assessed, the total income and outgo, and so on.

2. At the time of the village meeting he has to read what he has written, account for the money spent. Each Penyarikan who is absent from a meeting is fined 500 kèpèng. Further if, through carelessness, he loses the record, he is fined 1,100 kèpèng, and he has to make good any losses the loss of the record causes.

Sinomans

c.1. The *Sinomans (Sayas)* change monthly on the day of the *odalan pusèh* [i.e., that day in *each* 35-day Balinese month]. He is obligated to deliver all the messages given by the klians and penyarikans.

2. If he doesn't take the messages as instructed, he is to be fined 250 kèpèng plus the fines of all the people to whom he didn't deliver the messages [i.e., the fines they incur by not perform-

188 *Appendix C*

ing whatever the message instructed them to perform]. If he doesn't put up the water-clock [*janggi*] he is fined 66 kèpèng. He is obligated to note who comes [to a village work, etc.] and report same to the penyarikan.

3. The Sinomans must bring enough *sirih* [betel hut] at the time of the village meetings for everyone in the village group. If he fails to provide this he is fined 33 kèpèng. After the meeting he is paid out of the village treasury for the sirih he provided, and he stops as Sinoman.

Pemangku

d.1. Concerning the appointment of the *Pemangku* [village temple priest] when there is no male heir of the [deceased] Pemangku [i.e., no patrilineal heir], it is proper that village members choose a Pemangku collectively. He must be someone who knows how to serve the gods, male and female, how to lead the religious rituals. He may not have a jealous or deceitful heart, because he will be continually serving the gods. He must be unruffled [Darma; detached, not easily disturbed, angered, etc.] noble [*makerti*; pure etc.] i.e., like a priest who is filled with the gods [i.e., with holiness], a *Bujangga. Buja* means hand; *angga* means body. A Pemangku is entered by the gods, but he must have first had the proper rituals: *mepedengendengenan ring dewa* and *pewintenan*, and have writing put on his tongue by a Brahmana priest (*Sang Maha Pandita*).

2. A Pemangku may use the bell and wear *Sangkul Putih* [white robes]. He must know how to say all the *mantras* [chants]: those for putting up a *ceniga* ornament, for filling a water jug, for cleaning the jugs [all these are ritual activities he does over and over again, etc.]. If he cannot read, he may memorize them; but if he doesn't know the mantras and can only speak Balinese [i.e., does not know *Kawi*, the sacred language], his having been *mewinten* [consecrated] is meaningless.

3. If after he has become Pemangku he marries [i.e., if his first wife dies], he must *mewinten* himself [i.e., again] with his wife, and hold a cleansing ceremony for his *Pura*. [This means that he gets the first *mewinten* ceremony paid for by the village, but must pay for the second one, if it is necessary, himself.]

4. The man who is Pemangku should take care of the Pura faithfully and keep it clean and carry out all the ceremonies, *rahinans* and *pujawalis (odalans)*, and also the ceremonies on the full and dark of the moon, and on *Kajang Keliwon* [a day

in the Balinese calendar]. For large ceremonies the congregation of the Pura must also help the Pemangku in his work. Also the Pemangku may not be unclean, he may not, i.e., break the law, steal, have quarrels in the village [i.e., can't be *puik*]. If he does, he must stop as mangku.

5. Also, if the Pemangku is ordered to ask help and protection from the gods by the congregation, if he has not purified himself first, then he must be fined and must give a *penyapuhan* ["sweeping"] offering to the Pura.

6. Also if he is unclean, has dirty clothes, has not yet purified himself ritually, washed his teeth and hair, and blessed himself with holy water, and nevertheless goes to the Pura and gives offerings, then the congregation should arrest the Mangku and bathe and bathe and bathe him [three different words for bathing him] and then discharge him. Then the altar must be given the *rahayu* cleansing ceremony by the congregation because the Pemangku has made it filthy.

7. Also if a man makes a ritual for the fulfillment of vow [i.e., a *kaul* ritual in temple, in which he gives offerings after having made a vow he would do so if he got some blessing—cured of illness, etc.], the offering-food involved must be divided into three equal parts; one share for the Pemangku, one for the congregation as a whole, and one for the man who is giving the ritual. If the Pemangku takes all this food, he should be discharged, because he is greedy, won't divide the food, won't share with the congregation. If the man who is giving the vow ritual is able to and gives cloth or parasols to the temple, these must all be kept in the temple [i.e., not divided] because they are considered the property of the gods.

8. A Pemangku may not be affected by *sebel* [ritual uncleanness which prevents him from entering the temple] arising from the death of others [i.e., nonfamily members]. He may not go to the cremations of others. If his own patrirelative dies, he is sebel seven days. After seven days he must give a *meperascita* offering to be free of the sebel. Also if his *siwa* [*guru*; i.e., his Brahmana priest, pedanda] dies, he is sebel and is also obligated to give the meperascita offering. If he should make offerings in the Pura before the conclusion of his sebel he is to be fined 1,700 kèpèng and must give a *penyapuhan* offering in the Pura.

9. Also, if the Pemangku dies, whether male or female, he must be cremated by the whole village congregation. He may not be buried. The cost of the cremation is to be borne by the congregation.

Section 5. General rules for the village members of the congregation.

1. Regulations for length of the sebel [unclean] period resulting from death in relation to work of village people in the Pura for *rahinans* and *pujawalis* [calendrical ceremonies].
    a) For the whole banjar [hamlet], three days *sebel*.
    b) For those in houseyards immediately adjoining to the deceased, seven days sebel.
    c) For those related as close as third cousins through women, seven days.
    d) For those related as close as third cousins through men, fourteen days.
    e) For those who are one household (one yard and one door) with the deceased, twenty-one days. If a mother dies in childbirth, forty-two days. Sebel people may not give out material for offerings at ceremonies because they are unclean, but they must give money instead [to buy the material, etc.]

2. Also if a man asks blessings in the Pura but not using the Pemangku as a medium, and climbs up on the altar and stays there a long time, if he is a member of another congregation [i.e., not a member of this Pura], he is fined 4,500 kèpèng, because it is as if he has dirtied the gods. If he is from that congregation [i.e., is a member of the Pura] he is fined 1,700 kèpèng and also must give *pedudusan* and *merascita* offerings and a *mecaru* [sacrifice to the devils] using a Pedanda to *mewéda* [chant the wéda-s].

3. If a man climbs up on an altar without permission of the Pemangku, he is fined 4,900 kèpèng and must give pemerascita offerings.

4. When the Pemangku makes offerings for *Pujawali* ceremonies in the Pura, it is proper that the *Warga Sari* songs be sung. Anyone who says evil things or who swears at this time must be fined 500 kèpèng, each such person, and must give *penyapuhan* and *pengenteg* offerings at the appropriate altars.

5. Also if a man takes down the *Déwas* [the statues of the gods] or any of the paraphernalia of the gods who sit on the altar, without permission of the Pemangku, he has sinned and must give the *Manca Kelud* sacrifice, a *mesapuh* offering, and an extra-large perasascita offering, because this action is too rash [audacious, bold, etc.; the Balinese is *angunkul Serenggi*, a special phrase meaning literally "rise higher than God";

example: if you touch the head of a Brahmana without his permission].

6. Also, if a man falls into a trance and claims that he speaks as a god [i.e., that a god has entered him and is speaking], he must be made to grasp hot coconut-shell coals with both hands, one betel-nut chew length of time, and also to give an offering in front of the Pura. If he is not burned by the fire, then a Déwa has indeed entered him and should be worshipped. If he is burned [i.e., is deceiving] he must be fined and must sweep the Pura.

7. Also, if a man is crazy, if he is clearly insane, he may not enter the Pura during the time of odalan. It is proper that the congregation eject him with force; if he refuses to go, he may be tied up and given to those in charge of him [i.e., his family, etc.], and the congregation must give a pemerascita offering and those in charge of the insane man must be fined as above. If the insane man is a member of the pemaksan, he [i.e., his family] may not be fined but he must be ordered to go far away.

8. Also, if a man uses obscene language in the Pura during the time of odalan or rahinan or any time offerings are being made in the Pura, if he is inside the walls of the Pura he must be fined 700 kèpèng and give penyapuhan offerings, for it is as if this man has ordered the Déwas to leave the temple. If outside the Pura [i.e., in the yard, etc.], the Klian Pura must give advice to this man [i.e., tell him not to do it].

9. If a man fights within the walls of the Pura and is wounded so that blood flows, he must be fined, give penyapuhan and mepedudusan offerings, and the manca kelud sacrifice. Also, if a member of the congregation fights, along with swearing and cursing another's head [the phrase is *Luhuring apala*, "above the shoulders"; this is just about the worst thing you can say to someone] while there is a ceremony in the Pura, and in front of the whole congregation, if the man (or men) does not stop, does not pay any attention to the congregation, he may be tied up and delivered to the king, because his actions mean he is rebellious to the king. Also he must be fined 5,500 kèpèng and give pemerascita offerings in the Pura and any other fines or offerings as the congregation may decide.

10. Also, if a man steals property of the gods which is in the Pura (all the property of God), he must be fined according to the value of what has been lost: if it is of low value [*nista*], the fine is 500 kèpèng; if of middle value [*madiya*],

1,700 kèpèng; if of high value [*utama*], 4,500 *kèpèng*. Also if there is a theft or purposeful burning of the Pura, if the guilty one is not discovered and no clues are found, it is fitting that the whole congregation be made to swear an oath in front of the Pura. If any member refuses to swear, this is certain evidence that he is the guilty one and he may be tied up and delivered to the king. Also, this man must pay for the costs of all ceremonies, offerings needed. Also, such a Pura is called "hit by theft" [i.e., is in the state of *tampak pandung*], and so it is necessary to give *guru piduka* offerings, a meyawang ceremony, and a manca kelud sacrifice, because the Pura is extraordinarily defiled. Similarly if a man dies inside the Pura or if people have sexual intercourse in the Pura, the penalty is the same and the method of getting a confession the same. Also in these cases the Pura must be torn down and thrown into the sea.

11. Also, at the time of a ceremony in Pura or an odalan, when girls and boys (or men and women) must guard at night in the Pura, the Klian Pura must get sleeping places for them, putting the girls with the girls, the boys with the boys, and must come around three times during the night to make sure that the lamp is very bright.

   a) Also if people have intercourse in the Pura (a man with a woman), and another person knows it but doesn't report it to the Klian Pura, those who have performed the act are fined *werat pati* [heavy as death—the largest possible fine], 16,000 kèpèng, and must purify the Pura. The person who knows but did not report it to the Klian is fined 4,500 kèpèng, for it is a sin to keep quiet about evil.

   b) If persons are discovered having intercourse within the walls of the Pura, they are fined werat pati (the man is to be castrated for his offense, the girl to be taken to the graveyard and have a hot poker inserted in her vagina), and the fine used for the ceremonies in the Pura.

12. Also, if a girl who is menstruating wears a clean sarong [i.e., to hide the fact] and gives offerings in the Pura, with intent of concealing her actions, and another person knows this girl is menstruating and doesn't report to the Klian, both the menstruating girl and the one who did not report are fined 1,700 kèpèng and must give penyapuhan offerings in the Pura.

      a) Also, if a girl is unable to menstruate at all [i.e., because of malfunctioning, not because of pregnancy or age] she may not go into the Pura, for she is very unclean.

      b) Also, if a person is unclean (by unclean here is meant an adult person who evacuates or urinates, or shows his genitals, or is nude, within the walls of the Pura), he is sinful and must give the manca sata sacrifice.

13. Also, a person who is unclean can't go to the Pura at the time of odalan in Pura. Persons who have the sickness which cannot be named [leprosy] will insult the gods by their presence and will cause great calamities in the country and injure the king [i.e., there will be mice-plagues, epidemics, etc.] and such persons may not live in the country.

Section 6. Rules governing the behavior of members of the village.

If a member of the village doesn't follow all the true rules which bring about well-being, if he ignores them with the result that the old customs are ruined (destroyed), and if he persists in thus disobeying he should be fined 1,700 kèpèng per offense. If he still refuses to go along with the désa regulations, he should be expelled from the village. No one may talk to him, and his property is lost [confiscated]. He may not be aided either in good things or bad [i.e., in ceremonies of life-cycles, marriage, death, etc.]. If an odalan is held in the Pura désa and some other désa members support this man, or help him in good things or bad, he should be fined 1,000 kèpèng each such person, each day [i.e., each offense].

1. If a village member leaves for another village, and his moving is not caused by some wrong he has done to the village group, and then in the future he wishes to return and rejoin the village group, he is fined 1,700 kèpèng for treating the village lightly. If he leaves the village because of some wrong he has committed, he should be fined 4,900 kèpèng, plus the same fine as in the case of the man who quarrels with his heir in section 3, no. 6, above.

2. a) If a village member asks for holy water, and invites the gods to the Pura Désa [i.e., a personal invitation], he must provide the complete offerings, including 250 kèpèng ritual money for the holy water, plus 17,000 for the ceremony [i.e., to pay for the attendance of the gods].

    b) If he is not a member of the local village group and religious congregations, but of another such group within the kingdom, and he makes offerings in the village temple,

such as asking for holy water, begging forgiveness, ful-
filling a vow, inviting the village gods, he is to provide
complete offerings and is to pay as follows: for a *penan-
jung batu* offering, 1,700 kèpèng; for holy water, 2,500
kèpèng; and if he invited the gods he must pay 25,000
kèpèng, all this being witnessed by the village collectively.

3. The public temples [*Sadkahyangan Kahyang Tiga*] which the
   congregation [*pemaksan*] of the village are required to support are as follows:

   a) *Dalam Kaja (Dalam Agung)*, the primary responsibility
      lying with the *Dalam* congregation.
   b) *Dalam Kelod (Dalam Setera)*, the primary responsi-
      bility lying with the *Bukit* congregation.
   c) *Pusèh Gedé*, the primary responsibility lying with the
      Pusèh congregation.
   d) *Gunung Kawi Penataran* and (e) *Balé Agung*, the pri-
      mary responsibility lying with *Dalam, Pusèh* and *Bukit*
      congregations [i.e., together].

The congregation of village Aan is divided in thirds [to make three
subsections] [*tèmpèk*] along with the Puras and Pura rice land.

   a) Those who are members of the *Dalam* congregation
      are responsible for Pura Dalam Kaja, and for carrying
      out the ceremonies and doing all the necessary repairs.
   b) Those who are members of the Pusèh congregation
      are responsible for Pura Pusèh Gedé, and for carrying
      out the ceremonies and doing all the necessary repairs.
   c) Those who are members of the Bukit congregation are
      responsible for Pura Dalam Klod and for carrying out
      all the ceremonies and making all the necessary repairs.
   d, e) In *Pura Penataran, Gunung Kawi*, and *Balé Agung*,
      the responsibility for the ceremonies [*odalans*], rotates.
      Also responsibility for the *Pengusaba* [yearly ceremony
      for rice in Balé Agung] and responsibility for repairs
      in the temples rotates among all three divisions of the
      congregation.

4. When the place of the gods [in the temple] is set up anew
   [rebuilt], the seating place of the gods in the public temples,
   you have to give a *mesapuh-mesapuh* ceremony for setting up
   such a place of the gods, and the entire congregation is responsible for providing whatever paraphernalia is needed.

5.1. Also, all requests and other ceremonies in the Pura Dalam
   Setra, made at the time of a village cremation, are to be paid
   for by the man holding the cremation, according to the following rules. It is necessary that all the offerings [*banten*]

must be according to traditional custom. *Penebus atma in
Dalam Rajapati* [this is a banten the name of which literally
means to get the soul out of pawn; the conception is that
Rajapati has taken the soul in pawn while it is being kept in
the cemetery and you have to redeem the soul before you can
cremate it, etc.]; *pengulap* [a type of *banten*, meaning to call
someone to you, in this case the soul]; *pengenag* [another
banten, the same word as for clearing a *sawah*, used here for
digging bones out of the ground, etc.], asking for holy water
from the priest, and asking for holy water from the god of
the *Rajapati* temple, which is put on the corpses. These offerings can be enumerated as follows:

1) *Banten penubusan* [i.e., to get soul out of pawn].
2) *Banten nulapen pengenag* [i.e., to call the soul and open the
grave].
3) *Banten pengebet* [asking for holy water from Brahman priest].
4) *Banten pengabèn* [cremation offerings].

For the *penebus* ceremony each family [i.e., which is involved in cre-
mating someone] must pay 250 kèpèng, a pair of live ducks, and ten
coconuts per corpse; for the *pengabènan* ceremony they must pay
500 kèpèng, one live duck, and five coconuts per cremation tower.

2. Also, if a man dies and is buried in the Aan cemetery, but
members of another desa wish to cremate him, they must
follow the same village rules and payments as written above
in section 6, no. 2. If someone doesn't agree to these rules
(disagrees), it is fitting he be prevented from taking the
bones and the *Pemangku* refuse to make offerings, and the
klians and desa members guard carefully against theft. If this
outsider seizes the corpse, he is to be fined 16,000 kèpèng.
Also, he must be tied up and delivered to the king.

6. All things brought to the cremation, money or goods for offerings, are divided in three, one-third to the Pemangku, two-thirds
for the village members.

7. When making repairs in the public temples, the village may
seize any property needed, paying a just price as decided upon
by the village.

Section 7. Rules for village order.

1. If a member of the village has already been informed of a village work but he doesn't work (attend), he is fined 25 kèpèng
per offense. If he is late, as measured by the water clock, or
leaves work early to go home, so not contributing his full share,
he is to be fined just the same as a person who does not work
at all. Similarly if he loafs or doesn't do what he is told; if he

fails to bring something he has been told to bring, he is to be fined and must go home and get it. If he didn't get the message in the first place, the fines must be paid by the Sinoman [the man is given a refund].

2. If a village member is ordered to work but begs off by saying he is ill, he shall be fined the first three times a half-fine. If during this time anyone sees him go out of the house or work, even though he claims to be ill, the man should be fined in full according to the number of village works he has missed.

3. If a village member is absent from village work for illness, death [i.e., of a relative] or cremation, a visit to a relative or friend, work requested by his lord, and he fails to inform the Klian beforehand, he is fined as if he didn't work; if he does inform the Klian beforehand, the fine is one-half.

4. Village members must have a work meeting each month on the day already fixed in the rules [i.e., the day of the Pusèh Odalan in each month]. On this day [working on repairs in the Pura]:
   a) the Sinoman provides betel nut for everyone who attends.
   b) the Penyarikan opens the *lontar* [palm leaf manuscript] case and reads any letters [i.e., makes a report].
   c) The Klians announce all solutions of disagreements [decisions].
   d) The village members carry out what has been decided at the meeting.

5. Members who have been fined should pay their fines at this time. If they can't pay, they may give a pawn for a month [at ten percent interest, usually]. If they still don't pay after a month, the debt owed to the village is doubled. If after another month the debt is not paid, the village can seize the man's property in the amount of the interest owed. If he does not pay in another month, they may seize his property for the principal.

Notes

1. E.E. Evans-Pritchard, *The Nuer* (Oxford, 1940); cf. his *Kinship and Marriage Among the Nuer* (Oxford, 1951).

2. A full-scale analysis of the classical Balinese state, C. Geertz, *Negara: The Theatre State in Nineteenth Century Bali*, is in process of preparation.

3. For examples of the first view, see V.E. Korn, *Het Adatrecht van Bali*, 2d ed. (The Hague, 1932), esp. pp. 179–436; and M. Covarrubias, *Island of Bali* (New York, 1956). For the second view, see J. Belo, "The Balinese Temper," in D.G. Haring, ed., *Personal Character and Cultural Milieu* (Syracuse, New York, 1948), pp. 156–80; and G. Bateson and M. Mead, *Balinese Character: A Photographic Analysis* (New York, 1942).

4. For recent changes in kinship patterns, see J.A. Boon, "Dynastic Dynamics, Caste and Kinship in Bali Now," (Ph.D. dissertation, Department of Anthropology, University of Chicago, 1973).

5. For India, and the contrast generally, see R. Redfield, *The Primitive World and its Transformations* (Ithaca, New York: 1952); for Java, C. Geertz, *The Religion of Java* (Glencoe, Illinois: 1960).

6. For recent changes, still incipient, in this pattern, see C. Geertz, " 'Internal Conversion' in Contemporary Bali," in C. Geertz, *The Interpretation of Cultures* (New York, 1973), pp. 170–79.

7. For a full description of a temple ceremony, see J. Belo, *Bali: Temple Festival* (Locust Valley, New York: 1953).

8. On trance, see J. Belo, *Trance in Bali* (New York: 1960).

9. For a general summary of Balinese religious practices, see R. Goris and P.L. Dronkers, *Bali: Atlas Kebudayaan* (Jakarta, n.d. [ca. 1955]).

10. The 20,000 figure is from J.L. Swellengrebel, "Introduction," in J.L. Swellengrebel, ed., *Bali: Studies in Life, Thought, and Ritual* (The Hague and Bandung, 1960), p. 12.

11. In addition, one essentially administrative grouping, introduced by the Dutch and thus not focused on a temple, the *Perbekelan*, will be discussed.

12. The term *désa adat* is impossible to translate simply. *Désa* means "village" and *adat* here means, roughly, "traditional rules for behavior."

13. An example of such a charter, called *awig-awig désa*, appears in Appendix C.

14. R. Redfield, *The Little Community* (Chicago, 1955); V.E. Korn, *De Dorpsrepubliek Tnganan Pagringsingan* (Saantpoort, Netherlands, 1933); R. Goris, "The Religious Character of the Village Community," in Swellengrebel, *Bali*, pp. 77–100.

15. They include those with titles of the lowest value, *Sudra*, together with a very small number of so-called Bali Aga—persons considered to have no title at all but to be descendants of the "original" Balinese, meaning those who were living in Bali before the entry of the Hindu-Javanese in the thirteenth to fifteenth centuries. Some mountain villages are composed entirely of Bali Aga people, but most members of this titleless group live among the rest of the populace in the lowlands. In actual practice, the name Bali Aga is treated as if it were only another title in the commoner category. On Balinese titles generally, see V.E. Korn, *Het Adatrecht van Bali*, pp. 137–78.

16. For some recent changes in this situation, see Boon, *Dynastic Dynamics*.

17. The sources upon which this reconstruction of the Balinese state is based can be found in C. Geertz, *Negara*.

18. For this view, see Covarrubias, *Island of Bali*.

19. As noted, this organization, the government village, is the only one of the groups so far described which does not center on a temple—that is, it is the only strictly secular association of importance at the local level in Bali.

20. For another example of "village" organization, differing in some respects from these, see Appendix C. For yet other examples, and for the general problem of defining the term "village" in Bali, see C. Geertz, "Form and Variation in Balinese Village Structure," *American Anthropologist* 61 (1964): 1–33.

21. As kinship in the private or domestic domain is essentially the same for both commoners and gentry, it is treated here in a single integrated chapter. In the public or civil domain, however, the operation of kinship institutions is rather different in the two status groups, and thus is discussed in separate chapters.

22. *Kawitan* is also used to refer to sacred heirlooms, usually considered to have magical powers; and to founding, deified ancestors as such.

23. For further descriptions and drawings of these various buildings, see Covarrubias, *Island of Bali*, pp. 88–96.

24. See B. ter Haar, *Adat Law in Indonesia* (New York, 1948).

25. For a fuller description of Tihingan, see C. Geertz, "Tihingan, A Balinese Village," in R.M. Koentjaraningrat, ed., *Villages in Indonesia* (Ithaca, New York: 1967), pp. 210–43.

26. That is, this is the normatively—in fact, religiously—favored marriage. Actual preference is an outcome of more complex considerations. On this, see Boon, "Dynastic Dynamics."

27. See J. Belo, *Bali: Rangda and Barong* (Locust Valley, New York, 1949).

28. The term *dadia* refers both to the temple (usually spoken of as the *pura dadia*) and to the social group (usually called the *seka dadia*). There is considerable variation, and even some confusion, in the minds of the Balinese, as to terminology. What we here call the dadia is also variously termed *pemaksan, penjenengan, sanggah gdé* in different regions; *mrajan* or *mrajan gdé* for lower gentry; *batur* or *batur gdé* for higher gentry. Literally, dadia means "in" or "at" the direction "toward-the-mountain center of the island" (i.e., north in southern Bali, south in northern; the term for the direction as such is *kaja*), the sacred pole of Bali. On the highly developed Balinese direction cosmology, see Swellengrebel, *Bali*, pp. 36–53. We are indebted to J. Stephen Lansing for bringing this derivation to our attention.

29. J. Middleton and D. Tait, eds., *Tribes without Rulers*, (London, 1958).

30. Ibid.

31. For a partial, and actually only apparent exception with regard to upper-caste kinship, see below, Chapter 4, section 2.

32. For some recently arisen exceptions, see again Boon, "Dynastic Dynamics."

33. See V.E. Korn, *Het Adatrecht van Bali*, p. 119, for an example of all-Bali cohesiveness among the Pandé. For the Paseks, Boon, "Dynastic Dynamics."

34. Sometimes there is a short genealogy of divine and semidivine beings at the very top indicating the mythic origin of an all-Bali title-group, so that there may be a little genealogical structure at the top and a little more at the bottom, but nothing in between. This mythic genealogical charter is, in any case, but of peripheral importance to most people, enfolded in the general and diffuse notion of *kawitan*.

35. For the term "genealogical amnesia," see P.M. Gulliver, *The Family Herds* (London, 1955), pp. 113–17; and J. Barnes, "The Collection of Genealogies," *Rhodes-Livingston Journal* 5 (1947): 52–53.

36. For a fuller analytical description of the Balinese teknonymy system, see H. and C. Geertz, "Teknonymy in Bali: Parenthood, Age Grading and Genealogical Amnesia," *Journal of the Royal Anthropological Institute*, 94 (1964): 94–108.

37. The sex indicators are "I" for a male, "Ni" for a female; the birth-order titles are "Wayan" for the firstborn, "Madé" for the second, "Nyoman" for the third, "Ktut" for the fourth. For Balinese naming customs in general, see C. Geertz, "Person, Time, and Conduct in Bali," in C. Geertz, *The Interpretation of Cultures*, pp. 360–411.

38. The Balinese gentry exhibit in reverse the relationship between teknonymy and community social position. Most nobles are addressed not by teknonyms but by a single honorific title which persists throughout their lives, a title which is unaffected by either age or generation. There are, however, some instructive exceptions to the rule that gentry do not use teknonymy. Some low-ranking, impoverished nobles are, in fact, customarily addressed by teknonyms in place of their titles. These variations in mode of address appear to parallel the kinds of status the gentry may

have vis-a-vis the commoner hamlet community. Those of very high rank who also have considerable wealth or regional political position often live in the same settlement with commoners, but they are completely excluded from the hamlet government, or if they are accepted as citizens they have a very special status and certain specified privileges. These are the ones who are never addressed by teknonyms. On the other hand, the gentry of inferior rank who do use teknonymy also generally are accepted as nearly full and equal hamlet citizens. In such cases, the teknonyms employed are specially modified forms, terms which are more elegant than those employed by commoners, and which vary quite precisely with their rank within the gentry group.

39. In practice, of course, there are cases where husband and wife carry different teknonyms. At divorce and remarriage, a person may give up his or her former teknonym and take on a new one with the birth of a new child to the new marriage; but this is not always done, with the result that a man or woman may continue to be called by the name of a child from a former marriage. Similarly, in cases of polygamy, the husband has the teknonym of his first child, but his wives are indicated by the name of their first children. If one of the wives is barren, she may be called by the teknonym that her co-wife has, with the result that there are two women with the same teknonym. All of these situations, however, are relatively rare.

40. Belo's comment (J. Belo, "A Study of the Balinese Family," *American Anthropologist,* 38 [1936]: 12–31) that Balinese do not conceptually differentiate between parallel and cross cousins simply because they have a single reference term (*misan*) for (first) cousin is not quite accurate. When necessary, the parallel patri-cousin is distinguished as *misan kapurusa,* "cousin in the direct male line," as against *misan ulian luh,* "cousin through females" (i.e., MoSiChi, MoBrChi, and FaSiChi). For an argument, about which we have some reservations, that the cultural preference for first parallel cousin marriage actually works out in practice as a social preference for the second parallel cousin (*mindon*), see Boon, "Dynastic Dynamics."

41. This is the general rule, applicable to most Balinese. However, sometimes marriage with first cousins on either side is prohibited.

42. There are limits and prohibition within this endogamy rule. In addition to the prohibition of nuclear family incest, there is also a strong feeling that the couple should be of the same generation—that a man should not marry a woman to whom, under the Hawaiian terminology system, he might use the kin term "mother." Such marriages do occur, but they are thought to be magically dangerous. The reverse, marrying a girl from the next descending generation, one who might call the man "father," is not discouraged to the same degree. There is a similar dislike, or religiously based fear of marriages involving the direct exchange of sisters— i.e., two men each giving their sister in marriage to the other.

43. Tables 4 and 5—which are for commoners only—have been constructed on the basis of a written register of household heads for each of the three villages, supplied to us by the village chief of Tihingan. Working from this list, we gathered quantitative data on title-group, marriage,

land tenure, work patterns, political offices, and religious status. It thus represents a selection of the living adults in the three villages, a selection which was however made on a comparable basis—the criteria for "household head" being the same—in the three cases. The percentages of dadia membership and endogamy rates for Tihingan differ slightly in these tables from those in table 3, which were based on all marriages, past and present, that our informants could recall. The criteria for designating a title group a dadia are the same as in table 3.

44. In the past, and to a lesser extent today, the husband often had to pay a fairly heavy (money) fine in such a case. In some parts of Bali, e.g., Klungkung, this was paid to the king. In others, e.g., Gianyar, it was paid to the offended father-in-law. This payment, often misleadingly referred to as a "bride-price" in the literature (Korn, *Het Adatrecht van Bali*, pp. 486–88), was required only in the cases of those exogamous marriages which were by elopement (*ngerorod*) or kidnap (*melangan-dang*), and were much higher in the latter case. If good relations between the families were later restored, the father-in-law might return all or part of the fine to the son-in-law. Korn (p. 487) remarks that in earlier days this fine was set high—as much as 400–600 rijksdaalders in Buleleng—as a conscious effort to control elopements and kidnappings.

45. For a description of that context, see C. Geertz, *Negara*, and the references cited there.

46. Gentry terms for "dadia temple" are *batur dalem* or *batur agung* (for royalty) and *mrajan agung* (for other gentry). The terms for "houseyard," which are sometimes loosely applied to co-resident sections of the dadia kingroup, are *puri* ("palace," used for royal houses) and *jero* ("noble residence," used for gentry houses).

47. On the obverse side of these ties, however, on the commoner side, the dadia played no role whatsoever. In what was said to be a conscious effort to keep commoners from massing together into potentially powerful factions, affiliation to their lords was in terms of houseyards rather than villages or even familial groups. The result was that a number of lords would have subjects within any one hamlet, and within any one dadia, and that even a set of commoner brothers who did not reside together could easily have different lords. Few lords, with some local exceptions, ever "owned" an entire commoner dadia, or a whole hamlet.

48. In some accounts, the founding ancestor is said to be Arya Kenceng, a lower-ranking figure than Arya Damar. (Other accounts say Damar and Kenceng, are two names for the same man.) On all this, see Boon, "Dynastic Dynamics," and C. Geertz, *Negara*.

49. See note 37, above.

50. Thus, for gentry, the birth-order titles follow either of two sequences: (1) Putu (or Gdé), Madé, Nyoman, Ktut, then for the fifth child Madé again, then Nyoman, Ktut, Madé, Nyoman, etc.; (2) Putu (or Gdé), Madé, Nyoman, Ktut, then a series of Ktuts, for all subsequent children are called Ktut.

51. On this conception of "symbol," in which it is used to refer to "any object, act, event, quality, or relation which serves as a vehicle for a conception," see C. Geertz, "Religion as a Cultural System," in C.

Geertz, *The Interpretation of Cultures.* What follows in the next few pages owes much to A. Schutz, T. Parsons, and D.M. Schneider. See, in particular, the latter's *American Kinship: A Cultural Account* (Englewood Cliffs, N.J., 1968) and "What Is Kinship All About," in P. Reining, ed., *Kinship Studies in the Morgan Centennial Year* (Washington, D.C.: 1972), pp. 32–63.

52. On trading partnerships, M. Mead, *Kinship in the Admiralty Islands* (New York, 1934). On non co-residence, see R.F. Salisbury, *From Stone to Steel* (London, 1962). On central vs. marginal cases and family resemblance type definitions, see J. Searle, *Speech Acts* (Cambridge, 1970), pp. 4–12.

53. It is perhaps worthy of remark at this point, however, that the "kinship system" view of things—which sees extrafamilial kinship only where there are clans, or marriage rules, or inherited roles—has often inhibited the recognition of the degree to which such symbolization is widespread in "modern" societies, such as our own. For a provocative analysis of American kinship which sees the symbolism upon which it rests—a distinction between relations by "blood" and relations by "law"—as generally pervasive in our culture, see Schneider, *American Kinship.* For the concepts of the "scope" and "force" of a cultural pattern, see C. Geertz, *Islam Observed: Religious Development in Morocco and Indonesia* (New Haven, 1968), chap. 4.

54. See C. Geertz, "Religion as a Cultural System"; *Islam Observed,* chap. 4; "Ethos, World View and the Analysis of Sacred Symbols," in C. Geertz, *The Interpretation of Cultures,* pp. 126–41.

55. On this, see H. Geertz, "The Balinese Village," in G.W. Skinner, ed., *Local, National, and Regional Loyalties in Indonesia* (New Haven, 1959), pp. 24–33. The party system has now (1971) more or less dissolved, but the general divisions remain, and in a quite stable form.

Index